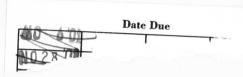

COLLECTED
POEMS
OF
HUGH
MacDIARMID

Photo Douglas MacAskill, Edinburgh

HUGH MACDIARMID

COLLECTED
POEMS
OF
HUGH
MacDIARMID

[pseud.]

NEW YORK

THE MACMILLAN COMPANY

1962

................................g

...........................y, New York
........................Galt, Ontario

........................ates of America

........................rd number: 61-13340

Most of the poems in this volume are reprinted from the following volumes by permission of the publishers: *Sangschaw, Penny Wheep, A Drunk Man Looks at the Thistle,* and *To Circumjack Cencrastus,* William Blackwood & Sons, Ltd.; *Stony Limits and Other Poems,* Victor Gollancz, Ltd.; *Lucky Poet,* Methuen & Co., Ltd.; *A Kist of Whistles and Other Poems, In Memoriam James Joyce, Poetry* (Scotland), Nos. 3 and 4, William Maclellan, Ltd.; *Honoured Shade,* W. & R. Chambers, Ltd.; *A Golden Treasury of Scottish Poetry,* Macmillan & Co., Ltd.; *Scots Unbound and Other Poems,* Messrs. Enaes MacKay, Scotland; *The Islands of Scotland,* Messrs. Botsford, London. "Happy on Heimaey" (a part of "My Heart Always Goes Back to the North") first appeared in *Poetry* (Chicago), and "Once in a Cornish Garden" in *Botteghe Oscure.* Some of the poems first appeared in *The Evening Dispatch,* Edinburgh, and in *The Voice of Scotland,* a quarterly. Also, a number of the poems appeared in the following volumes: *Annals of the Five Senses, First Hymn to Lenin and Other Poems, Second Hymn to Lenin and Other Poems, The Battle Continues.*

AUTHOR'S NOTE

This volume does not contain all the poems I have written, but all I think worth including in a definitive collection. The twelve volumes of poems I have so far published have all been drawn upon; some of them have been included entire; and, in addition, this collection includes a number of poems which have appeared in various periodicals but have not been included in any of my volumes. For some of these I have to make the customary grateful acknowledgments to the editors and proprietors of the periodicals in question, including my own quarterly, *The Voice of Scotland.*

HUGH MACDIARMID

Biggar, Lanarkshire

Contents

[ix]

[xi]

[xii]

From

Annals of the Five Senses

1923

A MOMENT IN ETERNITY

To George Ogilvie

The great song ceased
—Aye, like a wind was gone,
And our hearts came to rest,
Singly as leaves do,
And every leaf a flame.

My shining passions stilled
Shone in the sudden peace
Like countless leaves
Tingling with the quick sap
Of Immortality.

I was a multitude of leaves
Receiving and reflecting light,
A burning bush
Blazing for ever unconsumed,
Nay, ceaselessly,
Multiplying in leaves and light
And instantly
Burgeoning in buds of brightness,
—Freeing like golden breaths
Upon the cordial air
A thousand new delights,
—Translucent leaves
Green with the goodness of Eternity,
Golden in the Heavenly light,
—The golden breaths
Of my eternal life,

Like happy memories multiplied,
Shining out instantly from me
And shining back for ever into me,
—Breaths given out
But still unlost,
For ever mine
In the infinite air,
The everlasting foliage of my soul
Visible awhile
Like steady and innumerable flames,
Blending into one blaze
Yet each distinct
With shining shadows of difference.

A sudden thought of God's
Came like a wind
Ever and again
Rippling them as waters over stars,
And swiftlier fanning them
And setting them a-dance,
Upflying, fluttering down,
Moving in orderly intricacies
Of colour and of light,
Delaying, hastening,
Blazing and serene,
Shaken and shining in the turning wind,
Lassoing cataracts of light
With rosy boughs,
Or clamouring in echoing unequalled heights,
Rhythmical sprays of many-coloured fire
And spires chimerical
Gleaming in fabulous airs,
And suddenly
Lapsing again
To incandescence and increase.

And again the wind came
Blowing me afar
In fair fantastic fires,
—Ivies and irises invading

The upland garths of ivory;
Queen daisies growing
In the tall red grass
By pools of perfect peace;
And bluebells tossing
In transparent fields;
And silver airs
Lifting the crystal sources in dim hills
And swinging them far out like bells of glass
Pealing pellucidly
And quivering in faery flights of chimes;
Shivers of wings bewildered
In alleys of virgin dream;
Floral dances and revels of radiance
Whirling in stainless sanctuaries;
And eyes of Seraphim,
Shining like sunbeams on eternal ice,
Lifted toward the unexplored
Summits of Paradise.
And the wind ceased.
Light dwelt in me,
Pavilioned there.
I was a crystal trunk,
Columnar in the glades of Paradise,
Bearing the luminous boughs
And foliaged with the flame
Of infinite and gracious growth,
—Meteors for roots,
And my topmost spires
Notes of enchanted light
Blind in the Godhead!
—White stars at noon!

I shone within my thoughts
As God within us shines.

And the wind came,
Multitudinous and light
I whirled in exultations inexpressible
—An unpicturable, clear,

Soaring and glorying,
Swift consciousness,
A cosmos turning like a song of spheres
On apices of praise,
A separate colour,
An essential element and conscious part
Of successive and stupendous dreams
In God's own heart!
And the wind ceased
And like a light I stood,
A flame of glorious and complex resolve,
Within God's heart.

I knew then that a new tree,
A new tree and a strange,
Stood beautifully in Heaven.
I knew that a new light
Stood in God's heart
And a light unlike
The Twice Ten Thousand lights
That stood there,
Shining equally with me,
And giving and receiving increase of light
Like the flame that I was
Perpetually.
And I knew that when the wind rose
This new tree would stand still
Multiplied in light but motionless,
And I knew that when God dreamt
And His creative impulses
Ran through us like a wind
And we flew like clear and coloured
Flames in His dreams,
(Adorations, Gratitudes, and Joys,
Plenary and boon and pure,
Crystal and burning-gold and scarlet
Competing and co-operating flames
Reflecting His desires,
Flashing like epical imaginings
And burning virgin steeps

With ceaseless swift apotheoses)
One light would stand unmoved.

And when on pinnacles of praise
All others whirled
Like a white light deeper in God's heart
This light would shine,
Pondering the imponderable,
Revealing ever clearlier
Patterns of endless revels,
Each gesture freed,
Each shining shadow of difference,
Each subtle phase evolved
In the magnificent and numberless
Revelations of ecstasy
Succeeding and excelling inexhaustibly,
—A white light like a silence
Accentuating the great songs!
—A shining silence wherein God
Might see as in a mirror
The miracles that He must next achieve!

Ah, Light,
That is God's inmost wish,
His knowledge of Himself,
Flame of creative judgment,
God's interrogation of infinity,
Searching the unsearchable,
—Silent and steadfast tree
Housing no birds of song,
Void to the wind,
But rooted in God's very self,
Growing ineffably,
Central in Paradise!

When the song ceased
And I stood still,
Breathing new leaves of life
Upon the eternal air,
Each leaf of all my leaves

Shone with a new delight
Murmuring Your name.

O Thou,
Who art the wisdom of the God
Whose ecstasies we are!

THE FOOL

He said that he was God.
"We are well met," I cried,
"I've always hoped I should
Meet God before I died."

I slew him then and cast
   His corpse into a pool,
—But how I wish he had
   Indeed been God, the fool!

From
Sangschaw
1925

THE BONNIE BROUKIT BAIRN

Mars is braw in crammasy,
Venus in a green silk goun,
The auld mune shak's her gowden feathers,
Their starry talk's a wheen o' blethers,
Nane for thee a thochtie sparin',
Earth, thou bonnie broukit bairn!
—*But greet, an' in your tears ye'll droun*
The haill clanjamfrie!

THE WATERGAW

Ae weet forenicht i' the yow-trummle
I saw yon antrin thing,
A watergaw wi' its chitterin' licht
Ayont the on-ding;
An' I thocht o' the last wild look ye gied
Afore ye deed!

There was nae reek i' the laverock's hoose
That nicht—an' nane i' mine;
But I hae thocht o' that foolish licht
Ever sin' syne;
An' I think that mebbe at last I ken
What your look meant then.

THE SAUCHS IN THE REUCH
HEUCH HAUCH *

FOR GEORGE RESTON MALLOCH

There's teuch sauchs growin' i' the Reuch Heuch
Hauch.
Like the sauls o' the damned are they,
And ilk ane yoked in a whirligig
Is birlin' the lee-lang day.

O we come doon frae oor stormiest moods,
And licht like a bird i' the haun',
But the teuch sauchs there i' the Reuch Heuch
Hauch
As the deil's ain hert are thrawn.

The winds 'ud pu' them up by the roots,
Tho' it broke the warl' asunder,
But they rin richt doon thro' the boddom o' Hell,
And nane kens hoo fer under'

There's no' a licht that the Heavens let loose
Can calm them a hanlawhile,
Nor frae their ancient amplefeyst
Sall God's ain sel' them wile.

I HEARD CHRIST SING

FOR H. J. C. GRIERSON

I heard Christ sing quhile roond him danced
The twal' disciples in a ring,
And here's the dance I saw them dance,
And the sang I heard him sing.

* A field near Hawick.

[8]

Ane, twa, three, and their right feet heich,
Fower, five, six, and doon wi' them,
Seevin, aucht, nine, and up wi' the left,
Ten, eleevin, twal', and doon they came.

And Christ he stude i' the middle there,
And was the thirteenth man,
And sang the bonniest sang that e'er
Was sung sin' Time began.

And Christ he was the centrepiece,
Wi' three on ilka side.
My hert stude still, and the sun stude still,
But still the dancers plied.

O I wot it was a maypole,
As a man micht seek to see,
Wi' the twal' disciples dancin' roon',
While Christ sang like a lintie.

The twal' points o' the compass
Made jubilee roon' and roon',
And but for the click-click-clack o' the feet,
Christ's sang was the only soon'.

And there was nae time that could be tauld
Frae a clock wha's haun's stude still,
Quhile the figures a' gaed bizzin roon'
—I wot it was God's will.

Wersh is the vinegar,
And the sword is sharp.
Wi' the tremblin' sunbeams
Again for my harp,
I sing to Thee.

The spirit of man
Is a bird in a cage,
That beats on the bars

[9]

Wi' a goodly rage,
And fain'ud be free.

Twice-caged it is,
In life and in death,
Yet it claps its wings
Wi' a restless faith,
And sings as it may.

Then fill my mouth
Wi' the needfu' words,
That sall turn its wings
Into whirlin' swords,
When it hears what I say.

Hearken my cry,
and let me speak,
That when it hears
It sall lift its beak,
And sing as it should.

Sweet is the song
That is lost in its throat,
And fain'ud I hear
Its openin' note,
As I hang on the rood.

And when I rise
Again from the dead,
Let me, I pray,
Be accompanied
By the spirit of man.

Yea, as I rise
From earth to Heaven,
Fain'ud I know
That Thou has given
Consent to my plan—

Even as the stars
Sang here at my birth,
Let Heaven hear
The song of the earth
Then, for my sake.

The thorns are black,
And callous the nails.
As a bird its bars
My hand assails
Harpstrings . . . that break!

O I wot they'll lead the warl' a dance,
And I wot the sang sall be,
As a white sword loupin' at the hert
O' a' eternity.

Judas and Christ stude face to face,
And mair I couldna' see,
But I wot he did God's will wha made
Siccar o' Calvary.

MOONLIGHT AMONG
THE PINES

Thraw oot your shaddaws
Owre the heich hillsides,
A' ye lang trees
Quhair the white mune rides.

My spirit 'ud darken
The sun in the East
For aye, gin my luve
Laid bare her white breist.

O shaddaw that derns
In my hert till a sicht
O' Luve sends it plungin'
A' else into nicht! . . .

"YOU KNOW NOT WHO I AM"

After the German of Stefan George

Ye kenna wha I am—but this is fac'.
I ha'ena yet by ony word or ac'
Made mysel' human . . . an' sune I maun tak'
Anither guise to ony I've yet ta'en.
I'll cheenge; an' yet my ain true sel' I'll hain,
Tine only what ye ken as me. I' vain
Ye'll seek to haud me, an' ye needna murn,
For to a form ye canna ken I'll turn
'Twixt ae braith an' the neist: an' whan I'm gane
Ye'll ha'e o' me what ye ha'e haen o' a'
My kindred since licht on the earth 'good da'—
The braith that gi'es ye courage, an' the fain
Wild kiss that aye into yer saul maun burn.

OVERINZIEVAR

The pigs shoot up their gruntles here,
The hens staund hullerie,
And a' the hinds glower roond aboot
Wi' unco dullery.

Wi' sook-the-bluids and switchables
The grund's fair crottled up,
And owre't the forkit lichtnin' flees
Like a cleisher o' a whup!

[12]

EX VERMIBUS

Gape, gape, gorlin',
For I ha'e a worm
That'll gi'e ye a slee and sliggy sang
Wi' mony a whuram.

Syne i' the lift
Byous spatrils you'll mak',
For a gorlin' wi' worms like this in its wame
Nae airels sall lack.

But owre the tree-taps
Maun flee like a sperk,
Till it hes the haill o' the Heavens alunt
Frae dawin' to derk.

AU CLAIR DE LA LUNE

For W. B.

". . . She's yellow
An' yawps like a peany."
                    Anon.

"They mix ye up wi' loony fowk,
Wha are o' stars the mense,
The madness that ye bring to me,
I wadna change't for sense."
                    W. B.

- I -
Prelude to Moon Music

Earth's littered wi' larochs o' Empires,
Muckle nations are dust.
Time'll meissle it awa', it seems,
An' smell nae must.

[13]

But wheest!—whatna music is this,
While the win's haud their breath?
—*The Moon has a wunnerfu' finger*
For the back-lill o' Death!

- II -
Moonstruck

When the warl's couped soon' as a peerie
That licht-lookin' craw o' a body, the moon,
Sits on the fower cross-win's
Peerin' a' roon'.

She's seen me—she's seen me—an' straucht
Loupit clean on the quick o' my hert.
The quhither o' cauld gowd's fairly
Gi'en me a stert.

An' the roarin' o' oceans noo'
Is peerieweerie to me:
Thunner's a tinklin' bell: an' Time
Whuds like a flee.

- III -
The Man in the Moon

"Oh, lad, I fear that yon's the sea
Where they fished for you and me,
And there, from whence we both were ta'en,
You and I shall drown again."
                                        A. E. HOUSMAN

The moonbeams kelter i' the lift,
An' Earth, the bare auld stane,
Glitters beneath the seas o' Space,
White as a mammoth's bane.

An', lifted owre the gowden wave,
Peers a dumfoun'ered Thocht,

Wi' keethin' sicht o' a' there is,
An' bodily sicht o' nocht.

- IV -
The Huntress and Her Dogs

Her luchts o' yellow hair
Flee oot ayont the storm,
Wi' mony a bonny flaught
The colour o' Cairngorm.

Oot owre the thunner-wa'
She haiks her shinin' breists,
While th' oceans to her heels
Slink in like bidden beasts.

So sall Earth's howlin' mobs
Drap, lown, ahint the sang
That frae the chaos o' Thocht
In triumph braks or lang.

IN THE HEDGE-BACK

It was a wild black nicht,
But i' the hert o't we
Drave back the darkness wi' a bleeze o' licht,
Ferrer than een could see.

It was a wild black nicht,
But o' the snell air we
Kept juist eneuch to hinder the heat
Meltin' us utterly.

It was a wild black nicht,
But o' the win's roar we
Kept juist eneuch to hear oor herts beat
Owre it triumphantly.

[15]

It was a wild black nicht,
But o' the Earth we
Kept juist eneuch underneath us to ken
That a warl' used to be.

REID E'EN

Ilka hert an' hind are met
'Neath Arcturus gleamin' bonnie,
Bien the nicht owre a' the warl'.
Hey, nonny, nonny!

But my hert sall meet nae maik
This reid-e'en or ony.
Luve an' a' are left behind.
—Hey, nonny, nonny!

CROWDIEKNOWE

Oh to be at Crowdieknowe
When the last trumpet blaws,
An' see the deid come loupin' owre
The auld grey wa's.

Muckle men wi' tousled beards,
I grat as a bairn
'll scramble frae the croodit clay
Wi' feck o' swearin'.

An' glower at God an' a' his gang
O' angels i' the lift
—Thae trashy bleezin' French-like folk
Wha gar'd them shift!

Fain the weemun-folk'll seek
To mak' them haud their row
—*Fegs, God's no blate gin he stirs up*
The men o' Crowdieknowe!

THE EEMIS STANE

I' the how-dumb-deid o' the cauld hairst nicht
The warl' like an eemis stane
Wags i' the lift;
An' my eerie memories fa'
   Like a yowdendrift.

Like a yowdendrift so's I couldna read
The words cut oot i' the stane
Had the fug o' fame
An' history's hazelraw
No' yirdit thaim.

THE SCARLET WOMAN

For Alexander McGill

Black-burnin' shame is your garb, quo' they,
And syne gin you turn your face,
It lowes wi' a reid and laithly flame
That springs frae the evil place.

But noo I ha'e met you and seen for mysel'
Your face is the rare reid dawn,
And velvets o' nicht are the gouns you wear
To win the hert o' a man.

And a flame that springs frae the evil place,
And a flame that springs frae Heaven,

[17]

Are but as the thocht o' a man maun mak'
As his hert is richt or riven.

And glad I am that your face to me
Is the dawn, and no' dreadour,
Nor black affront but the bien nicht haps
Your bonnie form attour.

O burnin' rose o' the love o' God,
Pitch-darkness o' His will,
To Day and to Night, to Life and to Daith,
I gi'e me and fear nae ill.

THE FRIGHTENED BRIDE

Seil o' yer face! the send has come.
I ken, I ken, but awa' ye gan,
An' dinna fash, for what's i' yer hert
A' weemun ken an' nae man can.

Seil o' yer face! Ye needna seek
For comfort gin ye show yer plight.
To Gods an' men, coorse callants baith,
A fleggit bride's the seilfu' sicht.

THE LAST TRUMP

*Suggested by the Russian of
Dmitry Merezhkovsky*

Owre the haill warl' there's a whirrin'
An' a reishlin' an' a stirrin'
An' a muckle voice that cries:
"Let aal men rise!"

[18]

"Na, Na! Still the nicht is black.
I'll sleep on an' winna wauk.
Dinna reeze me. Dinna ca'.
Chapna' on my coffin-wa'."

"Fegs, ye canna sleep, for noo
Gabriel mak's a hullaballoo.
Hark his trumpet's awfu' toot.
A' the deid maun up an' oot."

Tootle-ootle-ootle-oo.
Tootle-oo.

"Gawa', gawa', an' let me lig,
Nae God 'ud awn me i' this rig
Or ha'e sic a rotten, stinkin'
Corpse as mine in's sunlicht blinkin'.

Gawa', gawa'." "Na, Na, my freen!
In yer grave ye're no' unseen.
Black affrontit tho' ye be
Up ye get—it's God's decree!

Up an' oot—an' say nae mair
Gleg or laith's no' here nor there.
Up—or God's begood to speir
Gin a'body's here!"

COPHETUA

OH! The King's gane gyte,
Puir auld man, puir auld man,
An' an ashypet lassie
Is Queen o' the lan'.

Wi' a scoogie o' silk
An' a bucket o' siller

[19]

She's showin' the haill Coort
The smeddum intil her!

WHEELRIG

There's a big black clood on the cantle o' Wheelrig,
And the waesome valley
'S fa'n like a dozened bird I'd fain tak' up i' my loof,
And ettle to rally.

Only a wee whiley-sin' it was fidgin' fu' fain
In its gowd and green—
Movin' i' the sun like a lassie,
Under her sweethert's een.

But the black clood grows on the cantle o' Wheelrig:
Wi' a cauld wund under't,
And the warld gaups at me like a saul frae its body,
Owre suddently sundered!

COUNTRY LIFE

OOTSIDE! . . . Ootside!
There's dooks that try tae fly
An' bum-clocks bizzin' by,
A corn-skriech an' a cay
An' guissay i' the cray.

Inside! . . . Inside!
There's golochs on the wa',
A cradle on the ca',
A muckle bleeze o' cones
An' mither fochin' scones.

O JESU PARVULE

"Followis ane sang of the birth of Christ, with the tune of Baw lu la law."
GODLY BALLATES

His mither sings to the bairnie Christ
Wi' the tune o' *Baw lu la law*.
The bonnie wee craturie lauchs in His crib
An' a' the starnies an' he are sib.
    Baw, baw, my loonikie, baw, balloo.

"Fa' owre, ma hinny, fa' owre, fa' owre,
A' body's sleepin' binna oorsels."
She's drawn Him in tae the bool o' her breist
But the byspale's nae thocht o' sleep i' the least.
    Balloo, wee mannie, balloo, balloo.

THE INNUMERABLE CHRIST

"Other stars may have their Bethlehem, and their Calvary too."
PROFESSOR J. Y. SIMPSON

Wha kens on whatna Bethlehems
Earth twinkles like a star the nicht,
An' whatna shepherds lift their heids
   In its unearthly licht?

'Yont a' the stars oor een can see
An' farther than their lichts can fly,
I' mony an unco warl' the nicht
   The fatefu' bairnies cry.

I' mony an unco warl' the nicht
The lift gaes black as pitch at noon,

[21]

An' sideways on their chests the heids
  O' endless Christs roll doon.

An' when the earth's as cauld's the mune
An' a its folk are lang syne deid,
On coontless stars the Babe maun cry
  An' the Crucified maun bleed.

GOD TAKES A REST

From "A Sea Suite"

As a man at nicht lets go o' life
And fa's into a sleep,
I cast me off frae the guid dry lan'
And turn yince owre to the deep.

I'll row the warl' like a plaid nae mair
For comfort roon' aboot me,
And the lives o' men sall be again
As they were lang, wi 'oot me.

For I sall hie me back to the sea
Frae which I broocht life yince,
And lie i' the stound o' its whirlpools, free
Frae a' that's happened since.

IN THE PANTRY

FOR N. M. GUNN

Knedneuch land
And a loppert sea
And a lift like a blue-douped
Mawkin'-flee.

I'm famished, but fegs!
What's here for a man
But a wheen rubbish that's lain
Sin' Time began?

The sun has a goût
And the mune's hairy-mouldit,
And wha but auld Daith
Has a stummack to hold it?

I'll thraw the lot oot
And lippen to get fresh,
For the sicht o'ts eneuch
To turn my soul nesh!

FARMER'S DEATH

FOR EDWIN MUIR

Ke-uk, ke-uk, ke-uk, ki-kwaik,
The broon hens keckle and bouk,
And syne wi' their yalla beaks
For the reid worms houk.

The muckle white pig at the tail
O' the midden slotters and slorps,
But the auld ferm hoose is lown
And wae as a corpse.

The hen's een glitter like gless
As the worms gang twirlin' in,
But there's never a move in by
And the windas are blin'.

Feathers turn fire i' the licht,
The pig's doup skinkles like siller,
But the auld ferm hoose is waugh
Wi' the daith intill her.

Hen's cries are a panash in Heaven,
And a pig has the warld at its feet;
But wae for the hoose whaur a buirdly man
Crines in a windin' sheet.

THE DISEASED SALMON

I'm gled it's no' my face,
But a fozie saumon turnin'
Deid-white i' the blae bracks o' the pool,
Hoverin' a wee and syne tint again i' the churnin'.

Mony's the face'll turn,
Like the fozie saumon I see;
But I hope that mine'll never be ane
And I can think o' naebody else's I'd like to be.

WHIP-THE-WORLD

Mountains and seas
Birl under his wings
Till a' gaes in a kink
O' skimmerin' rings.

He lays on wi' his sang,
The wullie wee chap,
Till he gars earth bizz
Like a dozened tap.

Syne he hings sidelins
Watchin' hoo lang
It tak's till it staggers
Oot o' his sang.

Aye it tak's langer
And ane o' thae days
"I'll thraw't in a whirl
It'll bide in," he says.

BALLAD OF THE FIVE SENSES

- I -

I wot there was nae sicht nor scent,
Nae savour, substance, soon',
I didna see, smell, taste, or feel
Or hear as I ga'ed roon'.

As I ga'ed roon' the divers warl'
That ony man can ken
Wi' een and nose and ears and haun's
And mou' as I ga'ed then.

The warl' o' Earth and sea and sky,
And eke o' Heaven and Hell,
That separate seemed, as separate seemed
The warl' wi'in mysel'.

And time and space and change and daith
Were neist to nocht to me,
At will I'd bring the distant near
At will the deid I'd see. . . .

O I wist it is a bonny warl'
That lies forenenst a' men,
And that ony man wi' his senses five
As weel's the neist may ken.

- II -

I was as blithe to be alive
As ony man could be,
And felt as gin the haill braid warl'
Were made yince-yirn for me.

[25]

I wot I kept my senses keen,
I wot I used them weel.
As God felt whan he made the warl'
I aye socht to feel.

Times are yin sees things as they'd ne'er
Been seen afore ava',
As gin a' men had erst been blin',
Or the a'e First Day 'good da'.

Times are yin sees things as they'd ne'er
Been seen afore ava',
I wot I saw things fresh and full,
As few men ever saw.

O I wist it is a bonny warl'
That lies forenenst a' men,
But it's naething but a shaddaw-show
To the warl' that I saw then.

There was nae movement on the earth
But frae my hert it came,
"Let there be licht," God said, and straucht
My een let oot the same.

Was it a tree? I couldna rest
Till 'neath my hert I kent
A pooer was pent gin it wan loose
Its boughs had heicher sent,

Had gi'en it bark 'gainst bolt and blast
Stranger than granite was,
And leaves sae green, a' ither greens
Were wan shaddaws.

I felt I could haud a' earth's trees
Dancin' upon my bluid,
As they were ba's that at a Fair
Stot in a loupin' flood. . . .

Yet sune I kent God or the warl'
Were no' for een to see,
Wi' body and saul I socht to staun'
As in Eternity.

Or bood I ha'e o' a' the warl'
But what my wits could mak',
And for the God made it and me
Nocht but my ain thochts tak'?

Oot o' the way, my senses five,
I ken a' you can tell,
Oot o' the way, my thochts, for noo'
I maun face God mysel'.

- III -

I cam' unto a place where there
Seemed nocht but naethingness,
Yet roon' and roon' me seemed to be
Things that were bodiless.

My senses there were nae mair use
Than gin I had had nane:
I felt their presence as they'd been
Thochts dernin' i' my brain,
Thochts no' like ony ither thochts
That ever I had ha'en.

They were like thochts for which a man
Can fin' nae words to tell,
Hoo' they compare wi' his ither thochts
E'en to his ain sel's sel.

And ilk ane differed frae the neist
As ilk ane did frae me:
And day and nicht, or life and daith
Mair like each ither be.

Water for stane micht weel be ta'en
Or Heaven and Hell seem yin,

A' differences men's minds can mak',
Maun end or ye begin. . . .

They were as blin' and deef and dumb,
They were as deid men be,
To a' that ony man alive
Can be or think or see.

And ilk ane differed frae the neist
As ilk ane did frae me:
And or ye 'good to coont them ye
Ga'ed 'yont infinity.

Yet weel I wot that life to each
Was bonny as to men,
Tho' I o' theirs as they o' mine
Could jot nor tittle ken.

Wae's me that thocht I kent the warl',
Wae's me that made a God,
My senses five and their millions mair
Were like banes beneath a sod.

For the warl' is like a flourishing tree,
And God is like the sun,
But they or I to either lie
Like deid folk i' the grun'.

- IV -

O gin ye tine your senses five,
And get ony o' theirs insteed,
Ye'll be as far frae what ye are
As the leevin' frae the deid.

And staun'in' as you're staun'in' noo,
And wi' things as they are
Ye'd be as gin ye stude upon
Anither kind o' star.

Leevin' quo' I and deid quo' I,
But daith may only be
A change o' senses so's a man
Anither warl' can see.

Or this warl' in anither way
For Heaven or Hell may be
But ither ways o' seein' the warl'
That ony man can see.

And God Himsel' sall only be
As far's a man can tell,
In this or ony ither life
A way o' lookin' at himsel'.

- V -

O I wist it is a bonny warl'
That lies forenenst a' men,
And that ony man wi' his senses five,
As weel's the neist may ken.

And I wist that that is a shaddaw show
To the warl's that can be seen
By men wha seek as I ha' socht
And keep their senses keen.

But O I'm fain for a gowden sun,
And fain for a flourishing tree,
That neither men nor the Gods they'll ken
In earth or Heaven sall see!

From
Penny Wheep
1926

TROMPE L'ŒIL

As I gaed doon the hedgeback
Five blue eggs I saw,
It was as gin you'd looked at me
Wi' five een for twa.

WHEESHT, WHEESHT

Wheesht, wheesht, my foolish hert,
For weel ye ken
I widna ha'e ye stert
Auld ploys again.

It's guid to see her lie
Sae snod an' cool,
A' lust o' lovin' by—
Wheesht, wheesht, ye fule!

EX EPHEMERIDE MARE

I ha'e seen the Egypt herrings
Eelyin' in an emeraud sea,
And it's fain I could ha'e gane
In their skinklan' company.

Sae in deeps Thocht canna faddom
Dern the dreams that glint a wee
Through Time's shawls, and syne are tint
In dowf immensity.

BLIND MAN'S LUCK

He juist sits oolin' owre the fire
And gin' a body speak t' him, fegs,
Turns up the whites o's een
Like twa oon eggs.

"I've riped the bike o' Heaven," quo' he,
"And whaur ma sicht s'ud be I've stuck
The toom doups o' the sun
And mune, for luck!"

THE CURRANT BUSH

There's no' ressum to the fore
Whaur the hoose stood.
—Only a'e wild cur'n' buss wags
Tossils o' forfochen blood.

It's a lass that deed in childing,
Puir thowless cratur,
Wha alane o' a' her race
Is still at odds wi' natur'.

CLOUDBURST AND
SOARING MOON

Cloodburst an' soarin' mune
And 'twixt the twa a taed
That loupit oot upon me
As doon the loan I gaed.

Noo I gang white an' lanely
But hoo I'm wishin', faith,
A clood aince mair cam' owre me
Wi' Jock the byreman's braith.

FEERY-O'-THE-FEET

"A deid man's never
Feery o' the feet,
Jock, five years buried
Maun be far frae fleet,
Sae, lad ye needna worry,
He'll no' hae's in a hurry."

Aye, lass! but Resurrection's
The danger that dings a',
We maun up braw an' early
Gin we're to win awa',
Else sune's the trumpet's blared
There'll be twa daiths in oor kirkyaird.

SOMERSAULT

I lo'e the stishie
O' Earth in space
Breengin' by
At a haliket pace.

A wecht o' hills
Gangs wallopin' owre,

Syne a whummlin' sea
Wi' a gallus glower.

The West whuds doon
Like the pigs at Gadara,
But the East's aye there
Like a sow at the farrow.

SONG

There's an unco tune
That ony wund wafts
Frae a piper playin'
Wantin' the chafts.

And an unborn man
Withooten a shape
Whiles sings a sang
You canna escape.

Tak' note o' the tune,
Gi'e words to the sang,
Or you'll ha'e nae peace
Whaurever you gang.

SEA-SERPENT

From "A Sea-Suite"

*"The soul grows clotted by contagion,
Imbodies, and imbrutes till she quite lose
The divine property of her first being."*
                    MILTON

It fits the universe man can ken
As a man's soul fits his body;

And the spirit o' God gaed dirlin' through't
In stound upon stound o' pride
Draughtin' his thick-comin' notions o' life
As fast as they flashed in owre'm
When there was sea and licht and little beside.

His joy in his wark gied it lint-white lines
Brichter than lichtnin's there.
Like starry keethins its fer-aff coils
Quhile the nearer rings
Ran like a raw o' siller girds
On the wan-shoggin' tap o' the waters
And soupled awa' like wings.

Round the cantles o' space Leviathan flickered
Like Borealis in flicht
Or eelied thro' the poorin' deeps o' the sea
Like a ca' o' whales and was tint to sicht,
But aye in its endless ups-and-doons
As it dwined to gleids or walloped in rings
God like a Jonah whirled in its kite
But blithe as a loon in the swings.

Syne it gethered in on itsel' again
And lowed like the plans o' Heaven,
A michty puzzle o' flames that mirrored
The ends o' the thocht
—For aince He had hit upon Life itsel'
Hoo c'u'd the mere mak'in o' lives
Keep gien'm the thrills He socht?

And the serpent's turned like a wud sin' syne
That canna be seen for the trees
Or's tint as the mid-day sun is tint
In the glory o' its rays,
And God has forgotten, it seems,
In the moniplied maze o' the forms
The a'efauld form o' the maze.

Whiles a blindin' movement tak's in my life
As a quick tide swallows a sea.
I feel like a star on a starry nicht,
A'e note in a symphony,
And ken that the serpent is movin' still,
A movement that a' thing shares,
Yet it seems as tho' it twines in a nicht
When God neither kens nor cares.

But mebbe yet the hert o' a man
When it feels the twist in its quick
O' the link that binds it to ilka life,
A'e stab in the nerves o' the stars,
'll raise a cry that'll fetch God back
To the hert o' His wark again?
—Though Nature and Man ha'e cried in vain
Rent in unendin' wars!

Or does the serpent dern wi' a mortal wound
Unseen in its unseen side,
And are the surges that still come owre us
Like the thraws o' a stricken man
—Wi' the pooer to inform undeemis lives
Wi' the single movement o' life nae mair,
But ebbin' fast—and ebbin' for aye—
Tho' we skinkle ahint like pools in the san'?

O Thou that we'd fain be ane wi' again
Frae the weary lapses o' self set free,
Be to oor lives as life is to Daith,
And lift and licht us eternally.
Frae the howe o' the sea to the heich o' the lift,
To the licht as licht to the darkness is,
Spring fresh and fair frae the spirit o' God
Like the a'e first thocht that He kent was His.

Loup again in His brain, O Nerve,
Like a trumpet-stang,
Lichtnin-clear as when first owre Chaos
Your shape you flang

—And swee his mind till the mapamound,
And meanin' o' ilka man,
Brenn as then wi' the instant pooer
O' an only plan!

LOCKED

The folk a' yammer that they've never seen
A corpse thraw owt like thine;
But e'en alive ye were byordinar thrawn
As we ken fine.

They've wide-flung ilka door and ilka drawer
But syne ye thraw like mad.
Nowt's lockit i' the hoose abies my hert.
—*Thraw on, my lad!*

THUNDERSTORM

I'se warran' ye're rawn for the yirdin'
An' no' muckle wunner,
When the lift's like a revelled hesp
I' the han's o' the thunner.

God's banes! when the haill warl' dirls
An' jows like a bell
An' the lichtnin's fleerin' atour
I'm waesome mysel'.

HUNGRY WATERS

For a Little Boy
at Linlithgow

The auld men o' the sea
Wi' their daberlack hair
Ha'e dackered the coasts
O' the country fell sair.

They gobble owre cas'les,
Chow mountains to san';
Or lang they'll eat up
The haill o' the lan'.

Lickin' their white lips
An' yowlin' for mair,
The auld men o' the sea
Wi' their daberlack hair.

TAM

Een that were blue as corncockles
  'll twinkle nae mair,
Nor a lauch like the simmer lichtnin'
Jouk i' the air.

A face that was reid as a cock's kaim
Is grey as a stane,
And a man for the weemun is lyin'
Himsel'—alane.

FOCHERTY

Duncan Gibb o' Focherty's
A giant to the likes o' me,
His face is like a roarin' fire
For love o' the barley-bree.

He gangs through this and the neebrin' shire
Like a muckle rootless tree
—And here's a caber for Daith to toss
That'll gi'e his spauld a swee!

His gain was aye a wee'r man's loss
And he took my lass frae me,
An wi' mony a quean besides
He's ta'en his liberty.

I've had nae chance wi' the likes o' him
And he's tramped me underfit
—Blaefaced afore the throne o' God
He'll get his fairin' yet.

He'll be like a bull in the sale-ring there,
And I'll lauch lood to see,
Till he looks up and canna mak' oot
Whether it's God—or me!

SABINE

A lass cam' to oor gairden-yett
An' ringle-e'ed was she,
And sair she spiered me for a leaf,
A leaf o' savin'-tree.

An' white as a loan soup was she,
The lass wha'd tint her snood,

[38]

But oot my gudewife cam' an' straucht
To rate the slut begood.

The lassie looked at her an' leuch,
"Och, plaise yersel!" said she,
"Ye'd better gi'e me what I seek
Than learn what I've to gi'e."

PARLEY OF BEASTS

Auld Noah was at hame wi' them a',
The lion and the lamb,
Pair by pair they entered the Ark
And he took them as they cam'.

If twa o' ilka beist there is
Into this room sud come,
Wad I cud welcome them like him,
And no' staun' gowpin' dumb!

Be chief wi' them and they wi' me
And a' wi' ane anither
As Noah and his couples were
There in the Ark thegither.

It's fain I'd mell wi' tiger and tit,
Wi' elephant and eel,
But noo-a-days e'en wi' ain's se
At hame it's hard to feel.

THE LOVE-SICK LASS

As white's the blossom on the rise
The wee lass was.
That 'bune the green risp i' the fu' mune
Cannily blaws.

Sweet as the cushie's croud she sang
Wi' 'r wee reid mou'—
Wha sauch-like i' the lowe o' luve
Lies sabbin' noo!

WILD ROSES

Wi' sae mony wild roses
Dancin' and daffin',
It looks as tho' a'
The countryside's laffin'.

But I maun ca' canny
Gin I'm no' to cumber
Sic a lichtsome warld
Wi' my hert's auld lumber.

Hoo I mind noo your face
When I spiered for a kiss
'Ud gae joukin' a' airts
And colourin' like this!

THE WIDOWER

Auld wife, on a nicht like this
Pitmirk and snell
It's hard for a man like me
To believe in himsel'.

A wheen nerves that hotch in the void,
And a drappie bluid,
And a buik that craves for the doonfa'
Like a guisand cude.

For Guid's sake, Jean, wauken up!
A word frae your mou'
Has knit my gantin' timbers
Thegither or noo.

THE LONG BLACK NIGHT

The nicht gangs stilpin' thwart the mune
A' stoichert up wi' starnies there.
Whaur are ye gan', O braw black nicht,
Wi' yer strawn o' beads sae fair?

"I dinna ken," says the lang black nicht,
Thringin' the starns on's shoulders there.
"I maun gang stilpin' thwart the mune,
But I kenna whaur—nor care."

TO ONE WHO URGES MORE
AMBITIOUS FLIGHTS

Dinna come tae bauld my glead,
It'll be a bear-meal-raik.
Wee bit sangs are a' I need,
Wee bit sangs for auld times' sake!
Here are ferlies nae yin sees
In a bensil o' a bleeze.

THE DEAD LIEBKNECHT

After the German
of Rudolf Leonhardt

His corpse owre a' the city lies
In ilka square and ilka street
His spilt bluid floods the vera skies
And nae hoose but is darkened wi't.

The factory horns begin to blaw
Thro' a' the city, blare on blare,
The lowsin' time o' workers a',
Like emmits skailin' everywhere.

And wi' his white teeth shinin' yet
The corpse lies smilin' underfit.

IN MYSIE'S BED

They ha'e laid the black ram i' Mysie's bed,
And keepit it frae baain'
Wi' a gude fotherin' O' kail-blades and a cloot
Soaken i' milk.

Quo Mysie, lauchin', "Gin I s'ud wed
He may be ca'd a man
But I'll haud him as dumb, ye maun ha'e nae doot,
As owt o' this ilk."

GUID CONCEIT

Fear not, my hert, and what can ail ye?
Be you ever free and prood
As yon bonnie capercailyie
Wingin' owre the winter clood!

MORNING

The Day loups up (for she kens richt weel
Owre lang wi' the Nicht she mauna lig)
And plunks the sun i' the lift aince mair
Like a paddle-doo i' the raim-pig.

UNDER THE GREENWOOD TREE

After the Cretan

A sodger laddie's socht a hoose,
A hoose and toon to bide in.
He's fund a road but never a hoose
Or toon the haill warld wide in.

And syne he's come to an auld green tree
—Then wae for a sodger loon
Wha's tint his way frae the battlefield
And here maun lay him doon.

There's brainches here for his graith o' war,
A root to tether his horse,
And a shaddaw for a windin' sheet
To row aboot his corse.

THE THREE FISHES

After the Cretan

I am a fisher lad and nane
Can better wield a gad than me,
And a'e day to the burn I've gane
And got me fishes three.

I've gi'en them to my minnie syne
And in the pan they're loupin',
When straucht they cheenge to lassies fine
And send my mither gowpin'.

O three braw queans, I see them plain
And a' as different as can be,
But noo they're ane, my mither's gane,
And Love's alane wi' me.

THE ROBBER

After the Cretan

A robber cam' to my hoose
And theft was a' his ploy,
Nor gowd nor siller could he find
And sae he stow my joy.

He stow the kisses frae my mou'
And mony a lauch and tear,
And syne begood upon my bluid
And toomed it vera near.

I gied him a' he wanted
And mebbe a wee thing mair,
I dinna ken what a' he took
But that's no' here nor there.

For aye he gied for a' he took,
And better gied than took,
And I've a bonnie laddie noo
And breists for him to sook.

- I -

Gin I resisted ill
I'd haud it in me still
Dernin' aneth my will
—*Resist not ill!*

Till nicht sall fa' nae mair,
Thunder nor lichtnin' there,
But a' thing grown fu' fair
And nae Daith there.

The fox has its hole
And in my soul
Room shall I gi'e
A' God let's be.

And sall resist nae ill
While ocht is made to kill
And ocht defenceless still
In token o' His will.

Gin Murder like a clood
Whiles comes owre my bluid
I'se warrant it is food
That's needfu' to my guid.

And Poverty and Daith
I need them as Earth needs
The winter's bitter braith
To lowse the simmer's seeds.

Sin' God has cherished us
Wi' carefu' cruelty
Let us wi' nae mair fuss
Follow his husbandry.

But wha 'ud follow God
Maun tak' a flegsome road!
It's time to try God's way
When we've his poo'er tae.

For we can kill, but wha
Can fetch to life ana'?
We mauna follow God
Afore we ken the road.

Christ descendit into Hell
And for a' that we can tell
A' that's guid on Earth may be
Gaen' like Him through devilry.

But he didna bide in Hell,
Didna' turn a Deil Himsel',
And gin we'd wun through it tae
We maun try to find His way.

O the Earth may be in Hell,
I may be a Deil mysel',
Mebbe Christ gaed through it but
Ithers in't foraye are shut.

A' that's guid on Earth may be
Gaen' like Christ through devilry?
—Then the devilry ser's God tae
Only in anither way?

Wha can say which is the better?
Wisna Christ the Devil's debtor?

V

Christ was sent to save mankind.
That's eneuch for us, you'll find
God Himsel'

May gang to Hell
To save the Deil
In time as weel.

That's no' for us—we're nocht but men,
The ways o' God we canna ken,
So let's
Leave'm alane
To square His debts
And mind oor ain.

- VI -
The sun pits oot a fire
And the flames o' Hell turn wan
As through the ugsome place
Passes the Son o' Man.

He looks aboot him syne,
Hell isna to be seen,
But ceases to exist
As it had never been.

- VII -
When foxes ettle
Hoose-dogs to be,
And eagles settle
In the hen-ree,

The meek may inherit
The Earth, but til then
We maun ha'e spirit
Gin we're to be men.

- VIII -
Earth's sma'-bookit
Under a clood
That gars't shine bricht
As ony star could.

[47]

O little I thocht
It could seem sae fair
Till my black mood
Kindled it there!

- IX -

Bonnie, Earth shines frae the heich o' the lift
But eagles rise frae't to begin wi'
And syne are nocht but dust o' its dust
When their wings are din' wi.

I rise and fa' in my restless way
And Earth seems big syne or sma'
But it'll be the same at the end as tho'
I'd never flown ava!

- X -

As the stane frae the sepulchre's
Mooth fell doon
I sall be shot
O' the warld's wecht soon.

The wecht o' my body,
The wecht o' my soul,
Like the stane frae the mooth
O' the sepulchre roll.

This is the tune
Fu' o' elation
That'll wauken the giants
In the cave o' creation.

SCUNNER

Your body derns
In its graces again
As the dreich grun' does

[48]

In the gowden grain,
And oot o' the daith
O' pride you rise
Wi' beauty yet
For a hauf-disguise.

The skinklan' stars
Are but distant dirt.
Tho' fer owre near
You are still—whiles—girt
Wi' the bonnie licht
You bood ha'e tint
—And I lo'e Love
Wi' a scunner in't.

SERVANT GIRL'S BED

The talla spales
And the licht loups oot,
Fegs, it's your ain creesh
Lassie, I doot
And the licht that reeled
Loose on't a wee
Was the bonny lowe
O' Eternity.

JIMSY: AN IDIOT

When Jimsy lauchs there's naething
But his lauchter to be seen,
As gin he'd flyped himsel'
Afore your vera een.

He tak's the licht o' Heaven
As a gargle for his mooth

And a'e movement o' his chafts
Mells the North and Sooth.

He owre's the Earth as a snake
Swallows an egg, and but
A glisk o' the lift's to be seen
Like a holin' rabbit's scut.

And afore God kens whaur He is
He's under the pap o' his hass
And his teeth are closin' ahint Him
And His pass is Jonah's pass.

EMPTY VESSEL

I met ayont the cairney
A lass wi' tousie hair
Singin' till a bairnie
That was nae langer there.

Wunds wi warlds to swing
Dinna sing sae sweet,
The licht that bends owre a' thing
Is less ta'en up wi't.

THE FAIRMER'S LASS

The fairmer's lass has kilted her coats
An's muckin' oot the byre,
Her hair is a' aboot her een
An' her braid face is fire.

*"The worms ha'e a' come oot o' the earth
An' streek their lengths a' airts.*

Their reid nebs eisen i' the sun
But wae's me for oor herts!

"The aidle-pool is a glory o' gowd
—My hert is black inside,
The worms may streek to their herts' content
But they ha'e nocht to hide."

THE BONNIE LOWE

Aboun the snaw-white channel
The bluid-reid roosies bleeze
—Ai, lassie, but I'd liefer hae
The mou' ye winna gie's.

Like greeshuckle the petals lie
O' roosies tashed to bits
—But a'e wee cheep for evermair
In flame has rowed my wits.

SUNNY GALE

The trees were like bubblyjocks
In the wild gowd wind,
The way that they fattened
And the way that they thinned
And the stramash they made.

Noo wi' taps streekit oot,
Eisenin' into the sun,
Their leafs scrauchin'; and syne
Swallin' back on the grun'
And tint in the shade.

But aye they raxed oot
Whustlin' heich in the lift
And aye loutit back
Wi' orra leafs left adrift
In their shaddaws' black whirlpools

Round my lugs the a'e meenit
In squabbles o' green
And the neist in a wan doze
Fer awa' they'd be seen
Or half-smoored i' the mools.

ON THE THRESHOLD

*Suggested by the French
of Gustave Kahn*

Guisers I ken
Your fause faces under
Hidena' the face
That has thrilled me wi' wunder.

Ye ships that rock
A' the seev'n seas owre
Through nane o' your keels
Need my een fash to glower.

By land nor water
Nor lift sall I find
The love I can never
Get oot o' my mind.

The warld canna haud
The quean that I seek
Yet nocht sall the door
That leads to her steek. . . .

Life keeks in the winda,
Daith tirls at the pin
—But she loups to the threshold
To welcome me in.

KRANG

Sideways hurled
The krang o' a warld
The sun has flensed
Is lyin' forenenst.

"Whirlwind, whirlwind
Cwa' and look sharp
And gi'e me a tune
On this white harp.

"And I sall sing
The kind o' sang
That roond the krang
O' a world s'ud ring."

SUPPER TO GOD

S'ud ye ha'e to gi'e
His supper to God
What like fare
'Ud ye set on the brod?

Lint-white linen
And siller-ware
And a tassie o' floo'ers
In the centre there?

Pot-luck 'ud be best,
I need ha'e nae fear
Gin God s'ud come
To's supper here.

Deal scrubbed like snaw
And blue-and-white delf
And let ilk ane
Rax oot for hisself.

A' that I'd ask
Is no' to ken whan,
Or gin it's Him
Or a trev'lin man.

Wi' powsoudie or drummock,
Lapper-milk kebbuck and farle,
We can aye wecht the wame
O' anither puir carle.

FROM "SONGS FOR CHRISTINE"

Aetat a year and a half

- I -
Fairy Tales

Ither folks' fairy tales
'll no' dae for you.
You maun ha'e your ain
As new as you're new.

In the licht o' the mune
We'll gang oot wi' a girn
And see if we canna
Catch them yince-yirn.

Fairy tales are aye best
When they're catched on the hop,
—There's naething worth ha'en
To be hed frae a shop.

- II -
Bubblyjock

It's hauf like a bird and hauf like a bogle
And juist stands in the sun there and bouks.
It's a wunder its heid disna burst
The way it's aye raxin' its chouks.

Syne it twists its neck like a serpent
But canna get oot a richt note
For the bubblyjock swallowed the bagpipes
And the blether stuck in its throat.

THE QUEST

- I -
I canna see you, lass,
For your face and your hair.
Are you mair than them
For they're ill to spare?

There's something I'd hear
Wert no' for your voice
Wert better worth hearin'
—But wow for the choice!

- II -
C'wa' into the darkness
—Whatever's to ken
Aiblins your flesh
'll no' hide frae me then!

[55]

But if need be I'll tak' ye
Through Daith to fin' oot
And be haud'n nae mair
Wi' a shaddaw o' doot.

And och! for your beauty
And och! for your braith
Gin you're the wumman I want
On the yon side o' Daith!

GAIRMSCOILE

Aulder than mammoth or than mastodon
Deep i' the herts o' a' men lurk scaut-heid
Skrymmorie monsters few daur look upon.
Brides sometimes catch their wild een, scansin' reid,
Beekin' abune the herts they thocht to lo'e
And horror-stricken ken that i' themselves
A like beast stan's, and lookin' love thro' and thro'
Meets the reid een wi' een like seevun hells.
. . . Nearer the twa beasts draw, and, couplin' brak
The bubbles o' twa sauls and the haill warld gangs black.

Yet wha has heard the beasts' wild matin'-call
To ither music syne can gi'e nae ear.
The nameless lo'enotes haud him in a thrall.
Forgot are guid and ill, and joy and fear.
. . . My bluid sall thraw a dark hood owre my een
And I sall venture deep into the hills
Whaur, scaddows on the skyline, can be seen
—Twinin' the sun's brent broo wi' plaited horns
As gin they crooned it wi' a croon o' thorns—
The beasts in wha's wild cries a' Scotland's destiny thrills.

The lo'es o' single herts are strays; but there
The herds that draw the generations are,
And whasae hears them roarin', evermair
Is yin wi' a' that gangs to mak' or mar

The spirit o' the race, and leads it still
Whither it can be led, 'yont a' desire and will.
Wergeland, I mind o' thee—for thy bluid tae
Kent the rouch dirl o' an auld Scots strain,
—A dour dark burn that has its ain wild say
Thro' a' the thrang bricht babble o' Earth's flood.
Behold, thwart my ramballiach life again,
What thrawn and roothewn dreams, royat and rude,
Reek forth—a foray dowless herts condemn—
While chance wi' rungs o' sang or silence renshels them.

(A foray frae the past—and future tae
Sin Time's a blindness will thraw aff some day!)
. . . On the rumgunshoch sides o' hills forgotten
Life bears beasts rowtin' that it deemed extinct,
And, sudden, on the hapless cities linked
In canny civilisation's canty dance
Poor herds o' heich-skeich monsters, misbegotten,
. . . Streets clear afore the scarmoch advance:
Frae every winnock skimmerin' een keek oot
To see what sic camsteerie cast-offs are aboot.
Cast-offs —But wha mak's life a means to ony end?
This sterves and that stuff's fu', scraps this and succours that?
The best survive there's nane but fules contend.
Na! Ilka daith is but a santit need.
. . . Lo! what bricht flames o' beauty are lit at
The unco' een o' lives that Life thocht deid
Till winnock efter winnock kindles wi' a sense
O' gain and glee—as gin a mair intense
Starn nor the sun had risen in wha's licht
Mankind and beasts anew, wi' gusto, see their plicht.

Mony's the auld hauf-human cry I ken
Fa's like a revelation on the herts o' men
As tho' the graves were split and the first man
Grippit the latest wi' a freendly han'
. . . And there's forgotten shibboleths o' the Scots
Ha'e keys to senses lockit to us yet
—Coorse words that shamble thro' oor minds like stots,
Syne turn on's muckle een wi' doonsin' emerauds lit.

[57]

I hear nae "hee-haw" but I mind the day
A'e donkey strunted doon a palm-strewn way
As Chesterton has sung; nae wee click-clack
O' hoofs but to my hert at aince comes back
Jammes' Prayer to Gang to Heaven wi' the Asses;
And shambles-ward nae cattle-beast e'er passes
But I mind hoo the saft een o' the kine
Lichted Christ's craidle wi' their canny shine.

Hee-Haw! Click-Clack! And Cock-a-doodle-doo!
—Wull Gabriel in Esperanto cry
Or a' the warld's undeemis jargons try?
It's soon', no' sense, that faddoms the herts o' men,
And by my sangs the rouch auld Scots I ken
E'en herts that ha'e nae Scots'll dirl richt thro'
As nocht else could—for here's a language rings
Wi' datchie sesames, and names for nameless things.

- II -
Wergeland, my warld as thine "ca' canny" cries,
And daurna lippen to auld Scotland's virr.
Ah, weel ye kent—as Carlyle quo' likewise—
Maist folk are thowless fules wha downa stir,
Crouse sumphs that hate nane 'bies wha'd wauken them.
To them my Pegasus tae's a crocodile.
Whummelt I tak' a bobquaw for the lift.
Insteed o' sangs my mou' drites eerned phlegm.
. . . Natheless like thee I stalk on mile by mile,
Howk'n up deid stumps o' thocht, and saw'in my eident gift.
Ablachs, and scrats, and dorbels o' a' kinds
Aye'd drob me wi' their puir eel-droonin' minds,
Wee drochlin' craturs drutling their bit thochts
The dorty bodies! Feech! Nae Sassunuch drings
'll daunton me. —Tak' ye sic things for poets?
Cock-lairds and drotes depert Parnassus noo.
A'e flash o' wit the lot to drodlich dings.
Rae, Martin, Sutherland—the dowless crew,
I'll twine the dow'd sheaves o' their toom-ear'd corn,
Bind them wi' pity and dally them wi' scorn.

Lang ha'e they posed as men o' letters here,
Dounhaddin' the Doric and keepin't i' the draiks,
Drivellin' and druntin', wi' mony a datchie sneer
. . . But soon we'll end the haill eggtaggle, fegs!
. . . The auld volcanoes rummle 'neath their feet,
And a' their shoddy lives 'll soon be drush,
Danders o' Hell! They feel th' unwelcome heat,
The deltit craturs, and their sauls are slush,
For we ha'e faith in Scotland's hidden poo'ers,
The present's theirs, but a' the past and future's oors.

A HERD OF DOES

Gildermorie

There is no doe in all the herd
Whose heart is not her heart,
O Earth, with all their glimmering eyes
She sees thee as thou art.

Like them in shapes of fleeting fire
She mingles with the light
Till whoso saw her sees her not
And doubts his former sight.

They come and go and none can say
Who sees them subtly run
If they indeed are forms of life
Or figments of the sun.

So is she one with Heaven here,
Confounding mortal eyes,
As do the holy dead who move
Innumerous in the skies.

But now and then a wandering man
May glimpse as on he goes
A golden movement of her dreams
As 'twere a herd of does.

YOUR IMMORTAL MEMORY, BURNS!

Thought may demit
Its functions fit
While still to thee, O Burns,
The punctual stomach of thy people turns.

Most folks agree
That poetry
Is of no earthly use
Save thine—which yields at least this Annual Excuse!

Other cults die:
But who'll deny
That you your mob in thrall
Will keep, O Poet Intestinal?

From wame to wame
Wags on your fame,
Once more through all the world
On fronts of proud abdomena unfurled.

These be thy train,
No-Soul and No-Brain,
And Humour-Far-From-It,
Bunkum and Bung, Swallow-All and Vomit.

Palate and Paunch,
Enthusiasts staunch,
Gladly aver again,
"Behold one poet did not live in vain!"

"But us no Buts!"
Cry Gullet and Guts
Whose parrots of souls
Resemble a clever ventriloquist's dolls.

Be of good cheer
Since once a year

Poetry is not too pure
A savoury for shopkeepers to endure!

And, dined and wined,
Solicitors find
Their platitudes assume
The guise of intuitions that illume

The hidden heart
Of Human Art
And strike in ignorance
On wonders of unpredicated chance.

A boozy haze
Enchants your lays
And Gluttony for a change
Finds Genius within accosting range,

And cottons on!
—Thy power alone
The spectacle attests
Of drunken bourgeois on the Muses' breasts!

Only thy star
Falls from afar
To swim into the ken
Of countless masses of befuddled men,

In their hearts' skies
Like barmaids' eyes
Glabrous to glitter till
Their minds like rockets shoot away and spill

These vivid clots
Of idiot thoughts
Wherewith our Scottish life
Is once a year incomparable rife!

* * *

Belly will praise
Thee all its days
And spread to all nations
Thy fame in belchings and regurgitations,

While mean minds soar
And hiccoughs adore
And butcher-meat faces
Triumphant, transfigured, example thy graces!

From

A Drunk Man Looks at the Thistle

1926

SIC TRANSIT GLORIA SCOTIA

I amna' fou' saw muckle as tired—deid dune.
It's gey and hard wark coupin' gless for gless
Wi' Cruivie and Gilsanquhar and the like,
And I'm no' juist as bauld as aince I wes.

The elbuck fankles in the coorse o' time,
The sheckle's no' sae souple, and the thrapple
Grows deef and dour: nae langer up and doun
Gleg as a squirrel speils the Adam's apple.

Forbye, the stuffie's no' the real Mackay,
The sun's sel' aince, as sune as ye began it,
Riz in your vera saul: but what keeks in
Noo is in truth the vilest "saxpenny planet."

And as the worth's gane doun the cost has risen.
Yin canna thow the cockles o' yin's hert
Wi'oot ha'en' cauld feet noo, jalousin' what
The wife'll say (I dinna blame her fur't).

It's robbin' Peter to pey Paul at least. . . .
And a' that's Scotch aboot it is the name,
Like a' thing else ca'd Scottish nooadays
—A' destitute o' speerit juist the same.

(To prove my saul is Scots I maun begin
Wi' what's still deemed Scots and the folk expect,
And spire up syne by visible degrees
To heichts whereo' the fules ha'e never recked.

But aince I get them there I'll whummle them
And souse the craturs in the nether deeps,
—For it's nae choice, and ony man s'ud wish
To dree the goat's weird tae as weel's the sheep's!)

Heifetz in tartan, and Sir Harry Lauder!
Whaur's Isadora Duncan dancin' noo?
Is Mary Garden in Chicago still
And Duncan Grant in Paris—and me fou'?

Sic transit gloria Scotia—a' the floo'ers
O' the Forest are wede awa'. (A blin' bird's nest
Is aiblins biggin' in the thistle tho'? . . .
And better blin' if'ts brood is like the rest!)

You canna gang to a Burns supper even
Wi'oot some wizened scrunt o' a knock-knee
Chinee turns roon to say "Him Haggis—velly goot!"
And ten to wan the piper is a Cockney.

No' wan in fifty kens a wurd Burns wrote
But misapplied is a'body's property,
And gin there was his like alive the day
They'd be the last a kennin' haund to gi'e—

Croose London Scotties wi' their braw shirt fronts
And a' their fancy freen's, rejoicin'
That similah gatherings in Timbuctoo,
Bagdad—and Hell, nae doot—are voicin'

Burns' sentiments o' universal love,
In pidgin' English or in wild-fowl Scots,
And toastin' ane wha's nocht to them but an
Excuse for faitherin' Genius wi' *their* thochts.

A' *they've* to say was aften said afore
A lad was born in Kyle to blaw aboot.
What unco fate mak's *him* the dumpin'-grun'
For a' the sloppy rubbish they jaw oot?

[64]

Mair nonsense has been uttered in his name
Than in ony's barrin' liberty and Christ.
If this keeps spreedin' as the drink declines,
Syne turns to tea, wae's me for the *Zeitgeist!*

Rabbie, wad'st thou wert here—the warld hath need,
And Scotland mair sae, o' the likes o' thee!
The whisky that aince moved your lyre's become
A laxative for a' loquacity.

O gin they'd stegh their guts and haud their wheesht
I'd thole it, for "a man's a man," I ken,
But though the feck ha'e plenty o' the "a' that,"
They're nocht but zoologically men.

I'm haverin', Rabbie, but ye understaun'
It gets my dander up to see your star
A bauble in Babel, bandied like a saxpence
'Twixt Burbank's Baedeker and Bleistein's cigar.

There's nane sae ignorant but think they can
Expatiate on *you,* if on nae ither.
The sumphs ha'e ta'en you at your wurd, and, fegs!
The foziest o' them claims to be a—Brither!

Syne "Here's the cheenge"—the star o' Rabbie Burns.
Sma' cheenge, "Twinkle, Twinkle." The memory slips
As G. K. Chesterton heaves up to gi'e
"The Immortal Memory" in a huge eclipse,

Or somebody else as famous if less fat.
You left the like in Embro in a scunner
To booze wi' thieveless cronies sic as me.
I'se warrant you'd shy clear o' a' the hunner

Odd Burns Clubs tae, or ninety-nine o' them,
And haud your birthday in a different kip
Whaur your name isna ta'en in vain—as Christ
Gied a' Jerusalem's Pharisees the slip,

—Christ wha'd ha'e been Chief Rabbi gin he'd lik't!—
Wi' publicans and sinners to foregather,
But, losh! the publicans noo are Pharisees,
And I'm no' shair o' maist the sinners either.

But that's aside the point! I've got fair waun'ert.
It's no' that I'm sae fou' as juist deid dune,
And dinna ken as muckle's whar I am
Or hoo I've come to sprawl here 'neth the mune.

That's it! It isna me that's fou' at a',
But the fu' mune, the doited jade, that's led
Me fer agley, or 'mogrified the warld.
—For a' I ken I'm safe in my ain bed.

Jean! Jean! Gin she's no' here it's no' *oor* bed,
Or else I'm dreamin' deep and canna wauken,
But it's a fell queer dream if this is no'
A real hillside—and thae things thistles and bracken!

It's hard wark haud'n by a thocht worth ha'en'
And harder speakin't, and no' for ilka man;
Maist Thocht's like whisky—a thoosan' under proof,
And a sair price is pitten on't even than.

As Kirks wi' Christianity ha'e dune,
Burns' Clubs wi' Burns—wi' a' thing it's the same,
The core o' ocht is only for the few,
Scorned by the mony, thrang wi'ts empty name.

And a' the names in History mean nocht
To maist folk but "ideas o' their ain,"
The vera opposite o' onything
The Deid 'ud awn gin they cam' back again.

A greater Christ, a greater Burns, may come.
The maist they'll dae is to gi'e bigger pegs
To folly and conceit to hank their rubbish on.
They'll cheenge folks' talk but no' their natures, fegs!

A VISION OF MYSELF

I maun feed frae the common trough ana'
Whaur a' the lees o' hope are jumbled up;
While centuries like pigs are slorpin' owre't
Sall my wee 'oor be cryin': "Let pass this cup?"

In wi' your gruntle then, puir wheengin' saul,
Lap up the ugsome aidle wi' the lave,
What gin it's your ain vomit that you swill
And frae Life's gantin' and unfaddomed grave?

I doot I'm geylies mixed, like Life itsel',
But I was never ane that thocht to pit
An ocean in a mutchkin. As the haill's
Mair than the pairt sae I than reason yet.

I dinna haud the warld's end in my heid
As maist folk think they dae; nor filter truth
In fishy gills through which its tides may poor
For ony *animalculae* forsooth.

I lauch to see my crazy little brain
—And ither folks'—tak'n itsel' seriously,
And in a sudden lowe o' fun my saul
Blinks dozent as the owl I ken't to be.

I'll ha'e nae hauf-way hoose, but aye be whaur
Extremes meet—it's the only way I ken
To dodge the curst conceit o' bein' richt
That damns the vast majority o' men.

I'll bury nae heid like an ostrich's,
Nor yet believe my een and naething else.
My senses may advise me, but I'll be
Mysel' nae maitter what they tell's. . . .

I ha'e nae doot some foreign philosopher
Has wrocht a system oot to justify

A' this: but I'm a Scot wha blin'ly follows
Auld Scottish instincts, and I winna try.

For I've nae faith in ocht I can explain,
And stert whaur the philosophers leave aff,
Content to glimpse its loops I dinna ettle
To land the sea serpent's sel' wi' ony gaff.

Like staundin' water in a pocket o'
Impervious clay I'pray I'll never be,
Cut aff and self-sufficient, but let reenge
Heichts o' the lift and benmaist deeps o' sea.

Water! Water! There was owre muckle o't
In yonder whisky, sae I'm in deep water
(And gin I could wun hame I'd be in het,
For even Jean maun natter, natter, natter). . . .

And in the toon that I belang tae
—What tho'ts Montrose or Nazareth?—
Helplessly the folk continue
To lead their livin' death! . . .

POET'S PUB *

*At darknin' hings abune the howff
A weet and wild and eisenin' air.
Spring's spirit wi' its waesome sough
Rules owre the drucken stramash there.*

*And heich abune the vennel's pokiness,
Whaur a' the white-weshed cottons lie;
The Inn's sign blinters in the mochiness,
And lood and shrill the bairnies cry.*

* From the Russian of Alexander Blok.

[68]

The hauflins 'yont the burgh boonds
Gang ilka nicht, and a' the same,
Their bonnets cocked; their bluid that stounds
Is playin' at a fine auld game.

And on the lochan there, hauf-herted
Wee screams and creakin' oar-locks soon'
And in the lift, heich, hauf-averted,
The mune looks owre the yirdly roon'.

And ilka evenin', derf and serious
(Jean ettles nocht o' this, puir lass),
In liquor, raw yet still mysterious,
A'e freend's aye mirrored in my glass.

Ahint the sheenin' coonter gruff
Thrang barmen ding the tumblers doun
"In vino veritas" cry rough
And reid-een'd fules that in it droon.

But ilka evenin' fey and fremt
(Is it a dream nae wauk'nin' proves?)
As to a trystin'-place undreamt,
A silken leddy darkly moves.

Slow gangs she by the drunken anes,
And lanely by the winnock sits;
Frae'r robes, atour the sunken anes,
A rooky dwamin' perfume flits.

Her gleamin' silks, the taperin'
O' her ringed fingers, and her feathers
Move dimly like a dream wi'in,
While endless faith aboot them gethers.

I seek, in this captivity,
To pierce the veils that darklin' fa'
—See white clints slidin' to the sea,
And hear the horns o' Elfland blaw.

I ha'e dark secrets' turns and twists,
A sun is gi'en to me to haud,
The whisky in my bluid insists,
And spiers my benmaist history, lad.

And owre my brain the flitterin'
O' the dim feathers gangs ance mair,
And, faddomless, the dark blue glitterin'
O' twa een in the ocean there.

My soul stores up this wealth unspent,
The key is safe and nane's but mine.
You're richt, auld drunk impenitent,
I ken it tae—the truth's in wine!

THE LOOKING GLASS

The munelicht's like a lookin'-glass,
The thistle's like mysel',
But whaur ye've gane, my bonnie lass,
Is mair than I can tell.

Were you a vision o' mysel',
Transmuted by the mellow liquor?
Neist time I glisk you in a glass,
I'se warrant I'll mak' siccar.

A man's a clean contrairy sicht
Turned this way in-ootside,
And, fegs, I feel like Dr. Jekyll
Tak'n guid tent o' Mr. Hyde. . . .

Gurly thistle—hic—you canna
Daunton me wi' your shaggy mien,
I'm sair—hic—needin' a shave,
That's plainly to be seen.

But what aboot it—hic—aboot it
Mony a man's been that afore.
It's no' a fact that in his lugs
A wund like this need roar! . . .

THE UNKNOWN GODDESS *

I ha'e forekent ye! O I ha'e forekent.
The years forecast your face afore they went.
A licht I canna thole is in the lift.
I bide in silence your slow-comin' pace.
The ends o' space are bricht: at last—oh swift!
While terror clings to me—an unkent face!

Ill-faith stirs in me as she comes at last,
The features lang forekent . . . are unforecast.
O it gangs hard wi' me, I am forspent.
Deid dreams ha'e beaten me and a face unkent
And generations that I thocht unborn
Hail the strange Goddess frae my hert's-hert torn! . . .

MY NATION'S SOUL

Or dost thou mak' a thistle o' me, wumman? But for thee
I were as happy as the munelicht, withoot care,
But thocht o' thee—o' thy contempt and ire—
Turns hauf the warld into the youky thistle there,

Feedin' on the munelicht and transformin' it
To this wanrestfu' growth that winna let me be.
The munelicht is the freedom that I'd ha'e
But for this cursèd Conscience thou has set in me.

* Freely adapted from the Russian of Alexander Blok.

It is morality, the knowledge o' Guid and Ill,
Fear, shame, pity, like a will and wilyart growth,
That kills a' else wi'in its reach and craves
Nae less at last than a' the warld to gi'e it scouth.

The need to wark, the need to think, the need to be,
And a'thing that twists Life into a certain shape
And interferes wi' perfect liberty—
These feed this Frankenstein that nae man can escape.

For ilka thing a man can be or think or dae
Aye leaves a million mair unbeen, unthocht, undune,
Till his puir warped performance is,
To a' that micht ha' been, a thistle to the mune.

It is Mortality itsel'—the mortal coil,
Mockin' Perfection, Man afore the Throne o' God
He yet has bigged himsel', Man torn in twa
And glorious in the lift and grisly on the sod! . . .

There's nocht sae sober as a man blin' drunk.
I maun ha'e got an unco bellyfu'
To jaw like this—and yet what I am sayin'
Is a' the apter, aiblins, to be true.

This munelicht's fell like whisky noo I see't
—Am I a thingum mebbe that is kept
Preserved in spirits in a muckle bottle
Lang centuries efter sin' wi' Jean I slept?

—Mounted on a hillside, wi' the thistles
And bracken for verisimilitude,
Like a stuffed bird on metal like a brainch,
Or a seal on a stump o' rock-like wood?

Or am I juist a figure in a scene
O' Scottish life A.D. one-nine-two-five?
The haill thing kelters like a theatre claith
Till I micht fancy that I was alive!

I dinna ken and nae man ever can.
I micht be in my ain bed efter a'.
The haill damned thing's a dream for ocht we ken,
—The Warld and Life and Daith, Heaven, Hell ana'.

We maun juist tak' things as we find them then,
And mak' a kirk or mill o' them as we can,
—And yet I feel this muckle thistle's staun'in'
Atween me and the mune as pairt o' a Plan.

It isna there—nor me—by accident.
We're brocht thegither for a certain reason,
Ev'n gin it's naething mair than juist to gi'e
My jaded soul a necessary *frisson*.

I never saw afore a thistle quite
Sae intimately, or a sic an 'oor.
There's something in the fickle licht that gi'es
A different life to't and an unco poo'er.

THE GOTHIC THISTLE *

*"Rootit on gressless peaks, whaur its erect
And jaggy leafs, austerely cauld and dumb,
Haud the slow scaly serpent in respect,
The Gothic thistle, whaur the insect's hum
Soon's fer aff, lifts abune the rock it scorns
Its rigid virtue for the Heavens to see.
The too'ering boulders gaird it. And the bee
Mak's honey frae the roses on its thorns."*

But that's a Belgian refugee, of coorse.
This Freudian complex has somehoo slunken
Frae Scotland's soul—the Scots aboulia—
Whilst a' its *terra nullius* is *betrunken*.

* From the Belgian poet, Georges Ramaeckers.

And a' the country roon' aboot it noo
Lies clapt and shrunken syne like somebody wha
Has lang o' seven devils been possessed;
Then when he turns a corner tines them a',

Or like a body that has tint its soul,
Perched like a monkey on its heedless kist,
Or like a sea that peacefu' fa's again
When frae its deeps an octopus is fished.

I canna feel it has to dae wi' me
Mair than a composite diagram o'
Cross-sections o' my forbears' organs
—And mine—'ud bring a kind o' freen'ly glow.

And yet like bindweed through my clay it's run,
And a' my folks'—it's queer to see't unroll.
My ain soul looks me in the face, as 'twere,
And mair than my ain soul—my nation's soul!

And sall a Belgian pit it into words
And sing a sang to't syne, and no' a Scot?
Oors is a wilder thistle, and Ramaeckers
Canna bear aff the gree—avaunt the thocht!

To meddle wi' the thistle and to pluck
The figs frae't is *my* métier, I think.
Awak' my muse, and gin you're in puir fettle,
We aye can blame it on th' inferior drink.

T. S. Eliot—it's a Scottish name—
Afore he wrote "The Waste Land" s'ud ha'e come
To Scotland here. He wad ha'e written
A better poem syne—like this, by gum!

Type o' the Wissenschaftsfeindlichkeit,
Begriffsmüdigkeit that has gar't
Men try Morphologies der Weltgeschichte,
And mad Expressionismus syne in Art.

THE OCTOPUS *

A shameless thing, for ilka vileness able,
It is deid grey as dust, the dust o' a man.
I perish o' a nearness I canna win awa' frae,
Its deidly coils aboot my buik are thrawn.

A shaggy poulp, embracin' me and stingin',
And as a serpent cauld agen' my hert.
Its scales are poisoned shafts that jag me to the quick
—And waur than them's my scunner's fearfu' smert!

O that its prickles were a knife indeed,
But it is thowless, flabby, dowf, and numb.
Sae sluggishly it drains my benmaist life
A dozent dragon, dreidfu', deef, and dumb.

In mum obscurity it twines its obstinate rings
And hings caressin'ly, its purpose whole;
And this deid thing, whale-white obscenity,
This horror that I writhe in—is my soul!

EBB AND FLOW

Is it the munelicht or a leprosy
That spreids aboot me; and a thistle
Or my ain skeleton through wha's bare banes
A fiendish wund's begood to whistle?

The devil's lauchter has a *hwll* like this.
My face has flown open like a lid
—And gibberin' on a hillside there
Is a' humanity sae lang has hid! . . .

My harns are seaweed—when the tide is in
They swall like blethers and in comfort float,

* Adapted from the Russian of Zinaida Hippius.

But when the tide is oot they lie like gealed
And runkled auld bluid-vessels in a knot!

The munelicht ebbs and flows and wi't my thocht,
Noo movin' mellow and noo lourd and rough.
I ken what I am like in Life and Daith,
But Life and Daith for nae man are enough. . . .

And O! to think that there are members o'
St. Andrew's Societies sleepin' soon',
Wha to the papers wrote afore they bedded
On regimental buttons or buckled shoon,

Or use o' England whar the U.K.'s meent,
Or this or that anent the Blue Saltire,
Recruitin', pedigrees, and Gude kens what,
Filled wi' a proper patriotic fire!

Wad I were them—they've chosen a better pairt,
The couthie craturs, than the ane I've ta'en,
Tyauvin' wi' this root-hewn Scottis soul;
A fer, fer better pairt—except for men.

Nae doot they're sober, as a Scot ne'er was,
Each tethered to a punctual-snorin' missus,
Whilst I, puir fule, owre continents unkent
And wine-dark oceans waunder like Ulysses. . . .

ALL THE INS AND OUTS *

The Mune sits on my bed the nicht unsocht,
And mak's my soul obedient to her will;
And in the dumb-deid, still as dreams are still,
Her pupils narraw to bricht threids that thrill
Aboot the sensuous windin's o' her thocht.

* Suggested by the German of Else Lasker-Schüler.

But ilka windin' has its coonter-pairt
—The opposite 'thoot which it couldna be—
In some wild kink or queer perversity
O' this great thistle, green wi' jealousy,
That breenges 'twixt the munelicht and my hert. . . .

TO THE MUSIC OF THE PIPES

Plant, what are you then? Your leafs
Mind me o' the pipes' lood drone
—And a' your purple tops
Are the pirly-wirly notes
That gang staggerin' owre them as they groan.

Or your leafs are alligators
That ha'e gobbled owre a haill
Company o' Heilant sodgers,
And left naethin' but the toories
O' their Balmoral bonnets to tell the tale.

Or a muckle bellows blawin'
Wi' the sperks a' whizzin' oot;
Or green tides sweeshin'
'Neth heich-skeich stars,
Or centuries fleein' doun a water-chute.

Grinnin' gargoyle by a saint,
Mephistopheles in Heaven,
Skeleton at a tea-meetin',
Missin' link—or creakin'
Hinge atween the deid and livin'. . . .

(I kent a Terrier in a sham fecht aince,
Wha louped a dyke and landed on a thistle.
He'd naething on ava aneth his kilt.
Schönberg has nae notation for his whistle.) . . .

OUR EDUCATIONAL SYSTEM

(Gin you're surprised a village drunk
Foreign references s'ud fool in,
You ha'ena the respect you s'ud
For oor guid Scottish schoolin'.

For we've the maist unlikely folk
Aye braggin' o' oor lear,
And, tho' I'm drunk, for Scotland's sake
I tak' my barrowsteel here!

Yet Europe's faur eneuch for me,
Puir fule, when bairns ken mair
O' th'ither warld than I o' this
—But that's no' here nor there!) . . .

Guid sakes I'm in a dreidfu' state.
I'll ha'e nae inklin' sune
Gin I'm the drinker or the drink,
The thistle or the mune.

I'm geylies feart I couldna tell
Gin I s'ud lay me doon
The difference betwixt the warld
And my ain heid gaen' roon'! . . .

THE CRYING OF THE FAIR

Drums in the Walligate, pipes in the air,
Come and hear the cryin' o' the Fair.

A' as it used to be, when I was a loon
On Common-Ridin' Day in the Muckle Toon.

The bearer twirls the Bannock-and-Saut-Herrin',
The Croon o' Roses through the lift is farin',

The aucht-fit thistle wallops on hie;
In heather besoms a' the hills gang by.

But noo it's a' the fish o' the sea
Nailed on the roond o' the Earth to me.

Beauty and Love that are bobbin' there;
Syne the breengin' growth that alane I bear;

And Scotland followin' on ahint
For threepenny bits spleet-new frae the mint.

Drums in the Walligate, pipes in the air,
The wallopin' thistle is ill to bear.

But I'll dance the nicht wi' the stars o' Heaven
In the Mairket Place as shair's I'm livin'.

Easy to cairry roses or herrin',
And the lave may weel their threepenny bits earn.

Devil the star! It's Jean I'll ha'e
Again as she was on her weddin' day. . . .

MAN AND THE INFINITE

Nerves in stounds o' delight,
Muscles in pride o' power,
Bluid as wi' roses dight
Life's toppin' pinnacles owre,
The thistle yet'll unite
Man and the Infinite!

Swippert and swith wi' virr
In the howes o' man's hert
Forever its muckle roots stir
Like a Leviathan astert

[79]

Till'ts coils like a thistle's leafs
Sweep space wi' levin sheafs.

Frae laichest deeps o' the ocean
It rises in flight upon flight,
And 'yont its uttermaist motion
Can still set roses alight,
As else unreachable height
Fa's under its triumphin' sight.

Here is the root that feeds
The shank wi' the blindin' wings
Dwinin' abuneheid to gleids
Like stars in their keethin' rings,
And blooms in sunrise and sunset
Inowre Eternity's yett.

Lay haud o' my hert and feel
Fountains ootloupin' the starns
Or see the Universe reel
Set gaen' by my eident harns,
Or test the strength o' my spauld
The wecht o' a' thing to hauld!

The howes o' Man's hert are bare,
The Dragon's left them for good,
There's nocht but naethingness there,
The hole whaur the Thistle stood,
That rootless and radiant flies
A Phoenix in Paradise! . . .

MAN'S CRUEL PLIGHT

Masoch and Sade
Turned into ane
Havoc ha'e made
O' my a'e brain.

Weel, gin it's Sade
Let it be said
They've made me mad
—That'll dae instead.

But it's no' instead
In Scots, but insteed,
—The life they've led
In my puir heid.

But aince I've seen
In the thistle here
A' that they've been
I'll aiblins wun clear.

Thistleless fule,
You'll ha'e nocht left
But the hole frae which
Life's struggle is reft! . . .

THE CHALLENGE OF THE ARTS

Reason ser's nae end but pleasure,
Truth's no' an end but a means
To a wider knowledge o' life
And a keener interest in't.

We wha are poets and artists
Move frae inklin' to inklin',
And live for oor antrin lichtnin's
In the haingles atweenwhiles.

Laich as the feck o' mankind
Whence we breenge in unkennable shapes
—*Crockats up, hair kaimed to the lift,*
And no' to cree legs wi'! . . .

OUTWARD BOUND

We're ootward boond frae Scotland.
Guid-bye, fare-ye-weel; guid-bye, fare-ye-weel.
—A' the Scots that ever wur
Gang ootward in a creel.

We're ootward boond frae Scotland.
Guid-bye, fare-ye-weel; guid-bye, fare-ye-weel.
The cross-tap is a monkey tree
That nane o' us can spiel.

We've never seen the Captain
But the first mate is a Jew.
We've shipped aboard Eternity.
Adieu, kind freends, adieu! . . .

THE INEDUCABLE

In the creel or on the gell
O' oor coutribat and ganien.
What gin ithers see or hear
Naething but a gowkstorm?

Gin you stop the galliard
To teach them hoo to dance,
There comes in Corbaudie
And turns their gammons up!

THE PSYCHO-SOMATIC
QUANDARY

You vegetable cat's melody!
Your *Concert Miaulant* is
A triumph o' discord shairly,

[82]

And suits my fancy fairly
—I'm shair that Scott'll * agree
He canna vie wi' this. . . .

Said my body to my mind,
"I've been startled whiles to find,
When Jean has been in bed wi' me,
A kind o' Christianity!"

To my body said my mind,
"But your benmaist thocht you'll find
Was 'Bother what I think I feel
—Jean kens the set o' my bluid owre weel,
And lauchs to see me in the creel
O' my courage-bag confined.' " . . .

I wish I kent the physical basis
O' a' life's seemin' airs and graces.

It's queer the thochts a kittled cull
Can lowse or splairgin' glit annul.

Man's spreit is wi' his ingangs twined
In ways that he can ne'er unwind.

A wumman whiles a bawaw gi'es
That clean abaws him gin he sees.

Or wi' a movement o' a leg
Shows'm his mind is juist a geg.

I'se warrant Jean 'ud no' be lang
In finding whence this thistle sprang.

Mebbe it's juist because I'm no'
Beddit wi' her that gars it grow! . . .

* F. G. Scott, a contemporary Scottish composer.

LOVE *

A luvin' wumman is a licht
That shows a man his waefu' plicht,
Bleezin' steady on ilka bane,
Wrigglin' sinnen an' twinin' vein,
Or fleerin' quick an' gane again,
And the mair scunnersome the sicht
The mair for love and licht he's fain
Till clear and chitterin' and nesh
Move a' the miseries o' his flesh. . . .

IN THE LAST ANALYSIS

O lass, wha see'st me
As I daur hardly see,
I marvel that your bonny een
Are as they hadna' seen.

Through a' my self-respect
They see the truth abject
—*Gin you could pierce their blindin' licht*
You'd see a fouler sicht! . . .

O WHA'S THE BRIDE?

O wha's the bride that cairries the bunch
O' thistles blinterin' white?
Her cuckold bridegroom little dreids
What he sall ken this nicht.

For closer than gudeman can come
And closer to'r than hersel',

* Suggested by the French of Edmond Rocher.

Wha didna need her maidenheid
Has wrocht his purpose fell.

O wha's been here afore me, lass,
And hoo did he get in?
—*A man that deed or was I born
This evil thing has din.*

And left, as it were on a corpse,
Your maidenheid to me?
—*Nae lass, gudeman, sin' Time began
'S hed ony mair to gi'e.*

*But I can gi'e ye kindness, lad,
And a pair o' willin' hands,
And you sall ha'e my breists like stars,
My limbs like willow wands.*

*And on my lips ye'll heed nae mair,
And in my hair forget,
The seed o' a' the men that in
My virgin womb ha'e met. . . .*

REPETITION COMPLEX

Millions o' wimmen bring forth in pain
Millions o' bairns that are no' worth ha'en.

Wull ever a wumman be big again
Wi's muckle's a Christ? Yech, there's nae sayin'.

Gin that's the best that you ha'e comin',
Fegs but I'm sorry for you, wumman!

Yet a'e thing's certain—Your faith is great.
Whatever happens, you'll no' be blate! . . .

THE PROBLEM CHILD

Mary lay in jizzen
As it were claith o' gowd,
But it's in orra duds
Ilka ither bairntime's row'd.

Christ had never toothick,
Christ was never seeck,
But Man's a fiky bairn
Wi' bellythraw, ripples, and worm-i'-the-cheek! . . .

THE SKELETON AT THE FEAST

Dae what ye wull ye canna parry
This skeleton-at-the-feast that through the starry
Maze o' the warld's intoxicatin' soiree
Claughts ye, as micht at an affrontit quean
A bastard wean!

Prood mune, ye needna thring your shouder there,
And at your puir get like a snawstorm stare,
It's yours—there's nae denyin't—and I'm shair
You'd no' enjoy the evenin' much the less
Gin you'd but openly confess!

Dod! It's an eaten and a spewed-like thing,
Fell like a little-bodies' changeling,
And it's nae credit t'ye that you s'ud bring
The like to life—yet, gi'en a mither's love,
—Hee, hee!—wha kens hoo't micht improve? . . .

Or is this Heaven, this yalla licht,
And I the aft'rins o' the Earth,
Or sic's in this wanchancy time
May weel fin' sudden birth?

[86]

The roots that wi' the worms compete
Hauf-publish me upon the air.
The struggle that divides me still
Is seen fu' plainly there.

The thistle's shank scarce holes the grun',
My grave'll spare nae mair, I doot.
—*The crack's fu' wide; the shank's fu' strong;*
A' that I was is oot.

My knots o' nerves that struggled sair
Are weel reflected in the herb;
My crookit instincts were like this,
As sterile and acerb.

My self-tormented spirit took
The shape repeated in the thistle;
Sma' beauty joiked my rawny banes
And maze o' gristle.

I seek nae peety, Paraclete,
And, fegs, I think the joke is rich
—*Pairt soul, pairt skeleton's come up;*
They kentna which was which! . . .

Thou Daith in which my life
Sae vain a thing can seem,
Frae whatna source d'ye borrow
Your devastatin' gleam?

Nae doot that hidden sun
'Ud look fu' wae ana',
Gin I could see it in the licht
That frae the Earth you draw! . . .

Shudderin' thistle, gi'e owre, gi'e owre!
A'body's gi'en in to the facts o' life;
The impossible truth'll triumph at last,
And mock your strife.

[87]

Your sallow leafs can never thraw,
Wi' a' their oorie shakin',
Ae doot into the hert o' life
That it may be mistak'n. . . .

THE BARREN FIG

O Scotland is
THE barren fig.
Up, carles, up
And roond it jig.

Auld Moses took
A dry stick and
Instantly it
Floo'ered in his hand.

Pu' Scotland up,
And wha can say
It winna bud
And blossom tae.

A miracle's
Oor only chance.
Up, carles, up
And let us dance!

TO BE YOURSELVES AND MAKE THAT WORTH BEING

Puir Burns, wha's bouquet like a shot kail blaws
—Will this rouch sicht no' gi'e the orchids pause?
The Gairdens o' the Muses may be braw,
But nane like oors can breenge and eat ana'!

And owre the kailyard-wa' Dunbar they've flung,
And a' their countrymen that e'er ha'e sung
For ither than ploomen's lugs or to enrichen
Plots on Parnassus set apairt for kitchen.

Ploomen and ploomen's wives—shades o' the Manse
May weel be at the heid o' sic a dance,
As through the polish't ha's o' Europe leads
The rout o' bagpipes, haggis, and sheep's heids!

The vandal Scot! Frae Branksome's deidly barrow
I struggle yet to free a' winsome marrow,
To show what Scotland micht ha'e hed instead
O' this preposterous Presbyterian breed.

(Gin Glesca folk are tired o' Hengler,
And still need breid and circuses, there's Spengler,
Or gin ye s'ud need mair than ane to teach ye,
Then learn frae Dostoevski and frae Nietzsche.

And let this lesson be—to be yersel's,
Ye needna fash gin it's to be ocht else.
To be yersel's—and to mak' that worth bein',
Nae harder job to mortals has been gi'en.

To save your souls fu' mony o' ye are fain
But deil a dizzen to mak' it worth the daein'.
I winda gi'e five meenits wi' Dunbar
For a' the millions o' ye as ye are.)

MY QUARREL WITH THE ROSE

I micht ha'e been contentit wi' the rose
Gin I'd had only reason to suppose
That what the English dae can e'er mak' guid
For what Scots dinna—and first and foremaist should.

[89]

I micht ha'e been contentit—gin the feck
O' my ain folk had grovelled wi' less respec',
But their obsequious devotion
Made it for me a criminal emotion.

I micht ha'e been contentit—ere I saw
That there were fields on which it couldna draw,
(While strang-er roots ran under't) and a'e threid
O't drew frae Scotland a' that it could need.

And left the maist o' Scotland fallow
(Save for the patch on which the kail-blades wallow),
And saw hoo ither countries' genius drew
Elements like mine that in a rose ne'er grew. . . .

Gin the threid haud'n us to the rose were snapt,
There's no' a'e petal o't that 'ud be clapt.
A' Scotland gi'es gangs but to jags or stalk,
The bloom is English—and 'ud ken nae lack!

TUSSLE WITH THE PHILISTINES

O drumlie clood o' crudity and cant,
Obliteratin' as the Easter rouk
That rows up frae the howes and droons the heichs,
And turns the country to a faceless spook.

Like blurry shapes o' landmarks in the haar
The bonny idiosyncratic place-names loom,
Clues to the vieve and maikless life that's lain
Happit for centuries in an alien gloom. . . .

Eneuch! For noo I'm in the mood,
Scotland, responsive to my thoughts,
Lichts mile by mile, as my ain nerves,
Frae Maidenkirk to John o' Groats!

[90]

What are the prophets and priests and kings,
What's ocht to the people o' Scotland?
Speak—and Cruivie'll goam at you,
Gilsanquhar jalouse you're dottlin'!

And Edinburgh and Glasgow
Are like ploomen in a pub.
They want to hear o' naething
But their ain foul hubbub. . . .

The fules are richt; an extra thocht
Is neither here nor there.
Oor lives may differ as they like
—The self-same fate we share.

And whiles I wish I'd nae mair sense
Than Cruivie and Gilsanquhar,
And envy their rude health and curse
My gnawin' canker.

Guid sakes, ye dinna need to pass
Only exam. to dee
—Daith canna tell a common flech
Frae a performin' flea! . . .

It sets you weel to slaver
To let sic gaadies fa'
—*The mune's the muckle white whale*
I seek in vain to kaa!

The Earth's my mastless samyn,
The thistle my ruined sail.
—Le'e go as you maun in the end,
And droon in your plumm o' ale! . . .

THE SPLORE

Clear keltie aff an' fill again
Withoot corneigh bein' cryit,
The drink's aye best that follows a drink.
Clear keltie aff and try it.

Be't whisky gill or penny wheep,
Or ony ither lotion,
We 'bood to ha'e a thimblefu' first,
And syne we'll toom an ocean! . . .

"To Luna at the Craidle-and-Coffin
To sof'n her hert if owt can sof'n:—

Auld bag o' tricks, ye needna come
And think to stap me in your womb.

You needna fash to rax and strain.
Carline, I'll *no* be born again

In ony brat you can produce.
Carline, gi' owre—O what's the use?

You pay nae heed but plop me in,
Syne shove me oot, and winna be din,

—Owre and owre, the same auld trick,
Cratur withoot climacteric! . . ."

"Noo Cutty Sark's tint that ana',
And dances in her skin—Ha! Ha!

I canna ride awa' like Tam,
But e'en maun bide juist whaur I am.

I canna ride—and gin I could,
I'd sune be sorry I hedna stude,

For less than a' there is to see
'll never be owre muckle for me.

[92]

Cutty, gin you've mair to strip,
Aff wi't, lass—and let it rip!" . . .

Ilka pleesure I can ha'e
Ends like a dram ta'en yesterday.

And tho' to ha'e it I am lorn
—What better 'ud I be the morn? . . .

My belly on the gantrees there,
The spigot frae my cullage,
And wow but how the fizzin' yill
In spilth increased the ullage!

I was an axious barrel, lad,
When first they tapped my bung.
They whistled me up, yet thro' the lift
My freaths like rainbows swung.

Waesucks, a pride for ony bar,
The boast o' barleyhood,
Like Noah's Ark abune the faem,
Maun float, a gantin' cude.

For I was thrawn fu' cock owre sune,
And wi' a single jaw
I made the pub a blindin' swelth,
And how'd the warld awa'! . . .

THE MORTAL FLAW

What forest worn to the backhauf's this,
What Eden brocht doon to a beanswaup?
The thistle's to earth as the man
In the mune's to the mune, puir chap.

The haill warld's barkin' and fleein',
And this is the echo and aiker,

[93]

A soond that arrears in my lug
Herrin'-banein' back to its maker,

A swaw like a flaw in a jewel
Or *nadryv* * jaloused in a man,
Or Creation unbiggit again
To the draucht wi' which it began. . . .

Abordage o' this toom houk's nae mowse.
It munks and's ill to lay haud o',
As gin a man ettled to ride
On the shouders o' his ain shadow.

I canna biel't; tho' steekin' an e'e
Tither's munkie wi' munebeam for knool in't,
For there's nae sta'-tree and the brute's awa'
Wi' me kinkin' like foudrie ahint. . . .

Sae Eternity'll buff nor stye
For Time, and shies at a touch, man;
Yet aye in a belth o' Thocht
Comes alist like the Fleein' Dutchman. . . .

As the worms'll breed in my corpse until
It's like a rice-puddin', the thistle
Has made an eel-ark o' the lift
Whaur elvers like skirl-in-the-pan sizzle.

Like a thunder-plump on the sunlicht,
Or the slounge o' daith on my dreams,
Or as to a fair forfochen man
A breedin' wife's beddiness seems,

Saragossa Sea, St. Vitus' Dance,
A *cafard* in a brain's despite,
Or lunacy that thinks a' else
Is loony—and is dootless richt! . . .

* Tragical crack (Dostoevski's term).

Gin my thochts that circle like hobby-horses
'Udna loosen to nightmares I'd sleep;
For nocht but a chowed core's left whaur Jerusalem lay
Like aipples in a heap! . . .

THE TRAGIC TRYST

It's a queer thing to tryst wi' a wumman
When the boss o' her body's gane,
And her banes in the wund as she comes
Dirl like a raff o' rain.

It's a queer thing to tryst wi' a wumman
When her ghaist frae abuneheid keeks,
And you see in the licht o't that a'
You ha'e o'r's the cleiks. . . .

REDUCTIO AD ABSURDUM

What forest worn to the backhauf's this,
What Eden brocht doon to a beanswaup?
—A' the ferlies o' natur' spring frae the earth,
And into't again maun drap.

Animals, vegetables, what are they a'
But as thochts that a man has ta'en?
And Earth sall be like a toom skull syne.
—Whaur'll its thochts be then?

THE SPUR OF LOVE

The munelicht is my knowledge o' mysel',
Mysel' the thistle in the munelicht seen,
And hauf my shape has fund itsel' in thee
And hauf my knowledge in your piercin' een.

E'en as the munelicht's borrowed frae the sun
I ha'e my knowledge o' mysel' frae thee,
And much that nane but thee can e'er mak' clear,
Save my licht's frae the source, is dark to me.

Your acid tongue, vieve lauchter, and hawk's een,
And bluid that drobs like haill to quicken me,
Can turn the mid-day black or midnicht bricht,
Lowse me frae licht or eke frae darkness free.

Bite into me forever mair and lift
Me clear o' chaos in a great relief
Till, like this thistle in the munelicht growin',
I brak' in roses owre a hedge o' grief. . . .

THE FEMININE PRINCIPLE

I am like Burns, and ony wench
Can ser' me for a time.
Licht's in them a'—in some a sun,
In some the merest skime.

I'm no' like Burns, and week I ken,
Tho' ony wench can ser',
It's no' through mony but through yin
That ony man wuns fer. . . .

I wedded thee frae fause love, lass,
To free thee and to free mysel';
But man and wumman tied for life
True can be and truth can tell.

[96]

Pit ony couple in a knot
They canna lowse and needna try,
And mair o' love at last they'll ken
—If ocht!—than joy'll alane descry.

For them as for the beasts, my wife,
A's fer frae dune when pleesure's owre,
And coontless difficulties gar
Ilk hert discover a' its power.

I dinna say that bairns alane
Are true love's task—a sairer task
Is aiblins to create oorsels
As we can be—it's that I ask.

Create oorsels, syne bairns, syne race.
Sae on the cod I see't in you
Wi' Maidenkirk to John o' Groats
The bosom that you draw me to.

And nae Scot wi' a wumman lies,
But I am he and ken as 'twere
A stage I've passed as he maun pass't,
Gin he grows up, his way wi' her! . . .

A'thing wi' which a man
Can intromit's a wumman,
And can, and s'ud, become
As intimate and human.

And Jean's nae mair my wife
Than whisky is at times,
Or munelicht or a thistle
Or kittle thochts or rhymes.

He's no' a man ava',
And lacks a proper pride,
Gin less than a' the warld
Can ser' him for a bride!

THE LIGHT OF LIFE

Use, then, my lust for whisky and for thee,
Your function but to be and let me be
And see and let me see.

If in a lesser licht I grope my way,
Or use't for ends that need your different ray
Whelm't in superior day.

Then aye increase and ne'er withdraw your licht.
—Gin it shows either o's in hideous plicht,
What gain to turn't to nicht?

Whisky mak's Heaven or Hell and whiles mells baith,
Disease is but the privy torch o' Daith,
—But sex reveals life, faith!

I need them a' and maun be aye at strife.
Daith and ayont are nocht but pairts o' life.
—Then be life's locht, my wife! . . .

LOVE OFTEN WUNS FREE

Love often wuns free
In lust to be strangled,
   Or love, o' lust free,
   In law's sairly tangled.

And it's ill to tell whether
Law or lust is to blame
When love's chokit up
—It comes a' to the same.

In this sorry growth
Whatna beauty is tint
That freed o't micht find
A waur fate than is in't? . . .

YANK OOT YOUR ORRA BOUGHS

Yank oot your orra boughs, my hert!

God gied man speech and speech created thocht,
He gied man speech but to the Scots gied nocht
Barrin' this clytach that they've never brocht
To onything but sic a Blottie O
As some bairn's copybook micht show,

A spook o' soond that frae the unkent grave
In which oor nation lies loups up to wave
Sic leprous chuns as tatties have
That cellar-boond send spindles gropin'
Towards ony hole that's open,

Like waesome fingers in the dark that think
They still may widen the ane and only chink
That e'er has gi'en mankind a blink
O' Hope—tho' ev'n in that puir licht
They s'ud ha'e seen their hopeless plicht.

This puir relation o' my topplin' mood,
This country cousin, streak o' churl-bluid,
This hopeless airgh 'twixt a' we can and should,
This Past that like Astarte's sting I feel,
This arrow in Achilles' heel.

Yank oot your orra boughs, my hert!

Mebbe we're in a vicious circle cast,
Mebbe there's limits we can ne'er get past,
Mebbe we're sentrices that at the last
Are flung aside, and no' the pillars and props
O' Heaven foraye as in oor hopes.

Oor growth at least nae steady progress shows,
Genius in mankind like an antrin rose
Abune a jungly waste o' effort grows,

But to Man's purpose it mak's little odds,
And seems irrelevant to God's. . . .

Eneuch? Then here you are. Here's the haill story.
Life's connached shapes too'er up in croons o' glory,
Perpetuatin', natheless, in their gory
Colour the endless sacrifice and pain
That to their makin's gane.

The roses like the saints in Heaven treid
Triumphant owre the agonies o' their breed,
And wag fu' mony a celestial heid
Abune the thorter-ills o' leaf and prick
In which they ken the feck maun stick.

Yank oot your orra boughs, my hert!

A mongrel growth, jumble o' disproportions,
Whirlin' in its incredible contortions,
Or wad-be client that an auld whore shuns,
Wardin' her wizened orange o' a bosom
Frae importunities sae gruesome.

Or new diversion o' the hormones
Mair fond o' procreation than the Mormons,
And fetchin' like a devestatin' storm on's
A' the uncouth dilemmas o' oor natur'
Objectified in vegetable maitter.

Yank oot your orra boughs, my hert!

And heed nae mair the foolish cries that beg
You slice nae mair to aff or pu' to leg,
You skitin' duffer that gars a'body fleg,
—What tho' you ding the haill warld oot o' joint
Wi' a skier to cover-point!

Yank oot your orra boughs, my hert!

There *was* a danger—and it's weel I see't—
Had brocht ye like Mallarmé to defeat:—

"Mon doute, amas de nuit ancienne s'achève
En maint rameau subtil, qui, demeuré les vrais
Bois même, prouve hélas! que bien seul je m'offrais
Pour triomphe la faute idéale des roses." *

Yank oot your orra boughs, my hert!

THE FORM AND PURPOSE OF THE THISTLE

I love to muse upon the skill that gangs
To mak' the simplest thing that Earth displays.
The eident life that ilka atom thrangs,
And uses it in the appointit ways,
And a' the endless brain that nocht escapes
That myriad moves them to inimitable shapes.

Nor to their customed form or ony ither
New to Creation, by man's cleverest mind,
A' needfu' particles first brocht thegither,
Could they wi' timeless labour be combined.
There's nocht that Science yet's begood to see
In hauf its deemless detail or its destiny.

Oor een gi'e answers based on pairt-seen facts
That beg a' questions, to ebb minds' content,
But hoo a'e feature or the neist attracts,
Wi' millions mair unseen, wha kens what's meant
By human brains and to what ends may tell
For naething's seen or kent that's near a thing itsel'!

Let whasae vaunts his knowledge then and syne
Sets up a God and kens *His* purpose tae

* The line which precedes these in Mallarmé's poem is "Aimai-je un rêve?" and
Wilfred Thorley translates the passage thus:

> *"Loved I Love's counterfeit?*
> *My doubts, begotten of the long night's heat,*
> *Dislimn the woodland till my triumph shows*
> *As the flawed shadow of a frustrate rose."*

Tell me what's gar't a'e strain o' maitter twine
In sic an extraordinary way,
And what God's purpose wi' the Thistle is
—I'll aiblins ken what he and his God's worth by this.

I've watched it lang and hard until I ha'e
A certain symp'thy wi' its orra ways
And pride in its success, as week I may,
In growin' exactly as its instinct says,
Save in sae fer as thwarts o' weather or grun'
Or man or ither foes ha'e'ts aims perchance fordone.

But I can form nae notion o' the spirit
That gars it tak' the difficult shape it does,
Nor judge the merit yet or the demerit
O' this detail or that sae fer as it goes
T' advance the cause that gied it sic a guise
As maun ha'e pleased its Maker wi' a gey surprise.

The craft that hit upon the reishlin' stalk,
Wi'ts gausty leafs and a' its datchie jags,
And spired it syne in seely flooers to brak
Like sudden lauchter owre its fousome rags
Jouks me, sardonic lover, in the routh
O' contrairies that jostle in this dumfoondrin' growth.

What strength 't'ud need to pit its roses oot,
Or double them in number or in size,
He canna tell wha canna plumb the root,
And learn what's gar't its present state arise,
And what the limits are that ha'e been put
To change in thistles, and why—and what a change
        'ud boot. . . .

BALLAD OF THE CRUCIFIED ROSE

I saw a rose come loupin' oot *
Frae a camsteerie plant.
O wha'd ha'e thocht yon puir stock had
Sic an inhabitant?

For centuries it ran to waste,
Wi' pin-heid flooers at times.
O'ts hidden hert o' beauty they
Were but the merest skimes.

Yet while it ran to wud and thorns,
The feckless growth was seekin'
Some airt to cheenge its life until
A' in a rose was beekin'.

"Is there nae way in which my life
Can mair to flooerin' come,
And bring its waste on shanks and jags
Doon to a minimum?

"It's hard to struggle as I maun
For scrunts o' blooms like mine,
While blossom covers ither plants
As by a knack divine.

"What hinders me unless I lack
Some needfu' discipline?
—I wis I'll bring my orra life
To beauty or I'm din!"

Sae ran the thocht that hid ahint
Thie thistle's ugsome guise,
"I'll brak' the habit o' my life
A worthier to devise."

"My nobler instincts sall nae mair
This contrair shape be gi'en.

* The General Strike (May, 1926).

[103]

I sall nae mair consent to live
A life no' fit to be seen."

Sae ran the thocht that hid ahint
The thistle's ugsome guise,
Till a' at aince a rose loupt oot
—I watched it wi' surprise.

A rose loupt oot and grew, until
It was ten times the size
O' ony rose the thistle afore
Hed heistit to the skies.

And still it grew till a' the buss
Was hidden in its flame.
I never saw sae braw a floo'er
As yon thrawn stock became.

And still it grew until it seemed
The haill braid earth had turned
A reid reid rose that in the lift
Like a ball o' fire burned.

The waefu' clay was fire aince mair,
As Earth had been resumed
Into God's mind, frae which sae lang
To grugous state 'twas doomed.

Syne the rose shrivelled suddenly
As a balloon is burst;
The thistle was a ghaistly stick,
As gin it had been curst.

Was it the ancient vicious sway
Imposed itsel' again,
Or nerve owre weak for new emprise
That made the effort vain,

A coward strain in that lorn growth
That wrocht the sorry trick?

—The thistle like a rocket soared
And cam' doon like the stick.

Like grieshuckle the roses glint,
The leafs like farles hing,
As roond a hopeless sacrifice
Earth draws its barren ring.

The dream o' beauty's dernin' yet
Ahint the ugsome shape.
—Vain dream that in a pinheid here
And there can e'er escape!

The vices that defeat the dream
Are in the plant itsel',
And till they're purged its virtues maun
In pain and misery dwell.

Let Deils rejoice to see the waste,
The fond hope brocht to nocht.
The thistle in their een is as
A favourite lust they've wrocht.

The orderin' o' the thistle means
Nae richtin' o't to them.
Its loss they ca' a law, its thorns
A fule's fit diadem.

And still the idiot nails itsel'
To its ain crucifix,
While here a rose and there a rose
Jaups oot abune the pricks.

Like connoisseurs the Deils gang roond
And praise its attitude,
Till on the Cross the silly Christ
To fidge fu' fain's begood!

Like connoisseurs the Deils gang roond
Wi' ready platitude.

It's no' sae dear as vinegar,
And every bit as good!

The bitter taste is on my tongue,
I chowl my chafts, and pray
"Let God forsake me noo and no'
Staund connoisseur-like tae!" . . .

THE THISTLE'S CHARACTERISTICS

The language that but sparely flooers
And maistly gangs to weed;
The thocht o' Christ and Calvary
Aye liddenin' in my heid;
And a' the dour provincial thocht
That merks the Scottish breed
—These are the thistle's characters,
To argie there's nae need.
Hoo weel my verse embodies
The thistle you can read!
—But will a Scotsman never
Frae this vile growth be freed?

O ilka man alive is like
A quart that's squeezed into a pint
(A maist unScottish-like affair!)
Or like the little maid that showed
Me into a still sma'er room.
What use to let a sunrise fade
To ha'e anither like't the morn,
Or let a generation pass
That ane nae better may succeed,
Or wi' a' Time's machinery
Keep naething new aneth the sun,
Or change things oot o' kennin' that
They may be a' the mair the same?

The thistle in the wund dissolves
In lichtin's as shook foil gi'e way
In sudden splendours, or the flesh
As Daith lets slip the infinite soul;
And syne it's like a sunrise tint
In grey o' day, or love and life,
That in a cloody blash o' sperm
Undae the warld to big't again,
Or like a pickled foetus that
Nae man feels ocht in common wi'
—But micht as easily ha' been!
Or like a corpse a soul set free
Scunners to think it tenanted
—And little recks that but for it
It never micht ha' been at a',
Like love frae lust and God frae man!

The wasted seam that dries like stairch
And pooders aff, that micht ha' been
A warld o' men and syne o' Gods;
They grey that haunts the vievest green;
The wrang side o' the noblest scene
We ne'er can whummle to oor een,
As 'twere the hinder pairts o' God.
His face aye turned the opposite road,
Or's neth the floowers the drumlie clods
Frae which they come at sicna odds,
As a' Earth's magic frae a spirt,
In shame and secrecy, o' dirt!

Then shak' nae mair in silly life,
Nor stand impossible as Daith,
Incredible as a'thing is
Inside or oot owre closely scanned.
As mithers aften think the warld
O' bairns that ha'e nae end or object,
Or lovers think their sweethearts made
Yince-yirn—wha thae'na waled the lave,
Maikless—when they are naebody,

Or men o' ilka sort and kind
Are prood o' thochts they ca' their ain,
That nameless millions had afore
And nameless millions yet'll ha'e,
And that were never worth the ha'en,
Or Cruivie's "latest" story or
Gilsanquhar's vows to sign the pledge,
Or's if I thocht maist whisky *was,*
Or failed to coont the cheenge I got,
Sae wad I be gin I rejoiced,
Or didna ken my place in thee.

O stranglin' rictus, sterile spasm
Thou stricture in the groins o' licht
Thou ootrie gangrel frae the wilds
O' chaos fenced frae Eden yet
By the unsplinterable wa'
O' munebeams like a bleeze o' swords!

Nae chance lunge cuts the Gordian knot,
Nor sall the belly find relief
In wha's entangled moniplies
Creation like a stoppage jams,
Or in whose loins the mapamound
Runkles in strawns o' bubos whaur
The generations gravel.
The soond o' water winnin' free,
The sicht o' licht that braks the rouk,
The thocht o' every thwart owrecome
Are in my ears and een and brain,
In whom the bluid is spilt in stour,
In whom a' licht in darkness fails,
In whom the mystery o' life
Is to a wretched weed bewrayed.

But let my soul increase in me,
God dwarfed to enter my puir thocht
Expand to his true size again,
And protoplasm's look befit

The nature o' its destiny,
And seed and sequence be nae mair
Incongruous to ane anither,
And liquor packed impossibly
Mak' pint-pot an eternal well,
And art be relevant to life,
And poets mair than dominies yet,
And ends nae langer tint in means,
Nor forests hidden by their trees,
Nor men be sacrificed alive
In foonds o' fate designed for them,
Nor mansions o' the soul stand toom
Their owners in their cellars trapped,
Nor a' a people's genius be
A rumple-fyke in Heaven's doup.
While Calvinism uses her
To breed a minister or twa!

A black leaf owre a white leaf twirls,
A grey leaf flauchters in atween,
Sae ply my thochts aboot the stem
O' loppert slime frae which they spring.
The thistle like a snawstorm drives,
Or like a flicht o' swallows lifts,
Or like a swarm o' midges hings,
A plague o' moths, a starry sky,
But's naething but a thistle yet,
And still the puzzle stands unsolved.
Beauty and ugliness alike,
And life and daith and God and man,
Are aspects o't but nane can tell
The secret that I'd fain find oot
O' this bricht hive, this sorry weed,
The tree that fills the universe,
Or like a reistit herrin' crines.

Gin I was sober I micht think
It was like something drunk men see!
The necromancy in my bluid

Through a' the gamut cheenges me
O' dwarf and giant, foul and fair,
But winna let me be mysel'
—My mither's womb that reins me still
Until I tae can prick the witch
And "Wumman" cry wi' Christ at last,
"Then what hast thou to do wi' me?"
The tug-o'-war is in me still,
The dog-hank o' the flesh and soul,
Faither in Heaven, what gar'd ye tak'
A village slut to mither me,
Your mongrel o' the fire and clay?
The trollop and the Deity share
My writhen form as tho' I were
A picture o' the time they had
When Licht rejoiced to file itsel'
And Earth upshuddered like a star.

A drucken hizzie gane to bed
Wi' three-in-ane and ane-in-three.
O fain I'd drink until I saw
Scotland a ferlie o' delight,
And fain bide drunk nor ha'e't recede
Into a shrivelled thistle syne,
As when a sperklin' tide rins oot,
And leaves a wreath o' rubbish there!

Wull a' the seas gang dry at last
(As dry as I am gettin' noo),
Or wull they aye come back again,
Seilfu' as my neist drink to me,
Or as the sunlicht to the mune,
Or as the bonny sangs o' men,
Wha're but puir craturs in themsels,
And save when genius mak's them drunk,
As donnert as their audiences,
—As dreams that mak' a tramp a king,
A madman sane to his ain mind,
Or what a Scotsman thinks himsel',
Tho' naethin' but a thistle kyths.

The mair I drink the thirstier yet,
And whiles when I'm alowe wi' booze,
I'm like God's sel' and clad in fire,
And ha'e a Pentecost like this.
O wad that I could aye be fou',
And no' come back as aye I maun
To naething but a fule that nane
'Ud credit wi' sic thochts as thae,
A fule that kens they're empty dreams!
Yet but fer drink and drink's effects,
The yeast o' God that barms in us,
We micht as weel no' be alive.
It maitters not what drink is ta'en,
The barley bree, ambition, love,
Or Guid or Evil workin' in's,
Sae lang's we feel like souls set free
Frae mortal coils and speak in tongues
We dinna ken and never wull,
And find a merit in oorsels,
In Cruivies and Gilsanquhars tae,
And see the thistle as ocht but that!

For wha o's ha'e the thistle's poo'er
To see we're worthless and believe't?

A' thing that ony man can be's
A mockery o' his soul at last.
The mair it shows't the better, and
I'd suner be a tramp than king,
Lest in the pride o' place and poo'er
I e'er forgot my waesomeness.
Sae to debauchery and dirt,
And to disease and daith I turn,
Sin' otherwise my seemin' worth
'Ud block my view o' what is what,
And blin' me to the irony
O' bein' a grocer 'neth the sun,
A lawyer gin Justice ope'd her een,
A pedant like an ant promoted,
A parson buttonholin' God,

Or ony cratur o' the Earth
Sma'-bookt to John Smith, High Street, Perth,
Or sic like vulgar gaffe o' life
Sub specie aeternitatis—
Nae void can fleg me hauf as much
As bein' mysel', whate'er I am,
Or, waur, bein' onybody else.

The nervous thistle's shiverin', like
A horse's skin aneth a cleg,
Or Northern Lichts or lustres o'
A soul that Daith has fastened on,
Or mornin' efter the nicht afore.

THE GRAVE OF ALL MANKIND

Shudderin' thistle, gi'e owre, gi'e owre. . . .

Grey sand is churnin' in my lugs
The munelicht flets, and gantin' there
The grave o' a' mankind's laid bare
—On Hell itsel' the drawback rugs!

Nae man can ken his hert until
The tide o' life uncovers it,
And horror-struck he sees a pit
Returnin' life can never fill! . . .

A STICK-NEST IN YGDRASIL

Thou art the facts in ilka airt
That breenge into infinity,
Criss-crossed wi' coontless ither facts
Nae man can follow, and o' which
He is himsel' a helpless pairt,

Held in their tangle as he were
A stick-nest in Ygdrasil!

The less man sees the mair he is
Content wi't, but the mair he sees
The mair he kens hoo little o'
A' that there is he'll ever see,
And hoo it mak's confusion aye
The waur confoondit till at last
His brain inside his heid is like
Ariadne wi' an empty pirn,
Or like a birlin' reel frae which
A whale has rived the line awa'.
What better's a forhooied nest
Than skasloch scattered owre the grun'?

O hard it is for man to ken
He's no' creation's goal nor yet
A benefitter by't at last—
A means to ends he'll never ken,
And as to michtier elements
The slauchtered brutes he eats to him
Or forms o' life owre sma' to see
Wi' which his heedless body swarms,
And a' man's thocht nae mair to them
Than ony moosewob to a man
His Heaven to them the blinterin' o'
A snail-trail on their closet wa'!

For what's an atom o' a twig
That tak's a billion to an inch
To a' the routh o' shoots that mak'
The bygrowth o' the Earth aboot
The michty trunk o' Space that spreids
Ramel o' licht that ha'e nae end,
—The trunk wi' centuries for rings,
Comets for fruit, November shooers
For leafs that in its Autumns fa'
—And Man at maist o' sic a twig
Ane o' the coontless atoms is!

[113]

My sinnens and my veins are but
As muckle o' a single shoot
Wha's fibres I can ne'er unwaft
O' my wife's flesh and mither's flesh
And a' the flesh o' humankind,
And revelled thrums o' beasts and plants
As gangs to mak' twixt birth and daith
A'e sliver for a microscope;
And a' the life o' Earth to be
Can never lift frae underneath
The shank o' which oor destiny's pairt
As heich's to stand forenenst the trunk
Stupendous as a windlestrae!

I'm under nae delusions, fegs!
The whuppin' sooker at wha's tip
Oor little point o' view appears,
A midget coom o' continents
Wi' blebs o' oceans set, sends up
The braith o' daith as weel as life,
And we maun braird anither tip
Oot owre us or we wither tae,
And join the sentrice skeleton
As coral insects big their reefs.
What is the tree? As fer as Man's
Concerned it disna maitter
Gin but a giant thistle 'tis
That spreids eternal mischief there,
As I'm inclined to think.
Ruthless it sends its solid growth
Through mair than he can e'er conceive,
And braks his warlds abreid and rives
His Heavens to tatters on its horns.

The nature or the purpose o't
He needna fash to speir, for he
Is destined to be sune owre grown
And hidden wi' the parent wud
The spreidin' boughs in darkness hap,

And a' its future life'll be
Ootwith'm as he's ootwith his banes.

Juist as man's skeleton has left
Its ancient ape-like shape ahint,
Sae states o' mind in turn gi'e way
To different states, and quickly seem
Impossible to later men,
And Man's mind in its final shape,
Or lang'll seem a monkey's spook,
And, strewth, to me the vera thocht
O' Thocht's already fell like that!
Yet still the cracklin' thorns persist
In fitba' match and peepy show,
To antic hay a dog-fecht's mair
Than Jacob v. the Angel,
And through a cylinder o' wombs,
A star reflected in a dub,
I see as 'twere my ain wild harns
The ripple o' Eve's moniplies.

And faith! Yestreen in Cruivie's een
Life rocked at midnicht in a tree,
And in Gilsanquhar's glower I saw
The taps o' waves 'neth which the warld
Ga'ed rowin' like a jeelyfish,
And whiles I canna look at Jean
For fear I'd see the sunlicht turn
Worm-like into the glaur again!

A black leaf owre a white leaf twirls,
My liver's shadow on my soul,
And clots o' bluid loup oot frae stems
That back into the jungle rin,
Or in the waters underneath
Kelter like seaweed, while I hear
Abune the thunder o' the flood,
The voice that aince commanded licht
Sing "Scots Wha Ha'e" and hyne awa'

Like Cruivie up a different glen,
And leave me like a mixture o'
A wee Scotch nicht and Judgment Day,
The bile, the Bible, and the *Scotsman*
Poetry and pigs—Infernal Thistle,
Damnition haggis I've spewed up,
And syne return to like twa dogs!
Blin' Proteus wi' leafs or hands
Or flippers ditherin' in the lift
—Thou Samson in a warld that has
Nae pillars but your cheengin' shapes
That dung doon, rise in ither airts
Like windblawn reek frae smoo'drin' ess!
—Hoo lang maun I gi'e aff your forms
O' plants and beasts and men and Gods
And like a doited Atlas bear
This steeple o' fish, this eemis warld,
Or, maniac heid wi' snakes for hair,
A maenad, ape Aphrodite,
And scunner the Eternal sea?

Man needna fash and even noo
The cells that mak' a'e sliver wi'm,
The threidy knit he's woven wi',
'Ud fain destroy what sicht he has
O' this puir transitory stage,
Yet though he kens the fragment is
O' little worth he e'er can view,
Jalousin' it's a cheatrice weed,
He tyauves wi' ai' his micht and main
To keep his sicht despite his kind
Conspirin' as their nature is
'Gainst ocht wi' better sicht than theirs.

What gars him strive? He canna tell—
It may be nocht but cussedness.
—At best he hopes for little mair
Than his suspicions to confirm,
To mock the sicht he hains sae weel
At last wi' a' he sees wi' it,

Yet, thistle or no' whate'er its end,
Aiblins the force that mak's it grow
And lets him see a kennin' mair
Than ither folk and fend his sicht
Agen their jealous plots awhile
'll use the poo'ers it seems to waste,
This purpose ser'd, in ither ways,
That may be better worth the bein'
—Or sae he dreams, syne mocks his dream
Till Life grows sheer awa' frae him,
And bratts o' darkness plug his een.

It may be nocht but cussedness,
But I'm content gin a' my thocht
Can dae nae mair than let me see,
Free frae desire o' happiness,
The foolish faiths o' ither men
In breedin', industry, and War,
Religion, Science, or ocht else
Gang smash—when I ha'e nane mysel',
Or better gin I share them tae,
Or mind at least a time I did!

Aye, this is Calvary—to bear
Your Cross wi'in you frae the seed,
And feel it grow by slow degrees
Until it rends your flesh apairt,
And turn, and see your fellow-men
In similar case but sufferin' less
Thro' bein' mair wudden frae the stert! . . .

THE FORK IN THE WALL

I'm fu' o' a sticket God.
THAT'S what's the maitter wi' me.
Jean has stuck sic a fork in the wa'
That I row in agonie.

[117]

Mary never let dab.
SHE was a canny wumman.
She hedna a gaw in Joseph at a'
But, wow, this seecund comin'! . . .

THE GOAL OF SCOTTISH HISTORY

Narodbogonosets * are my folk tae,
But in a sma' way nooadays—
A faitherly God wi' a lang white beard,
Or painted Jesus in a haze
O' blue and gowd, a gird aboot his heid
Or some sic thing. It's been a sair come doon,
And the trade's nocht to what it was.
Unnatural practices are the cause.
Baith bairns and Gods'll be obsolete soon
(The twaesome gang thegither), and forsooth
Scotland turn Eliot's waste—the land o' Drouth.

But even as the stane the builders rejec'
Becomes the corner-stane, the time may be
When Scotland sall find oot its destiny,
And yield the *vse-chelovek*.†
—At a' events, owre Europe flaught atween
My whim (and mair than whim) it pleases
To seek the haund o' Russia as a freen'
In workin' oot mankind's great synthesis. . . .

Melville ‡ (a Scot) kent weel hoo Christ's
Corrupted into creeds malign,
Begotten strife's pernicious brood
That claims for patron Him Divine.
(The Kirk in Scotland still I cry
Crooks whaur it canna crucify!)

* God-bearers.
† The All-Man or Pan-Human.
‡ Herman Melville.

Christ, bleedin' like the thistle's roses,
He saw—as I in similar case—
Maistly, in beauty and in fear,
'Ud "paralyse the nobler race,
Smite or suspend, perplex, deter,
And, tortured, prove the torturer."

And never mair a Scot sall tryst,
Abies on Calvary, wi' Christ,
Unless, mebbe, a poem like this'll
Exteriorise things in a thistle,
And gi'e him in this form forlorn
What Melville socht in vain frae Hawthorne. . . .

Spirit o' strife, destroy in turn
Syne this fule's Paradise, syne that;
In thee's in Calvaries that owrecome
Daith efter Daith let me be caught,

Or in the human form that hauds
Us in its ignominious thrall,
While on brute needs oor souls attend
Until disease and daith end all,

Or in the grey deluded brain,
Reflectin' in anither field
The torments o' its parent flesh
In thocht-preventin' thocht concealed,

Or still in curst impossible mould,
Last thistle-shape men think to tak',
The soul, frae flesh and thocht set free,
On Heaven's strait if unseen rack.

There may be heicher forms in which
We can nae mair oor plicht define,
Because the agonies involved
'll bring us their ain anodyne.

Yet still we suffer and still sall,
Altho', puir fules, we mayna kent

As lang as like the thistle we
In coil and in recoil are pent.

And ferrer than mankind can look
Ghast shapes that free but to transfix
Twine rose-crooned in their agonies,
And strive agen the endless pricks.

The dooble play that bigs and braks
In endless victory and defeat
Is in your spikes and roses shown,
And a' my soul is haggar'd wi't. . . .

Be like the thistle, O my soul,
Heedless o' praise and quick to tak' affront,
And growin' like a mockery o' a'
Maist life can want or thole,
And manifest forevermair
Contempt o' ilka goal.

O' ilka goal—save ane alane;
To be yoursel', whatever that may be,
And as contemptuous o' that,
Kennin' nocht's worth the ha'en,
But certainty that nocht can be,
And hoo that certainty to gain.

For this you still maun grow and grope
In the abyss wi' ever-deepenin' roots
That croon your scunner wi' the grue
O' hopeless hope
—And gin the abyss is bottomless,
Your growth'll never stop! . . .

What earthquake chitters oot
In the Thistle's oorie shape,
What gleids o' central fire
In its reid heids escape,
And whatna coonter forces
In growth and ingrowth graip

In an eternal clinch
In this ootcuissen form
That winna be outcast,
But triumphs at the last
(Owre a' abies itsel'
As fer as we can tell,
Sin' frae the Eden o' the world
Ilka man in turn is hurled,
And ilka garden rins to waste
That was ever to his taste?)

O keep the Thistle 'yont the wa'
Owre which your skeletons you'll thraw.

LETTER TO DOSTOEVSKI

I, in the Thistle's land,
As you * in Russia where
Struggle in giant form
Proceeds for evermair,
In my sma' measure 'bood
Address a similar task,
And for a share o' your
Appallin' genius ask.

Wha built in revelations
What maist men in reserves
(And only men confound!)
A better gift deserves
Frae ane wha like hissel
(As ant-heap unto mountain)
Needs bigs his life upon
The everloupin' fountain
That frae the Dark ascends
Whaur Life begins, Thocht ends

* Dostoevski.

—A better gift deserves
Than thae wheen yatterin' nerves!

For mine's the clearest insicht
O' man's facility
For constant self-deception,
And hoo his mind can be
But as a floatin' iceberg
That hides aneth the sea
Its bulk; and hoo frae depths
O' an unfaddomed flood
Tensions o' nerves arise
And humours o' the blood
—Keethin's nane can trace
To their original place.

*Hoo mony men to mak' a man
It tak's he kens wha kens Life's plan.*

But there are flegsome deeps
Whaur the soul o' Scotland sleeps
That I to bottom need
To wauk Guid kens what deid,
Play at stertle-a-stobie,
Wi' nation's dust for hobby,
Or wi' God's sel' commerce
For the makin' o' a verse.

*"Melville, sea-compelling man,
Before whose wand Leviathan
Rose hoary-white upon the Deep,"* *
*What thou hast sown I fain 'ud reap
O' knowledge 'yont the human mind
In keepin' wi' oor Scottish kind,
And, thanks to thee, may aiblins reach
To what this Russian has to teach,
Closer than ony ither Scot,
Closer to me than my ain thocht,
Closer than my ain braith to me,*

* Quoted from Robert Buchanan.

As close as to the Deity
Approachable in whom appears
This Christ o' the neist thoosand years.

As frae your baggit wife
You turned whenever able,
And often when you werena,
Unto the gamin' table,
And opened wide to ruin
Your benmaist hert, aye brewin',
A horror o' whatever
Seemed likely to deliver
You frae the senseless strife
In which alane is life,
—As Burns in Edinburgh
Breenged arse-owre-heid thoro'
A' *it* could be the spur o'
To pleuch his sauted furrow,
And turned frae a' men honour
To what could only scunner
Wha thinks that common-sense
Can e'er be but a fence
To keep a soul worth ha'en
Frae what it s'ud be daein'
—Sae I in turn maun gie
My soul to misery,
Daidle disease
Upon my knees,
And welcome madness
Wi' exceedin' gladness
—Aye, open wide my hert
To a' the thistle's smert.

And a' the hopes o' men
Sall be like wiles then
To gar my soul betray
Its only richtfu' way,
Or as a couthie wife
That seeks nae mair frae life
Than domesticity

E'en wi' the likes o' me—
As gin I could be carin'
For her or for her bairn
When on my road I'm farin'
—O I can spend a nicht
In ony man's Delicht
Or wi' ony Wumman born
—But aye be aff the morn!

In a' the inklin's cryptic,
Then, o' an epileptic,
I ha'e been stood in you
And droukit in their grue
Till I can see richt through
Ilk weakness o' my frame
And ilka dernin' shame,
And can employ the same
To jouk the curse o' fame,
Lowsed frae the dominion
O' popular opinion,
And risen at last abune
The thistle like a mune
That looks serenely doon
On what queer things there are
In an inferior star
That couldna be, or see,
Themsel's, except in me.

Wi' burnt-oot hert and poxy face
I sall illumine a' the place,
And there in ne'er a found o' grace
That isna in a similar case.

Let a' the thistle's growth
Be as a process, then,
My spirit's gane richt through,
And needna threid again,
Tho' in it sall be haud'n
For aye the feck o' men
Wha's queer contortions there

As memories I ken,
As memories o' my ain
O' mony an ancient pain.
But sin' wha'll e'er wun free
Maun tak' like coorse to me,
A fillip I wad gi'e
Their eccentricity,
And leave the lave to dree
Their weirdless destiny.

It's no withoot regret
That I maun follow yet
The road that led me past
Humanity sae fast,
Yet scarce can gi'e a fate
That is at last mair fit
To them wha tak' that gait
Than theirs wha winna ha'e't,
Seein' that nae man can get
By ony airt or wile,
A destiny quite worth while
As fer as he can tell
—Or even you yoursel'!

And O! I canna thole
Aye yabblin' o' my soul,
And fain I wad be free
O' my eternal me,
Nor fare mysel' alane
—Withoot that tae be gane,
And this, I ha'e nae doot,
This road'll bring aboot.

The munelicht that owre clear defines
The thistle's shrill cantankerous lines
E'en noo whiles insubstantialises
Its grisly form and 'stead devises
A maze o' licht, a siller-frame,
As 'twere God's dream frae which it came,
Ne'er into bein' coorsened yet,

The essence lowin' pure in it,
As tho' the fire owrecam' the clay,
And left its wraith in endless day.

These are the moments when a' sense
Like mist is vanished and intense,
Magic emerges frae the dense
Body o' bein' and beeks immense
As, like a ghinn oot o' a bottle,
Daith rises frae's when oor lives crottle.

These are the moments when my sang
Clears its white feet frae oot amang
My broken thocht, and moves as free
As souls frae bodies when they dee.
There's naething left o' me ava'
Save a' I'd hoped micht whiles befa'.

Sic sang to men is little worth.
It has nae message for the earth.
Men see their warld turned tapsalteerie,
Drookit in a licht owre eerie,
Or sent birlin' like a peerie—
Syne it turns a' they've kent till then
To shapes they can nae langer ken.

Men canna look on nakit licht.
It flings them back wi' darkened sicht,
And een that canna look at it,
Maun draw earth closer roond them yet
Or, their sicht tint, find nocht insteed
That answers to their waefu' need.

And yet this essence frae the clay
In dooble form aye braks away,
For, in addition to the licht,
There is an e'er-increasin' nicht,
A nicht that is the bigger, and
Gangs roond licht like an airn band

That noo and then mair tichtly grips,
And snuffs it in a black eclipse,
But rings it maistly as a brough
The mune, till it's juist bricht enough—
O wull I never lowse a licht
I canna dowse again in spite,
Or dull to haud within my sicht?
The thistle canna vanish quite.
Inside a' licht its shape maun glint,
A spirit wi' a skeleton in't.

The world, the flesh, 'll bide in us
As in the fire the unburnt buss,
Or as frae sire to son we gang
And coontless corpses in us thrang.

And e'en the glory that descends
I kenna whence on *me* depends,
And shapes itsel' to what is left
Whaur I o' me ha'e me bereft,
And still the form is mine, altho'
A force to which I ne'er could grow
Is movin' in't as 'twere a sea
That lang syne drooned the last o' me
—That drooned afore the warld began
A' that could ever come frae Man.

And as at sicna times am I,
I wad ha'e Scotland to my eye
Until I saw a timeless flame
Tak' Auchtermuchty for a name,
And kent that Ecclefechan stood
As pairt o' an eternal mood.
Ahint the glory comes the nicht
As Maori to London's ruins,
And I'm amused to see the plicht
O' Licht as't in the black tide droons,
Yet even in the brain o' Chaos
For Scotland I wad hain a place,
And let Tighnabruaich still

Be pairt and paircel o' its will,
And Culloden, black as Hell,
A knowledge it has o' itsel'.

Thou, Dostoevski, understood,
Wha had your ain land in your bluid,
And into it as in a mould
The passion o' your bein' rolled,
Inherited in turn frae Heaven
Or sources fer abune it even.

Sae God retracts in endless stage
Through angel, devil, age on age,
Until at last his infinite natur'
Walks on earth a human cratur'
(Or less than human as to my een
The people are in Aiberdeen);
Sae man returns in endless growth
Till God in him again has scouth.

For sic a loup towards wisdom's croon
Hoo fer a man maun base him doon,
Hoo plunge aboot in Chaos ere
He finds his needfu' fittin' there,
The matrix oot o' which sublime
Serenity sall soar in time!

Ha'e I the cruelty I need,
Contempt and syne contempt o' that,
And still contempt in endless meed
That I may never yet be caught
In ony satisfaction, or
Bird-lime that winna let me soar?

Is Scotland big enough to be
A symbol o' that force in me,
In wha's divine inebriety
A sicht abune contempt I'll see?

For a' that's Scottish is in me,
As a' things Russian were in thee
And I in turn 'ud be an action
To pit in a concrete abstraction
My country's contrair qualities,
And mak' a unity o' these
Till my love owre its history dwells,
As owretone to a peal o' bells.
And in this heicher stratosphere
As bairn at giant at thee I peer. . . .

IN THE PECULIAR LIGHT OF LOVE

O Jean, in whom my spirit sees,
Clearer than through whisky or disease,
Its dernin' nature, wad the searchin' licht
Oor union raises poor'd owre me the nicht.

I'n faced wi' aspects o' mysel'
At last wha's portent nocht can tell,
Save that sheer licht o' life that when we're joint
Loups through me like a fire a' else i' aroint.

Clear my lourd flesh, and let me move
In the peculiar licht o' love,
As aiblins in Eternity men may
When their swack souls nae mair are clogged wi' clay.

Be thou the licht in which I stand
Entire, in thistle-shape, as planned,
And no' hauf-hidden and hauf-seen as here
In munelicht, whisky, and in fleshly fear,

In fear to look owre closely at
The grisly form in which I'm caught,
In sic a reelin' and imperfect licht
Sprung frae incongruous elements the nicht!

But wer't by thou they were shone on,
Then wad I ha'e nae dreid to con
The ugsome problems shapin' in my soul,
Or gin I hed—certes, nae fear you'd thole!

Be in this fibre like an eye
And ilka turn and twist descry,
Hoo here a leaf, a spine, a rose—or as
The purpose o' the poo'er that brings't to pass.

Syne liberate me frae this tree
As wha had there imprisoned me,
The end achieved—or show me at the least
Mair meanin' in't, and hope o' bein' released.

METAPHYSICAL PICTURES OF THE THISTLE

I tae ha'e heard Eternity drip water
(Aye water, water!), drap by drap
On the a'e nerve, like lichtnin', I've become,
And heard God passin' wi' a bobby's feet
Ootby in the lang coffin o' the street
—Seen stang by chitterin' knottit stang loup oot
Uncrushed by the echoes o' the thunderin' boot,
Till a' the dizzy lint-white lines o' torture made
A monstrous thistle in the space aboot me,
A symbol o' the puzzle o' man's soul
—And in my agony been pridefu' I could still
Tine nae least quiver or twist, watch ilka point
Like a white-het bodkin ripe my inmaist hert,
And aye wi' clearer pain that brocht nae anodyne,
But rose forever to a fer crescendo
Like eagles that ootsoar wi' skinklan wings
The thieveless sun they blin'
                    —And pridefu' still
That 'yont the sherp wings o' the eagles fleein'
Aboot the dowless pole o' Space,

Like leafs aboot a thistle-shank, my bluid
Could still thraw roses up
            —And up!

O rootless thistle through the warld that's pairt o' you,
Gin you'd withstand the agonies still to come,
You maun send roots doon to the deeps unkent,
Fer deeper than it's possible for ocht to gang,
Savin' the human soul,
Deeper than God himsel' has knowledge o',
Whaur lichtnin's canna probe that cleave the warld,
Whaur only in the entire dark there's founts of strength
Eternity's poisoned draps can never file,
And muckle roots thicken, deef to bobbies' feet.
A mony-brainchin' candelabra fills
The lift and's lowin' wi' the stars;
The Octopus Creation is wallopin'
In coontless faddoms o' a nameless sea.
I am the candelabra, and burn
My endless candles to an Unkent God.
I am the mind and meanin' o' the octopus
That thraws its empty airms through a' th' Inane.

And a' the bizzin' suns ha'e bigged
Their kaims upon the surface o' the sea.
My lips may feast for ever, but my guts
Ken naething o' the Food o' Gods.

"Let there be licht," said God, and there was
A little: but he lacked the poo'er
To licht up mair than pairt o' space at aince,
And there is lots o' darkness that's the same
As gin he'd never spoken
—Mair darkness than there's licht,
And dwarfin' to a candle-flame,
A spalin' candle that'll sune gang oot.
—Darkness comes closer to us than the licht,
And is oor natural element. We peer oot frae't
Like cat's een bleezin' in a goustrous nicht
(Whaur there is nocht to find but stars

That look like ither cats' een),
Like cat's een, and there is nocht to find
Savin' we turn them in upon oorsels;
Cats canna.

Darkness is wi' us a' the time, and Licht
But veesits pairt o' us, the wee-est pairt
Frae time to time on a short day atween twa nichts.
Nae licht is thrawn on *them* by ony licht.
Licht thraws nae licht upon itsel';
But in the darkness them wha's een
Nae fleetin' lichts ha'e dazzled and deceived
Find qualities o' licht, keener than ony licht
Keen and abidin';
That show the nicht unto itsel',
And syne the licht,
That queer extension o' the dark,
That seems a separate and a different thing,
And, seemin' sae, has lang confused the dark,
And set it at cross-purposes wi' itsel'.

O little Life
In which Daith guises and deceives itsel',
Joy that mak's Grief a Janus,
Hope that is Despair's fause-face,
And Guid and Ill that are the same,
Save as the chance licht fa's!
And yet the licht is there,
Whether frae within or frae withoot.
The conscious Dark can use it, dazzled nor deceived.
The licht is there, and th'instinct for it,
Pairt o' the Dark and o' the need to guise,
To deceive and be deceived,
But let us then be undeceived
When we deceive,
When we deceive oorsels.
Let us enjoy deceit, this instinct in us.
Licht cheenges naething.
And gin there is a God wha made the licht
We are adapted to receive,

He cheenged naething.
And hesna kythed Hissel!
Save in this licht that fa's whaur the Auld Nicht was,
Showin' naething that the darkness didna hide,
And gin it shows a pairt o' that
Confoondin' mair than it confides
Ev'n in that.

The epileptic thistle twitches
(A trick o' wund or mune or een—or whisky).
A brain laid bare,
A nervous system,
The skeleton wi' which men labour
And bring to life in Daith
—I, risen frae the deid, ha'e seen
My deid man's eunuch offspring.
—The licht frae bare banes whitening evermair,
Frae twitchin' nerves thrawn aff,
Frae nakit thocht,
Works in the Darkness like a fell disease,
A hungry acid and a cancer,
Disease o' Daith-in-Life and Life-in-Daith.

O for a root in some untroubled soil,
Some cauld soil 'yont this fevered warld,
That 'ud draw darkness frae a virgin source,
And send it slow and easefu' through my veins,
Release the tension o' my grisly leafs,
Withdraw my endless spikes,
Move coonter to the force in me that hauds
Me raxed and rigid and ridiculous
        And let my roses drap
Like punctured ba's that at a Fair
Fa' frae the loupin' jet!
        —Water again! . . .

THE THISTLE AS A SPIDER'S WEB

Omsk and the Calton turn again to dust,
The suns and stars fizz oot with little fuss,
The bobby booms away and seems to bust,
And leaves the world to darkness and to us.

The circles of our hungry thought
Swing savagely from pole to pole.
Death and the Raven drift above
The graves of Sweeney's body and soul.

My name is Norval. On the Grampian Hills
It is forgotten, and deserves to be.
So are the Grampian Hills and all the people
Who ever heard of either them or me.

What's in a name? From pole to pole
Our interlinked mentality spins.
I know that you are Deosil, and suppose
That therefore I am Widdershins.

Do you reverse? Shall us? Then let's.
Cyclone and Anti?—how absurd!
She should know better at her age.
Auntie's an ass, upon my word.

This is the sort of thing they teach
The Scottish children in the school.
Poetry, patriotism, manners—
No wonder I am such a fool. . . .

Hoo can I graipple wi' the thistle syne,
Be intricate as it and up to a' its moves?
A' airts its sheenin' points are loupin' 'yont me,
Quhile still the firmament it proves.

And syne it's like a wab in which the warld
Squats like a spider, quhile the mune and me
Are taigled in an endless corner o't
Tyauvin' fecklessly. . . .

FAREWELL TO DOSTOEVSKI

The wan leafs shak' atour us like the snaw.
Here is the cavaburd in which Earth's tint.
There's naebody but Oblivion and us,
Puir gangrel buddies, waunderin' hameless in't.

The stars are larochs o' auld cottages,
And a' Time's glen is fu' o' blinnin' stew.
Nae freen'ly lozen skimmers: and the wund
*Rises and separates even me and you.**

I ken nae Russian and you ken nae Scots.
We canna tell oor voices frae the wund.
The snaw is seekin' everywhere: oor herts
At last like roofless ingles it has fund.

And gethers there in drift on endless drift,
Oor broken herts that it can never fill;
And still—its leafs like snaw, its growth like **wund**—
The thistle rises and forever will! . . .

The thistle rises and forever will,
Getherin' the generations under't.
This is the monument o' a' they were,
And a' they hoped and wondered.

THE BARREN TREE

The barren tree, dry leafs and cracklin' thorns,
This is the mind o' a' humanity,
—The empty intellect that left to grow
'll let nocht ither be.
Lo! It has choked the sunlicht's gowden grain,
And strangled syne the white hairst o' the mune.

* Dostoevski.

Thocht that mak's a' the food o' nocht but Thocht
Is reishlin' grey abune. . . .

O fitly frae oor cancerous soil
May this heraldic horror rise!
The Presbyterian thistle flourishes,
And its ain roses crucifies. . . .

No Edinburgh Castle or the fields
O' Bannockburn or Flodden
Are dernin' wi' the miskent soul
Scotland sae lang has hod'n.

It hauds nae pew in ony kirk,
The soul Christ cam' to save;
Nae R.S.A.'s hae pentit it,
F.S.A.'s fund its grave.

Is it alive or deid? I show
My hert—wha will can see.
The secret clyre in Scotland's life
Has brust and reams through me.

A whummlin' sea in which is heard
The clunk o' nameless banes;
A grisly thistle dirlin' shrill
Abune the broken stanes.

Westminster Abbey nor the Fleet,
Nor England's Constitution, but
In a' the michty city there,
You mind a'e fleggit slut,

As Tolstoi o' Lucerne alane
Minded a'e beggar minstrel seen!
The woundit side draws a' the warld.
Barbarians ha'e lizards' een.

Glesca's a gless whaur Magdalene's
Discovered in a million crimes.

Christ comes again—wheesht, whatna bairn
In backlands cries betimes?

Hard faces prate o' their success
And pickle-makers awn the hills.
There is nae life in a' the land
But this infernal thistle kills. . . .

Nae mair I see
As aince I saw
Mysel' in the thistle
Harth and haw!

Nel suo profondo vidi che s'interna
Legato con amore in un volume
(Or else by Hate, fu' aft the better Love)
Ciò che per l'universo si squanderna

Sustanzia ed accidenti, e lor costume,
Quasi conflati insieme fer tal modo.
(The michty thistle in wha's boonds I rove)
Ché ciò ch'io dico è un semplice lume.*

And kent and was creation
In a' its coontless forms,
Or glitterin' in raw sunlicht,
Or dark wi' hurrying storms.

But what's the voice
That sings in me noo?
—A'e hauf o' me tellin'
The tither it's fou!

It's the voice o' the Sooth
That's held owre lang
My Viking North
Wi' its siren sang. . . .

* Wicksteed's translation of Dante's Italian (*Paradiso,* canto xxxiii, 85–90) is as follows: "Within its depths I saw ingathered bound by love in one volume, the scattered leaves of all the universe; substance and accidents and their relations, as though together fused, after such fashion that what I tell of is one simple flame."

FIER COMME UN ECOSSAIS

Fier comme un Ecossais

If a' that I can be's nae mair
Than what mankind's been yet, I'll no'
Begink the instincts thistlewise
That dern—and canna show.

Damned threids and thrums and skinny shapes
O' a' that micht, and su'd, ha' been
—Life onyhow at ony price!—
In sic I'll no' be seen!

Fier comme un Ecossais

The wee reliefs we ha'e in booze,
Or wun at times in carnal states,
May hide frae us but canna cheenge
The silly horrors o' oor fates.

Fier—comme un Ecossais!

THE EMPTINESS AT THE END

There's muckle in the root,
That never can wun oot,
Or't owre what is 'ud sweep
Like a thunderstorm owre sheep.

But shadows whiles upcreep,
And heavy tremors leap. . . .
C'wa', Daith, again, sned Life's vain shoot,
And your ain coonsel keep! . . .

Time like a bien wife,
Truth like a dog's gane—

The bien wife's gane to the aumrie
To get the puir dog a bane.

Opens the aumrie door,
And lo! the skeleton's there,
And the gude dog, Truth, has gotten
Banes for evermair. . . .

IN THE KEEL OF HEAVEN

Maun I tae perish in the keel o' Heaven,
And is this fratt upon the air the ply
O' cross-brath'd cordage that in gloffs and gowls
Brak's up the vision o' the warld's bricht gy?

Ship's tackle and an eemis cairn o' fraucht
Darker than clamourin' veins are roond me yet,
A plait o' shadows thicker than the flesh,
A fank o' tows that binds me hand and fit.

What gin the gorded fullyery on hie
And a' the fanerels o' the michty ship
Gi'e back mair licht than fa's upon them ev'n
Gin sic black ingangs haud us in their grip?

CREATION'S WHIRLIGIG

Grugous thistle, to my een
Your widdifow ramel evince,
Sibness to snakes wha's coils
Rin coonter airts at yince,
And fain I'd follow each
Gin you the trick'll teach.

Blin' root to bleezin rose,
Through a' the whirligig
O' shanks and leafs and jags
What sends ye sic a rig?
Bramble yokin' earth and heaven,
Till they're baith stramulyert driven!

Roses to lure the lift
And roots to wile the clay
And wuppit brainches syne
To claught them 'midyards tae
Till you've the precious pair
Like hang'd men dancin' there.

Wi' mony a seely prickle
You'll fleg a sunburst oot,
Or kittle earthquakes up
Wi' an amusin' root,
While, kilted in your tippet,
They still can mak' their rippit.

MY QUARREL WITH ENGLAND

And let me pit in guid set terms
My quarrel wi' th'owre sonsy rose,
That roond about its devotees
A fair fat cast o' aureole throws
That blinds them, in its mirlygoes,
To the necessity o' foes.

Upon their King and system I
Glower as on things that whiles in pairt
I may admire (at least for them),
But wi' nae claim upon my hert,
While a' their pleasure and their pride
Ootside me lies—and there maun bide.

Ootside me lies—and mair than that,
For I stand still for forces which
Were subjugated to mak' way
For England's poo'er, and to enrich
The kinds o' English, and o' Scots,
The least congenial to my thoughts.

Hauf his soul a Scot maun use
Indulgin' in illusions,
And hauf in gettin' rid o' them
And comin' to conclusions
Wi' the demoralisin' dearth
O' onything worth while on Earth. . . .

THE GREAT WHEEL

I'm weary o' the rose as o' my brain,
And for a deeper knowledge I am fain
Than frae this noddin' object I can gain.

Beauty is a'e thing, but it tines anither
(For, fegs, they never can be f'und thegither),
And 'twixt the twa it's no' for me to swither.

As frae the grun' sae thocht frae men springs oot,
A ferlie that tells little o' its source, I doot,
And has nae vera fundamental root.

And cauld agen my hert are laid
The words o' Plato when he said,
"God o' geometry is made."

Frae my ain mind I fa' away,
That never yet was feared to say
What turned the souls o' men to clay,

Nor cared gin truth frae me ootsprung
In ne'er a leed o' ony tongue
That ever in a heid was hung.

I ken hoo much oor life is fated
Aince its first cell is animated,
The fount frae which the flesh is jetted.

I ken hoo lourd the body lies
Upon the spirit when it flies
And fain abune its stars 'ud rise.

And see I noo a great wheel move,
And a' the notions that I love
Drap into stented groove and groove?

It maitters not my mind the day
Nocht maitters that I strive to dae,
—For the wheel moves on in its ain way.

I sall be moved as it decides
To look at Life frae ither sides:
Rejoice, rebel, its turn abides.

And as I see the great wheel spin
There flees a licht frae't lang and thin
That Earth is like a snaw-ba' in.

(To the uncanny thocht I clutch
—The nature o' man's soul is such
That it can ne'er wi' life tine touch.

Man's mind is in God's image made,
And in its wildest dreams arrayed
In pairt o' Truth is still displayed.

Then suddenly I see as weel
As me spun roon' within the wheel,
The helpless forms o' God and Deil.

And on a birlin' edge I see
Wee Scotland squattin' like a flea,
And dizzy wi' the speed, and me!)

I've often thrawn the warld frae me,
Into the Pool o' Space, to see
The Circles o' Infinity.

Or like a flat stone gar'd it skite,
A Morse code message writ in licht
That yet I couldna read aricht.

The skippin' sparks, the ripples, rit
Like skritches o' a grain o' grit
'Neth Juggernaut in which I sit.

Twenty-six thoosand years it tak's
Afore a'e single roond it mak's,
And syne it melts as it were wax.

The Phoenix guise 't'll rise in syne
Is mair than Euclid or Einstein
Can dream o' or's in dreams o' mine.

Upon the huge circumference are
As neebor points the Heavenly War
That dung doun Lucifer sae far,

And that upheaval in which I
Sodgered 'neth the Grecian sky
And in Italy and Marseilles,

And there isna room for men
Wha the haill o' history ken
To pit a pin twixt then and then.

Whaur are Bannockburn and Flodden?
—O' a'e grain like facets hod'n,
Little wars (twixt that which God in

Focht and won, and that which He
Took baith sides in hopelessly),
Less than God or I can see

By whatna cry o' mine oottopped
Sall be a' men ha'e sung and hoped
When to a'e note they're telescoped?

And Jesus and a nameless ape
Collide and share the selfsame shape
That nocht terrestrial can escape?

But less than this nae man need try.
He'd better be content to eye
The wheel in silence whirlin' by.

Nae verse is worth a ha'et until
It can join issue wi' the Will
That raised the Wheel and spins it still,

But a' the music that mankind,
'S made yet is to the Earth confined,
Poo'erless to reach the general mind,

Poo'erless to reach the neist star e'en,
That as a pairt o'ts sel' is seen,
And only men can tell between.

Yet I exult oor sang has yet
To grow wings that'll cairry it
Ayont its native speck o' grit.

And I exult to find in me
The thocht that this can ever be,
A hope still for humanity.

For gin the sun and mune at last
Are as a neebor's lintel passed,
The wheel'll tine its stature fast,

And birl in time inside oor heids
Till we can thraw oot conscious gleids
That draw an answer to oor needs,

Or if nae answer still we find
Brichten till a' thing is defined
In the huge licht-beams o' oor kind,

And if we still can find nae trace
Ahint the Wheel o' ony Face,
There'll be a glory in the place,

And may we aiblins swing content
Upon the wheel in which we're pent
In adequate enlightenment.

Nae ither thocht can mitigate
The horror o' the endless Fate
A'thing's whirled in predestinate.

O whiles I'd fain be blin' to it,
As men wha through the ages sit,
And never move frae aff the bit,

Wha hear a Burns or Shakespear sing,
Yet still their ain bit jingles string,
As they were worth the fashioning.

Whatever Scotland is to me,
Be it aye pairt o' a' men see
O' Earth and o' Eternity

Wha winna hide their heids in't till
It seems the haill o' Space to fill,
As 'twere an unsurmounted hill.

He canna Scotland see what yet
Canna see the Infinite,
And Scotland in true scale to it.

Nor blame I muckle, wham atour
Earth's countries blaw, a pickle stour,
To sort wha's grains they ha's nae poo'er.

E'en stars are seen thegither in
A'e skime o' licht as grey as tin
Flyin' on the wheel as 'twere a pin.

Syne ither systems ray on ray
Skinkle past in quick array
While it is still the self-same day,

A'e day o' a' the million days
Through which the soul o' man can gaze
Upon the wheel's incessant blaze,

Upon the wheel's incessant blaze
As it were on a single place
That twinklin' filled the howe o' space.

A'e point is a' that it can be,
I wis nae man'll ever see
The rest o' the rotundity.

Impersonality sall blaw
Through me as 'twere a bluffert o' snaw
To scour me o' my sense o' awe,

A bluffert o' snaw, the licht that flees
Within the Wheel, and freedom gi'es
Frae Dust and Daith and a' Disease,

—The drumlie doom that only weighs
On them wha ha'ena seen their place
Yet in creation's lichtnin' race,

In the movement that includes
As a tide's resistless floods
A' their movements and their moods,—

Until disinterested we,
O' a' oor auld delusions free,
Lowe in the wheel's serenity

As conscious items in the licht,
And keen to keep it clear and richt
In which the haill machine is dight,

The licht nae man has ever seen
Till he has felt that he's been gi'en
The stars themsels insteed o' een,

And often wi' the sun has glowered
At the white mune until it cowered,
As when by new thocht auld's o'erpowered.

Oor universe is like an e'e
Turned in, man's benmaist hert to see,
And swamped in subjectivity.

But whether it can use its sicht
To bring what lies withoot to licht
To answer's still ayont my micht.

But when that inturned look has brocht
To licht what still in vain it's socht
Ootward maun be the bent o' thocht.

And organs may develop syne
Responsive to the need divine
O' single-minded humankin'.

The function, as it seems to me,
O' Poetry is to bring to be
At lang, lang last that unity. . . .

But wae's me on the weary wheel!
Higgledy-piggledy in't we reel,
And little it cares hoo we may feel.

Twenty-six thoosand years 't'll tak'
For it to threid the Zodiac;
—A single roond o' the wheel to mak'!

Lately it turned—I saw mysel'
In sic a company doomed to mell.
I micht ha'e been in Dante's Hell.

It shows hoo little the best o' men
E'en o' themsels at times can ken,
—I sune saw that when I gaed ben

The lesser wheel within the big
That moves as merry as a grig
Wi' mankind in its whirligig

And hasna turned a'e circle yet
Tho' as it turns we slide in it,
And needs maun tak' the place we get,

I felt it turn, and syne I saw
John Knox and Clavers in my raw,
And Mary Queen o' Scots ana',

And Rabbie Burns and Weelum Wallace,
And Carlyle lookin' unco gallus,
And Harry Lauder (to enthrall us).

And as I looked I saw them a',
A' the Scots baith big and sma',
That e'er the braith o' life did draw.

"Mercy o' Gode, I canna thole
Wi' sic an orra mob to roll."
—"Wheesht! It's for the guid o' your soul."

"But what's the meanin', what's the sense?"
—"Men shift but by experience,
'Twixt Scots there is nae difference.

They canna learn, sae canna move,
But stick for aye to their auld groove
—The only race in History who've

Bidden in the same category
Frae stert to present o' their story,
And deem their ignorance their glory.

The mair they differ, mair the same.
The wheel can whummle a' but them,
—They ca' their obstinacy 'Hame,'

And 'Puir Auld Scotland' bleat wi' pride,
And wi' their minds made up to bide
A thorn in a' the wide world's side.

There ha'e been Scots wha ha'e ha'en thochts
They're strewn through maist o' the various lots
—Sic traitors are nae langer Scots!"

"But in this huge ineducable
Heterogeneous hotch and rabble,
Why am *I* condemned to squabble?"

"A Scottish poet maun assume
The burden o' his people's doom,
And dee to brak' their livin' tomb.

Mony ha'e tried, but a' ha'e failed.
Their sacrifice has nocht availed.
Upon the thistle they're impaled.

You maun choose but gin ye'd see
Anither category ye
Maun tine your nationality."

And I look at a' the random
Band the wheel leaves whaur it fand 'em.
         "Auch, to Hell,
I'll tak' it to avizandum." . . .

O wae's me on the weary wheel,
And fain I'd understand them!

And blessin' on the weary wheel,
Whaurever it may land them! . . .

But aince Jean kens what I've been through
The nicht, I dinna doot it,
She'll ope her airms in welcome true,
And clack nae mair aboot it. . . .

THE STARS LIKE THISTLE'S
ROSES FLOWER

The stars like thistle's roses floo'er
The sterile growth o' Space ootour,
That clad in bitter blasts spreids oot
Frae me, the sustenance o' its root.

O fain I'd keep my hert entire,
Fain hain the licht o' my desire,
But ech! the shinin' streams ascend,
And leave me empty at the end.

For aince it's toomed my hert and brain,
The thistle needs maun fa' again.
—But a' its growth 'll never fill
The hole it's turned my life intill! . . .

YET HA'E I SILENCE LEFT

Yet ha'e I Silence left, the croon o' a'.

No' her, wha on the hills langsyne I saw
Liftin' a foreheid o' perpetual snaw.

No' her, wha in the how-dumb-deid o' nicht
Kyths, like Eternity in Time's despite.

No' her, withooten shape, wha's name is Daith,
No' Him, unkennable abies to faith

—God whom, gin e'er He saw a Man, 'ud be
E'en mair dumfooner'd at the sicht than he.

—But Him, whom nocht in man or Deity,
Or Daith or Dreid or Laneliness can touch,
Wha's deed owre often and has seen owre much.

O I ha'e Silence left,

            —"And weel ye micht,"
Sae Jean'll say, "efter sic a nicht!"

From

To Circumjack Cencrastus

1930

THE DAY OF THE CRUCIFIXION

Hunters were oot on a Scottish hill
A'e day when the sun stude suddenly still
At noon and turned the colour o' port
A perfect nuisance, spoilin' their sport.
Syne it gaed pitch black a'thegither.
Isn't that juist like oor Scottish weather!

SHADOWS THAT FEED ON THE LIGHT

Shaddows that feed on the licht for aye
Hauntin' the waters that canna win free,
The wild burn loups but you haud it fast
As the hands o' the past haud me.

A burn may dream o' a warld aince mair
O' water and licht and nocht beside,
But has aye as faur to gang as it's gane,
And a burn in the dark roots' clutch'll bide.

Tint in a windhaw or siller swirl
Bigger and blacker the roots strike back,
As whiles through a high-falutin' o' love
I hear my body mockin' my talk. . . .

THE SHEILING OF THE BROKEN HEART

Yet wae for the poet wi' nocht but his bluid
   For a bardic goon.
Like the last dark reid crawberries under the firs
   His life'll be sune.
     Bodach cleoncain deirg.

For he that's aince lain in the Yellow Stag's Couch
   —Leabaidh an Daimhe Bhuide—
'll never sing frae the Ruigh Bristidh Cridhe *
   The sangs he s'ud to ye.
     Bodach cleancain deirg . . .

THE MAVIS OF PABAL

I am the mavis o' Pabal
   Back on the tap o' the hill,
My voice and wings still wantin'
   A wee thing in strength and skill.
I am the mavis o' Pabal, lang
I've lain wi' my heid on my breist
In a day that was dark, my sang
Forgotten like licht in the East,
   But the dawn is breakin' at last
   And I'm back on the tap o' the hill
   And I'll sing as I sang in the past
   —If singin' depends upon will!

I am the mavis o' Pabal,
   A pool cut aff frae the sea,
A tree withoot roots that stands
   On the ground unsteadily.
I should ha'e stayed wi' the rest
Doon in Coille Ghrumach still

* The Sheiling of the Broken Heart.

And no' ettled to be on the crest
O' this bricht impossible hill,
   For poetry's no' made in a lifetime
   And I lack a livin' past;
   I stand on the tap o' the hill
   —But the miracle canna last!

Maun I flee the Atlantic tae
   Whaur ten thoosand o' the clan
Host whaur the first ane landit
   —I'd leifer ha'e seen nae dawn.
Can I sing them back hame again?
The nicht has lasted owre lang,
And I doot if American clansmen
Are worth the orts o' a sang.
   —O it's fine to be back in the sun
   And the shoots are tender and green
   But I'm lanely, and flute as I will,
   There's nae sign o' a mate to be seen!

THE PARROT CRY

Tell me the auld, auld story
O' hoo the Union brocht
Puir Scotland into being
As a country worth a thocht.
England, frae whom a' blessings flow
What could we dae withoot ye?
Then dinna threip it doon oor throats
As gin we e'er could doot ye!
   My feelings lang wi' gratitude
   Ha'e been sae sairly harrowed
   That dod! I think it's time
   The claith was owre the parrot!

Tell me o' Scottish enterprise
And canniness and thrift,

And hoo we're baith less Scots and mair
Than ever under George the Fifth,
And hoo to "wider interests"
Oor ain we sacrifice
And yet tine naething by it
As aye the parrot cries.
    Syne gi'e's a chance to think it oot
    Aince we're a' weel awaur o't,
    For, losh, I think it's time
    The claith was owre the parrot!

Tell me o' love o' country
Content to see't decay,
And ony ither paradox
Ye think o' by the way.
I doot it needs a Hegel
Sic opposites to fuse;
Oor education's failin'
And canna gi'e's the views
    That were peculiar to us
    Afore oor vision narrowed
    And gar'd us think it time
    The claith was owre the parrot!

A parrot's weel eneuch at times
But whiles we'd liefer hear
A blackbird or a mavis
Singin' fu' blythe and clear.
Fetch ony native Scottish bird
Frae the eagle to the wren,
And faith! you'd hear a different sang
Frae this painted foreigner's then.
    The marine that brocht it owre
    Believed its every word
    —But we're a' deeved to daith
    Wi' his infernal bird.

It's possible that Scotland yet
May hear its ain voice speak
If only we can silence

[155]

This endless-yatterin' beak.
The blessing wi' the black
Selvedge is the clout!
It's silenced Scotland lang eneuch,
Gi'e England turn aboot.
    For the puir bird needs its rest—
    Wha else'll be the waur o't?
    And it's lang past the time
    The claith was owre the parrot!

And gin that disna dae, lads,
We e'en maun draw its neck
And heist its body on a stick
A' ither pests to check.
I'd raither keep't alive, and whiles
Let bairns keek in and hear
What the Balliol accent used to be
Frae the Predominant Pairtner here!
    —But save to please the bairns
    I'd absolutely bar it
    For fegs, it's aye high time
    The claith was owre the parrot!

FROM THE SCOTS ANTHOLOGY

- I -

We're a'e clan here; I micht as weel
Ha'e been a Campbell as a MacNeill.

- II -

Alas that life is past
Noo I'm a laird at last.

- III -

I'm deid, no' daft, and dinna need
A folly o' flooers aboot my heid.

- IV -

Here lie MacDonalds glad to tine
A' that's become o' Scotland syne.

- V -

Croon me wi' blackthorn noo; in life
Droighneach * resisted a' my strife.

- VI -

Nae man that wants to ha'e ideas
Aboot life efter daith sud wait till he dees.

- VII -

The warld has fadit frae view
As Benbecula used to
And nae seagull follows my curragh noo.

- VIII -

My grave's no' bad; they've put intill't
Twa o' the Sassenachs I kill't.
I'll kill them again as sune as the horn
Toots on the Resurrection Morn.

- IX -

You've taen frae me the man that I loved.
Hoo do you think that in Heaven I'll ken
Him noo that you've made him ane o' your saints?
Keep him; I'd leifer no' see him again.

- X -

I'm deid. That's a' that's aboot it.
If you werena livin' you wadna doot it.

- XI -

Here in this forhooied nest
To a cauld egg I pit my breast,
And may Eternity dae the rest.
                              I canna mair.

* A metre called "blackthorny" because of its intricacy.

[157]

A FOOL SINGS

A fool sings "O it's braw to see
The mortal coil come adder-like
Oot o' the heather at yin's feet
And owre the glintin' water strike
In corkscrew style and instant glide
Frae sicht again on yonder side.

"Wad that the Zeitgeist, progress, a'
The warld's perplexities thegither
Micht as sma-bookit slide across
Oor vision in the sunny weather,
And leave the gowden warld ahint
Withoot a single crinkle in't." . . .

FROM THE GERMAN OF
RAINER MARIA RILKE *

I have been frequently astonished, letting go
My dead at last, to see them so at home
In death, so unexpectedly at rights,
So in their element that in a trice
'Twas ill to fathom they had ever lived. . . .
You only, you come back, and seem to try
To come in touch with something that will ring
Out suddenly, and show that you are here. . . .
O rob me not of what I've hardly learnt,
For I am right and you are wrong if still
You covet anything of so-called life.
We change all this, and see there's nothing here
In the clear light of our perfected selves.

I had more faith in you, and it confounds
All my ideas to find you here again,
You who changed most abysmally of all.

* Translation of Rilke's *Requiem—Für eine Freundin* (Requiem: To Paula Modersohn-Becker).

Not that your death is still incredible
(Although the manner of it tore apart
All we had been from aught we since could be
And made it difficult for us to find
Ourselves again). The trouble is that you
Were terrified to die, and keep your fear
Where fear is out of question, and so lose
A bit of your eternity, and lapse
Back here where nothing is as yet itself
—That broken, merged for the first time in the All,
You cannot see as even here you could
Life's upward irreversible way, and fall
By the dead weight of grievance from the spheres
To which you now belong to this poor past.
—*That* wakes me often like a thief at night.

Would I could think that you came sportively,
Because you are too certain of yourself,
O'erspilling your abundance, like a child
Going careless where grown folks must needs have care.
But ah! You ask for something. In my bones
That fact goes back and forward like a saw.
You ask for something. Though you were a dream
Tormenting me, pursuing me at nights,
When I retreat into my lungs and bowels
And the last poorest chamber of my heart.
E'en that were easier borne. . . . What do you ask?

What can I do for you? Is something, left
Behind you inadvertently, crying
Incessantly to find where you have gone
And vainly craving to be after you?
Where is it? Must I seek it in some part
Of life you never knew you had at all—
And failed to reckon with before you died.
Then I'll go there at once, and watch the ways
Of women about the doors and with their young,
Converse with all and sundry, and secure
An audience of the King, suborn the priests
To let me enter their holy places—yea,

And above all I will, when I've learned much,
Look simply at the animals until
An essence from them imperceptibly
Glides into me—stand in their eyes awhile
And witness how they put me out again
Gently, incuriously, and unjudged.

I'll get the gardeners to name their flowers
That in what I remember I may bring
Some faint suggestions of their myriad scents;
And fruits—I'll buy fruits till that country's like
Our old idea of what Heaven would be.
Full fruits! Ah, these you understand, set them
On plates before you, counterbalancing
Their weights with colours; and like fruits you saw
Women and children driven hither from within
Into their lives, and naked bore yourself
Fruit-like at last before the mirror here
Looking at yourself till like a pool your look
Closed over you, insubstantialised
(And no more saying: "This am I, no that is")
In those pure depths from which it had no wish
That you should ever re-emerge. Blessed!

Thus had I kept you, as you steeped yourself
Deep in the mirror. Why come differently?
What to recant? To tell me what? Is there
A sacrificial weight in amber beads
A visual recollection fails to show?
My memory cannot tell the purport now
Of looks so urgent and discharactered,
Or why your body's graces all appear
Like lines of destiny on an outheld palm.

Come to the candle. I don't fear the dead.
If they are to be seen my eyes will see
Them naturally enough. Come hither then.
See this cut rose. The light's as shy of it
As 'tis of you. It, too, need not be here.
But if't had stayed outside, unmixed with me,

It would have kept on growing and ere this
Have fallen apart—whereas it lingers here;
And yet—what is my consciousness to it?

Do not be frightened if I understand,
(Ah, there! It comes to me) for I must know
Even though the knowledge kills. I know you're here.
Even as a blind man fumbles round a thing
I feel your plight and have no name for it.
Let us lament together—the broken mirror
And you found naked in your hiding place.

Can you still weep? You cannot. All your tears
Contributed to ripen you and sent
The saps within you mounting in a life
That climbed and circled—to that height from which
Your fate reclaimed you, taking bit by bit
And daily more, till nothing but the core
Was left, full of the green seeds of your death;
And these you tasted in your hunger too
And found an after-sweetness in your mouth.
From this self-sacrifice your life returned
All trembling and mistrustful to its tasks.
How strange your most familiar organs seemed
(All save that one, exigent and estranged)
To your blood refluent from that secret source
Whether you had to drive it, make it eat,
Again and yet again, the while it looked,
The ingrate thing, as though you poisoned it.
You forced it finally—and lo! it ran
Too fast, too fast, it ran. You sought to cry:
"Whoa there! You're far enough. Too far for me
To herd you back"—but suddenly you knew
'Twas gone too far indeed, beyond recall.
The time to drive it back would come no more
Like a recurrent illness. You were free.

How short your life was, put against the hours
You sat surrendering all you might have been
To that blind germ of destiny again.

O tragic task! O task beyond all power!
How day by day you undid all you'd grown,
Made yourself down to other ends and still
Had courage to be proud of doing it well,
And then you looked for your reward at last
As children do when they take medicine,
But you'd to do your own rewarding too.
You were too far away from us even then.
No one could think of anything to please.
You knew it, and sat up in childhood there
And from the mirror that was you received
Your own self back, eager as a woman is
Dressing for visitors and doing her hair.
And so you died, as other women died
Before you in that cosy home, the death
Of women lying-in, who'd close themselves
Again, and only be themselves, but ah!
Cannot because the darkness enters in
And will not be denied—the darkness that
Women give birth to with—the outer dark.

Surely the keening women should have keened
In truth—women who weep for pay and whine
The whole night through, if they are paid enough,
When there's no other sound. Customs, hither.
We need more customs. Let us show our grief.
We acquiesce too readily—and so
You, dead, come back that you and I may mourn
Your death more adequately. Hear me then.
Fain would I throw my voice as 'twere a cloth
Over your remains, and have all I am
Torn into rags for ever, were mourning all.
Beyond all lamentation I accuse—
Not him who drew you back out of yourself
(I do not know him—he is all mankind)
But I impeach the world in him the Man.

If my life holds a state of having been
A child I can't recall—the purest state
Of being a child my earliest childhood knew,

I do not want to know it—I want to make
An angel of it without seeing it
And send it into the very front rank
Of shouting angels who remember God.
The agony has lasted far too long.
It is beyond us—this anachronism
Of false love spawning out of habit,
And claiming as its rights the wrongs it does.
Where is the man who has the right to own
What only snatches itself up at nights
Blissfully as a child might snatch a ball?

Are you still here, unseen? You knew as much
Of all this and might have had so much,
Open for everything, like a dawning day.
Women can suffer. To love's to be alone.
Poets know love's a readiness to change.
You were both woman and poet, and both form part
Of what our memories distort as you.
You grew so homely, taking in your looks
Like flags the morning after a fête—and all
You wanted was a long day's work, but ah!
The work was never done—is not done yet!

If you're still here—if in this darkness there's
A place in which your spirit hovers still
About the tired sounds of my lonely voice
Hear me, help me, for see we disappear,
Not knowing when, into anything beyond our thought
Even as a landsman's eyesight fails to hold
The Deity on the shoulders of a ship,
When its own lightness lifts it suddenly
Up and away into the bright sea wind. . . .

SCOTLAND'S FOUR
UNIVERSITIES

Oor four Universities
Are Scots but in name;
They wadna be here
If ither folk did the same
—Paid heed tae a' lear
Exceptin' their ain,
For they'd cancel oot syne
And leave us wi' nane.

I summoned the students
And spiered them to tell
Where Trenmor triumphed
Or Oscar fell.
"Dammit," I cried,
"But here is a mystery—
That nane o' ye ken
The first word in history!"

I tested them neist
In geography and there
Their ignorance was such
As gar'd me despair
Innis Fada and Rosnat
Made them look green as
I'd spoken o' places
On the faur side o' Venus!

But, och, when I cam'
To Arts and Letters,
The gomerils gapit
And shamed their begetters!
—Even Muireadach Albannach,
Lachlan Mor of his stem,
And Finlay Macnab
Meant nothing to them!

The professors were waur
Than the students were even,
And yattered in Sanscrit
Or Czech—wi' a leaven
O' some kind o' English,
A leid o' their ain;
God grant I may never
Hear the like o't again!

"I'm beggin your pardon
A mistake has been made.
It was SCOTS Universities
I was seekin'," I said.
"To condemn your ignorance
'Ud indeed be to wrang you
When in Hell here there isna
A Scotsman amang you!"

LOURD ON MY HERT

Lourd on my hert as winter lies
The state that Scotland's in the day.
Spring to the North has aye come slow
But noo dour winter's like to stay
  For guid,
  And no' for guid!

O wae's me on the weary days
When it is scarce grey licht at noon;
It maun be a' the stupid folk
Diffusin' their dullness roon and roon
  Like soot
  That keeps the sunlicht oot.

Nae wonder if I think I see
A lichter shadow than the neist

I'm fain to cry: "The dawn, the dawn!
I see it brakin' in the East."
    But ah
    —It's juist mair snaw!

HISTORIA ABSCONDITA

The Muse to whom his hert is given,
Historia Abscondita,
's already workin' like a leaven
To manifest her law.

The Gaelic sun swings up again
And to itself doth draw
A' kindlin' things, while a' the lave
Like rook is blawn awa'. . . .

THE IRISH IN SCOTLAND *

"Come tell me more of Scotland
—I know its many poets,
Byron, Lermontov and Wergeland,
And how Kant and Satie show its
Blood in their diverse ways;
And how Jean Rictus lived
In Edinburgh—Chopin too;
And what Stendhal says
            Of Scottish airs,
And now I'd fain hear you. . . ."

I asked him if he'd heard
Of Burns or Sir Walter Scott,

* These verses were published as a separate poem in *The Irish Statesman* under the
title of "The Irish in Scotland (to a visitor from France)."

Of Carlyle or R.L.S.
He said that he had not.
"Some people think that these
Are representative. . . . I don't.
At least, you've little to forget,
And should assimilate with ease,
        From that false Scotland free,
All that's worth knowing yet."

I took him to the islands
Where the wells are undefiled
And folk sing as their fathers sang
Before Christ was a child,
Then by gask and laggan and coul
To Aigas in Strathglass
Where he heard a port on the golden chanter
That can never be heard by a fool,
        And lastly to Lochan na Mna
That will respond, I believe,
To me, if I want her
As Lake Saima couldn't to Soloviev.

"On aird tuaidh tig in chabhair"
I said as we turned south,
And quoted "A theachlain thig ón Róimh,"
With blessings on the honey mouth
That loved the forests of Alba,
Cut down now, that may grow again
Thanks to the branch of Ireland
Growing among us with might and main
And "Dhia libh a laochradh Ghaoidheal"
And "curse the Sassenachs"
And left him, twenty miles from Carlisle,
        On his way back to France. . . .

Wad that I held Staoiligary
    And the four pennies o' Drimisdale,
And had never seen a news-sheet,
    No' even "The Daily Mail,"
The fifteen generations afore me

Could lippen me no' to fail
Into the darkness o' alien time,
    To carry my sang and sgeul
As the duck when she hears the thunder
    Dances to her ain Port a' Beul! . . .

At dawn the heid o' Clais Linneach
    A mile frae Fuaran Dhe
I saw a wee clood that awa doon
    In Glen Guisachan lay.
It grew as the sun's strength grew
Till it filled ilka glen and corrie
And covered o' but the heichmaist taps
O' the Cairngorms billowin' hoary.

The sun's licht on the clood reflected
    As on the waves o' a sea,
And as frae the Ark on Ararat
    The warld then was to me;
Syne fifty miles owre the mist-ocean
Wha but Alasdair MacMhaighstir stude?
Pricked oot in the blue and gowd there
In his maist idiosyncratic mood!

Faurer awa', steeply, oot o' the sun-bathed
    Distant Atlantic's waters
The great poets o' Gaelic Ireland
    Soared up frae the rags and tatters
O' the muckle grey mist o' Englishry—
Phoenix-flight frae the ashes upbeatin'—
Raifteri, O Rathaille, O Suilleabhain,
Feiriter, Haicead, and Ceitinn!

No' muckle's been tint in the Deluge
    Suppose it subsides nae mair.
I'm brawly content wi' what's left,
    And the ignorance flowin' doon there
Emphasises by way o' contrast

The glorious music abune
—Great poems manifestin' at aince
Ilka phase o' the sun and mune! . . .

TO ALASDAIR MacMHAIGHSTIR ALASDAIR *

Sall moudiewarps like eagles thrill
   Wi' a' the warld at view?
Blether o' Burns and Tannahill
   Wha kenna you
And roost their mice what never saw
   The Lion ava'?

Puir Rimbaud in his Bateau Ivre
   Gaed skitin' roond a dub;
O' Earth and no' juist Hell un livre
   The puir bit cub
Had aiblins made, gin he'd survived
Whaur your boat thrived.

Jaupin' the stars, or thrawin' lang strings
   O' duileasg owre the sun
Till like a jeely fish it swings
   In depths rewon,
And in your brain as in God's ain
   A'thing's ane again!

Auld Noah in his sea-barn was
   Your canny prototype;
Moses juist halved a burn, whereas
   You'd seas to flype,
And Melville sailed to jouk the world
   Through which you hurled.

* Great Scottish Gaelic poet, Alexander MacDonald (1700?–1780?).

As in his lines Valéry tries
To keep but their ain life,
Whereas in yours sea, earth and sky's
  A' hotchin' rife,
Your genius copes wi' a' that is
In endless ecstasies.

The blythe broon wren and viein' linnet
  Tune up their pipes in you,
The blackcock craws, the reid hen's in it,
  Swan and cuckoo;
Fishes' and bees' and friskin' calves'
  Acutes and graves! . . .

O time eneuch for Heaven or Hell
  Efter a man is deid,
But while we're here it's life itsel',
  And meikle o't we need,
And, certes, coupin' up the Earth,
  You f'und nae dearth!

Praisin' Morag or dispraisin',
  What does a poet care?
Sugar Brook's tune, sea's diapason,
  A's grist that's there.
Sodger, sailor, and poet chiel
  —And man as weel!

Wad that in thae thrang modern times
  I micht inherit,
And manifest in a' my rhymes,
  Your dowless spirit,
That balks at nought—aye competent
  To be—and ken't!

Like Leontiev and you I'd keep
  A' Earth's variety,
And to the endless challenge leap
  O' God's nimiety

—*Aiblins, like Him and you, great* Gael
  Whiles see Life haill,

As in yon michty passage in
  The Bhagavad-Gita where
A' Nature casts its ooter skin
  And kyths afore us, bare,
Compliqué, nombreaux, . . . et chinois!
  The airmy o' the Law!

SCOTLAND

Scotland's cauld and grey, you say,
But it's no' ill to prove
Oor dourest hills are only
Rainbows at a'e remove.

Gowdfinches were rife on the Borders
Till the eighteen-forties but syne
Disappeared and didna come back
Till the new century started,
But wherever there's thistles and hardheids
There's charms o' them noo.
Wad the Borders could mak' good a'
  Their losses like this!

A cock siskin sings in a spruce,
Crossbills are thrang wi' the rowans,
And a big crap o' beechmast has brocht
Mair bramblings aboot than ever,
I'll hear them breezin' afore
They leave for the North again,
And aiblins I'll follow them there
  And aiblins I'll no'.

A'e winter thirteen waxwings, hungry
Wi' their crossin' frae Europe, stript

Yon brier o' its hips in a hurry,
And I aince saw a yellow-browed warbler
Near by; and four grey shrikes in the Dale;
And there's nae sayin' what I'll no' see
In the neighbourhood yet, nae maitter
    Hoo lanely and quiet it looks. . . .

(Yet it'll gie me mair joy to see
Ocht natural tho' rare
—A honey-buzzard, or peregrine—
Than a Roc or Moa there. . . .)

TYUTCHEV WAS RIGHT

You say it isna lawfu'
To speir frae whence it springs,
As 'twere to place and motion
Subject like ither things
For it neither comes here
Nor yet can gang awa'
Tho' whiles we see't and whiles
It canna be seen at a'.

You say that we maun wait
As men wait for the dawn,
But the sun's way by nicht
Is plain to Everyman,
And tho' we mauna seek
This secret source, you say,
Some o's 'll find it yet
—At least in the same way.

When Wordsworth saw Lucy row'd
In Earth's diurnal course
Wi' rocks and stanes and trees
He saw by science perforce,

And contrair to human sense;
We gang mair contrair still
Wi' ideas we canna express
Except by a miracle.

The trouble is that words
Are a' but useless noo
To span the gulf atween
The human and "highbrow" view
—Victims at ilka point
O' optical illusions,
Brute Nature's limitations,
And inherited confusions.

Silence is the only way,
Speech squares aye less wi' fact.
Silence—like Chaos ere the Word
That gar'd the Play enact
That sune to conscious thocht
Maun seem a foolish dream.
Nae Word has yet been said,
Nae Licht's begun to gleam.

Tyutchev was richt and men maun gang
Awa' frae life to find
Haill worlds o' magic thochts
Day's licht can only blind,—
Thochts that they ne'er can share
Sin' each man's faurer are
Frae ony ither man's
Than star frae wide-set star
And faurer frae his usual sel'
Than Heaven is frae Hell.

But a' the stream o' consciousness
In maitter as in a tunnel lost
'll yet win free and jaw
Owre the warld's edge tost
Like a gowden waterfall

Naething can backward turn,
Nor spin in a vicious roond
Like yon apodeictic burn.

O wad that men could think
No' rationalise insteed
Mere preconceptions till
Nae real thocht's in their heid
And wad that they kent hauf
As muckle o' themsels
And things that maitter mair
As Science o' chemicals.

I'm gratefu' for the stream
That rids us o' vain dreams
And thraws us back upon
Oorsel's i' its clear gleams,
And yet we mauna be
Objective like the Greeks
Blind o' a'e e'e—and no' the ane
That humour steeks!

As Wordsworth shair o' his ain mind
The precipice whiles socht
Whaur a' else fa's awa'
And vanishes into thocht
Sae I repudiate here
As treachery to mankind
Contentment wi' the graces men
Like beasts or floo'ers may find.

And look to see the fountain
That loups to a certain height
And fa's again and rises,
As tho' were the sun's delight
To brak' its shaft and glitter
Frae abune on its scattered sparks,
Flee oot, autonymous as art,
Through a' the Heaven's arcs.

[174]

But that's no' yet and tho' I'm flegt
When there's nae gleam to see
I ken fu' weel that Chaos still
Freedom and pooer maun gie
To organisin' Reason that else
'Ud lack a' life and beauty,
And that Ignorance, Pain and Daith,
Are needit—yet a wee.

Man's curse has never been
His disregard o' the past
But the way in which he's let
It haud his spirit fast,
And next to the Past the Present
Binds him hand and fit,
And but for his surrender
He could ha' been heicher yet
Frae ocht that ony man is
Than men frae the brutes, I wis.

The way that maist men think
And feel 's beneath contempt
And frae a' that seems established
We canna be owre quick exempt—
Tho' the theory o' "Historic patience"
Applies to a'thing as to nations
And I maun gie a special section
To Scotland's case in this connection!
The day is comin' when ilka stane
'll hae as guid as a human brain

And frae what they are noo men
Develop in proportion then
    (At least it's hoped they will
    And no' be owretaen still)
While sex and ither hauf way stages
Perish wi' the barbarous Ages,
Tho' maist folk then as noo nae doot
'll hae "the misfortune no' t' exist,"

And the feck o' the rest'll lead a life
That to ocht worth while 'ud never be missed.

For the eternal evil's no'
Tragedy, but the absence o't,
No senseless extremes but the sordid mean,
No pooer but a pooerless lot,
No' the sharp and deep, but the dull and flat,
No' Hell but no' ha'en even that,
And the triviality o' a'
But the haill o' human thocht.

O the Devil is naething strange.
His face is the crood's or oor ain
When we cease to be oorsel's
And become "like abody" again—
When we cease to be oorsels
And try to be English insteed
And o' oor distinctive Scots
Tradition see but a gleid
—Tho' I see a' its morse code whiles
In the Anglophile night
As compared wi' Cencrastus
Gin' that's glintin' bright
As Blake at times descried
The showery form o' Enion
At the loved Terror's side. . . .

AODHAGAN O RAHAILLE SANG
THIS SONG*

Aodhagan O Rahaille sang this sang
That I maun sing again;
For I've met the Brightness o' Brightness

* Aodhagan O Rahaille, Irish poet, 1670–1726.

Like him in a lanely glen,
And seen the hair that's plaited
Like the generations o' men.

"Wha'e'er she is, I daurna look,
Eidolon o' a fallen race,
Wi' lifted e'en, as fain I wad,
Upon her noonday face
—Tholin' my ancestors' assize
For centuries in a minute's space!

And yet as tho' she didna see
The hopeless boor I was
She's taen me to her white breists there,
Her bricht hair owre us fa's.
She canna blame me gin I fail
To speir my fortune's cause.

O wad at least my yokel words
Some Gaelic strain had kept
As in Othello's sobs the oaths
O' Thames, no' Venice, leapt,
And aye in puir Doll Tearsheet's shift
The Queen o' Egypt slept.*

The modest daisy like the Rose
O' a' the Warld repetalled
—Fain through Burns' clay MacMhaighstir's fire
To glint within me ettled.
It stirred, alas, but couldna kyth,
Prood, elegant and mettled.

Nor owre my life's accursed acre
Dunvegan threw a bough,
To look as it had flourished there,
Nane seekin' to speir how.
Nae borrowed grace in this puir place
The particular Fates allow.

* With acknowledgments to Georges Lafourcade.

[177]

Illustrious, cardinal, aulic, curial
—Can e'er my tongue be these?
I ken fu' weel I ha'e nae words
To match Divine Philosophy's
Yet aiblins, tho' they canna last,
She needs her misalliances!

And yet . . . and yet . . . it isna richt
To waste hersel' on me;
Fu' mony a belted earl 'ud fain
Ha'e sic fair company.
I doot that when I ope my mooth
In horror yet she'll flee.

And yet . . . and yet . . . nae doot she kens
Better than me her need,
And gin I aped the gentry's tongue
'Ud flee wi' greater speed,
—Or is't a freak o' humour gars
Her dally wi' my leid?

And will she lauch ahint her haund
At my uncouth demeanour,
Comparin' my orra love wi' that
Some popinjay has gien her?
—At least by tryin' to seem refined
It's clear I'd juist chagrin her.

Chagrin her—and chagrin mysel,
For, certes, I'm alowe.
Whether she loves me, guid kens why,
Or needs rouch hoose, I trow
Or thocht to tease and jink me syne,
Maitters fell little—now!

Aodhagan O Rahaille sang this sang
That aince mair I sing here.
It's oh my dear, and oh my dear,
And oh my dear, my dear.

Time to love is short, is short.
We'll love—afore we speir.

. . . But tho' I'm blinded in her licht
The hardy doot's still rife
That aiblins I am sair beginked
Thro' sma' experience o' life,
And favoured here wi' nae King's dochter,
But juist . . . a minister's rinawa wife. . . .

EL REY DE ESCOCIA NO ES NADA

El Rey de Escocia no es nada.

For nane was king o' ocht but pairts,
And Bruce, a hero in certain airts,
Was Norman first and Scotsman second
And aye o' self, no' Scotland, reckoned.

El Rey de Escocia no es nada.

And Chairlie o' the gowden heid
Won little support till he was deid
And maist that's left's frae folks wha'd tak'
The ither side gin' he cam' back.

El Rey de Escocia no es nada.

And Rosebery, "oor uncrooned King,"
His fiky wits could never bring
To bother lang wi' the race o' Scots.
The Derby oftener claimed his thochts.

El Rey de Escocia no es nada.

And as for ony Wettin or Windsor
—But oh, losh me, if I begin, sir!
They're juist as like bein' Scottish Kings
As Scotland's Scottish in ither things.

[179]

El Rey de Escocia no es nada.

Imagine Burns, Scott, Carlyle, Lauder
Kings—Could onything be madder?
God micht ha' dune, gin he'd been livin'
But he played safe, preferrin' Heaven!

El Rey de Escocia no es nada.

FRAE ANITHER WINDOW IN THRUMS

Here in the hauf licht waitin' till the clock
Chops: while the winnock
Hauds me as a serpent hauds a rabbit
Afore it's time to grab it
—A serpent faded to a shadow
In the stelled een its een ha'e haud o'

Here in the daurk, while like a frozen
Scurl on Life's plumm the lozen
Skimmers—or goams in upon me
Wan as Dostoevski
Glowered through a wudden dream to find
Stavrogin in the corners o' his mind,

—Or I haud it, a 'prentice snake, and gar
Heaven dwine to a haunfu' haar
Or am like cheengeless deeps aneth
Tho' ice or sunshine, life or death,
Chequer the tap; or like Stavrogin
Joukin' his author wi' a still subtler grin. . . .

And yet I canna for the life o' me see
That I'd write better poetry
If like the feck o' Scots insteed
I read the books they read

And drew my thochts o' God and Man
Frae Neil Munro and Annie Swan!

Fu' weel I ken I would mak' verses which
'Ud notably enrich
"Oor Scots tradition"—in the minds
O' ministers and hinds;
And fain I'd keep as faur frae that
As Proust frae Johnnie Gibb—that's flat!

—Can I get faurer frae't than here
Whaur a' life's fictions disappear
And I'm left face to face wi' nocht
But sicna drab splash as brocht
My life to be, to mak' wi't what I can,
Back at the stert whaur a' began?

Seed in my womb, I ken nae mair
Than ony wife what bairn I'll bear
—Christ or a village idiot there
A thronèd king, or corpse i' the air? . . .

Nature to Art is still a witch
Confinin't by waefu' metamorphosis
To Life, a memory mindin' which
It bairnlies itsel' again like this. . . .

For if it's no' by thocht that Poetry's wrocht
It's no' by want o' thocht
The verse that flatters ignorance maun seem
To ignorant folk supreme
Sin' nane can read the verse that disna
The damned thing bides as if it isna!

Maun I tae sing a useless sang
            "La chanson grise
Où l'Indécis au Précis se joint."
Naebody else can listen to
—Like shades o' music missin' to
A' but ane in a listenin' thrang,

And perfect it forever mair
Like Proust wha thocht he couldna sleep
Sae lang that, sleepin', he'd still a deep
Unsleepin' sense o' sleeplessness there,

And borrowed frae that in turn the thocht
That he'd been soond asleep frae the stert;
And syne—but och! the sang in my hert
Coonts ilka shadow frae nicht to nocht!

—Like Proust, or the Glesca man wha deed
And said to Charon: "It's unco queer;
I dreamt I was deid, and no' juist here
At hame on a Sawbath day insteed!" . . .

Enclosed in silence, Earth's sang, unhurried
Dwines through the endless stages it needs
As 'twere the kind o' life Daith leads
In the deid aince they are buriet. . . .

That's the condition o't or near
Grey glumshin' o' the winda here,
—As fit a subject for immortal sang
As ocht wi' which men's minds are thrang. . . .

Here at the heicht o' her dance
Athikte's off in a dwam
—Gane in a kink
And no' able to think
By what mischance
She's tint her "I am,"
Or hoo to win back
Her knowledge and knack.

As ane that wauks in the nicht
Oot o' a croodit dream
* Openin' blin' een*
* On a toom black scene*
* Till life in a fricht*
* Like Daith 'bood seem*

Gantin' at her
A fish oot o' water.

Athikte withoot avail,
Drooned, 'ud dance on the plain
  O' the oorie sea
  But the nimbleness she
  Had in feet in a tail
  Is no' to capture again,
And even the art o' McDiarmid
Leaves her a connached mermaid.

Here in the hauf licht waitin' till the clock
Chops: while the winnock
Hauds me, as a serpent hauds a rabbit
Afore it's time to grab it
—A serpent faded to a shadow
In the stelled een its een hae haud o'. . . .

I WHO ONCE IN HEAVEN'S HEIGHT

I wha aince in Heaven's height
Gethered to me a' the licht
Can nae mair reply to fire,
'Neth deid leafs buriet in the mire.

Sib to dewdrop, rainbow, ocean,
No' for me their hues and motion.
This foul clay has filed me till
It's no' to ken I'm water still.

Here in the hauf licht hoo I've grown!
Seconds but centuries hae flown
Sin I was a reporter here
Chroniclin' the toon's sma' beer
Tinin' the maist o' life to get
The means to hain the least wee bit.

Pars aboot meetins, weddins, sermons, a'
The crude events o' life-in-the-raw
Vanish like snowflakes on this river. . . .
Dans le flot sans honneur de quelque noir mélange . . .
On wha's black bank I stand and shiver;
Nakit!—What gin the boss, as weel he micht,
Comes in and switches on the licht?

The Twentieth Century at Eternity
Gapes—and the clock strikes: Tea!
And sombrous I arise
Under his silly eyes
And doon the stairs, the devil at my back.
I doot the morn I'll get the sack!

"What was I da'en sittin' in the dark?"
"Huntin' like Moses for the vital spark,
—A human mole
Wi' a hole for a soul?"
"I sud think o' my wife and faimly"
I listen to him tamely.

"Cut oot this poetry stuff, my lad. Get on
Wi' advts. and puffs, and eident con
The proofs; it's in you gin you care
To dae't and earn (your maister) mair.
    Furth Fortune fill the fetters!
Apply yersel' to what's worth while
And I'll reward ye: that's my style."

"Yessir, I'm sorry. It'll no'
Heppen again. The clock was slow
And I was slower still, I'm sorry,
In gettin' back again afore ye
To sicna state as fits the job
O ane wha's brains you lout to rob."

Curse on the system that can gie
A coof like this control o' me
—No' that he's in the least bit waur
Or better, than ither bosses are—
And on the fate that gars a poet
Toady to find a way to show it!

Curse his new hoose, his business, his cigar,
His wireless set, and motor car
Alsatian, gauntlet gloves, plus fours and wife,
—A'thing included in his life;
And, abune a', his herty laughter,
And—if he has yin—his hereafter.

Owre savage? Deil the bit! That's nocht
To what men like the Boss deserve;
Maist men that is—anon I'll gie
Them a' their paiks, wit muckle verve.

He has an angry birthmark on his cheek,
    . . . *Le roy Scotiste*
    Qui demy face ot, ce dit-on,
    Vermeille comme une amathiste
    Depuys le front jusqu'au menton. . . .
A purple pig's fit—a' his skin
Sud lowe forever in black burnin' shame
To mak' his ootside like his in.
I'd send it owre him like a flypin knife
Till like a carcase in a butcher's shop
He fronts the world—affrontin' it;
A rinnin' wound that nocht'll stop.

[185]

For sae the will to ignorance o' his kind,
Their line o' least resistance, ruins life
As wha maun tine through foul disease
The heich ideas wi' which he's rife. . . .

Curse a'thing that gars me pretend or feel
That life as maist folk hae't is real
Or waste my time on their ideas
Or silly sociabilities,
Service, meanin' or ocht that'll tak'
My mind off ony verse it'll mak.
    I'm no' the kind o' poet
    That opens sales o' work. . . .
Curse on my dooble life and dooble tongue,
—Guid Scots wi' English a' hamstrung—

Speakin' o' Scotland in English words
As it were Beethoven chirpt by birds;
Or as if a Board school teacher
Tried to teach Rimbaud and Nietzsche.

And on this curst infirmity o' will
That hauds me bletherin' this way still
On things that like a midge-swarm pass
Sub specie aeternatatis.

Athikte I hae sung
Wi' a loose and gallus tongue,
Made a clamour better-suited,
To the Trollop, Life, I doot it,
Than to ane wha's never set fit
In a vulgar spirit yet.

Dulcinea aye turns oot to be
Aldonsa to a man like me
Yirdit in this plight alive
A' in vain I shout and strive
—And, gin I gied owre, my hert's beat
Faurer still 'ud fleg your feet.

Gin but the oor 'ud chop and set me free
Frae this accursed drudgery
Aiblins—aince I had my tea—
I could address mysel' to poetry,
Sufferin' nae mair th' embarrassment o' riches
Wi' which desire brute circumstance bewitches
Till my brain reels and canna faddom which is,
'Mid endless cues, the ane for which it itches.

Thrang o' ideas that like fairy gowd
'll leave me the "Review" reporter still
Waukenin' to my clung-kite faimly on a hill
O' useless croftin' whaur naething's growed
But Daith, sin Christ for an idea died
On a gey similar but less heich hillside.
Ech, weel for Christ: for he was never wed
And had nae weans clamourin' to be fed!

As 'tis I ken that ilka instant gies,
If I could haud it lang eneuch to seize
Them, coontless opportunities
For reams o' verse in as mony different keys,
—And that's damned nonsense for they canna a'
Lead t'owt worth while—gin owt's worth while ava'.

> (*Hell tak this improvisin'*
> *That leads a' airts and nane;*
> *A kind o' anti-poetry*
> *That is true poetry's bane!*)

Athikte I dreamt that you were here
Lyin' by me like a wumman in the daurk.
I heard the breathin' o' the seven seas
Faint as the matins o' a licht-lost lark,
—Or was it my ain hapy hert that passed
My hearin', and was tint in sleep at last . . .
Athikte, I thocht I kent I didna ken
Which o's was you and which me, then.
The haill warld pillowed on my shouder, licht.
As gin I'd been the sun by nicht.

Athikte I dreamt that you were here
But I am as a man wha's love is deid.
She comes in a' her beauty to his bed
But when he wauks, the toom nicht's there insteed
Sae a' the poet's moods I hae
Look in the cruel licht o' day
As silly as an effort to
Cuddle a ghaist my airms gang through.
And ilka sang is like a moon
That hings, a bonny aught, at noon. . . .

I'm weary o' the shapes mere chance can thraw
In this technique and that; and seek that law
To pit the maitter on a proper basis
My faith in which a feature o' the case is
I canna deal wi' here but efter tea
Will—if the wife and bairns—we'll wait and see. . . .
A' this is juist provisional and 'll hae
A tea-change into something rich and Scots
When I wha needs use English a' the day
Win back to the true language o' my thochts.

Stars are equal in wecht
Tho' they differ in size:
Betelgeuse, tight as the sun,
'ud draw in the skies
As Earth recovers a stane
Thrawn up frae the lift again.

Space 'ud fauld up and leave
Us ootside it (i.e.
Naewhaur)—as, whiles, I feel
A thocht o' Dunbar in me
Grow heavy until it has brocht
A' Shakespeare's sequence to nocht.

Scots letters, Dunbar, are juist names
For the effects o' a star
O' Finality deep in my mind
Pu'in' things asklent frae afar

—Fegs! English 'll look a gey fool
If this bias seizes the bool!

"Scots is a thing o' the Past"
Maist folk say: and "There's nae
Pittin' back the hands o' the clock"
And "History nane can undae."
—Can they no? In the darkness here
My coorse, either way, is fell clear.

And a' the day lang as I wark
In the office here
I feel the drag on my mind
O' a star that ettles to veer
The way o' life—till at nicht
I sit blin' in its licht! . . .

O Knowledge, wha can say
What benefit it is
To think o' China in Milngavie?
Felis demulta mites.

A man ranges through the ages
But kens his stature yet is
Nae cubit mair than erst it was.
Felis demulta mites.

And a' he comprehends
O' life and love and ditties
Is—ony cat'll purr if stroked;
Felis demulta mites.

A' men can ken and think
Depends on what their wit is;
Procrustes plays at Proteus;
Felis demulta mites.

O Knowledge, wha can tell
That o' ye ilka bit is

No' juist a dodge to hide faur mair?
Felis demulta mites. . . .

"There's owre mony yads in the fire,"
Cries my Muse, and her taengs hae taen
A'thing but Godheid and Scottishness
Oot o' my sang again!

ME

I'm the original
Plasm o' the ocean.
Feebly amused
At God's last notion

He ettles to use me
Like a conjurer's hat
And gar me evolve
He disna ken what—

Countries wi' their flora
And fauna—but lor!
He forgets hoo often
He's dune it afore.

I couldna thole
The process again
If he didna aye think
It has juist dawned on his brain,

If he didna aye wonder
Hoo faur he could cairry it
—Losh me when he canna
As muckle as vary it!

I'm the original
Plasm o' the ocean;
Humour accoonts
For my ditherin' motion.

NIL NISI DIVINUM

Nil nisi divinum stabile est; caetera fumus. . . .
Sall Jewry breed a Christ
Gaeldom canna equal,
Or India wi' a Buddha
Prevein anither sequel? . . .

He'll ca' nocht else a Heaven if he'd fain
Hae's fit insteed upon the heathery miles
Or wi' the lobster-fishers sail again
To Fladda Chuain and the Ascrib Isles.

If there's a Heaven it maun vie
Wi' this auld land o' his wha's hillsides lirk
Like elephant skins as he gangs by
Aince mair 'twixt John o' Groats and Maidenkirk. . . .

The Jews wha aince set oot to big
A new Jerusalem by the Forth
Stopt—Auld Reekie ser'd their turn;
They kent to come nae faurer North.

Sae faur their Asian madness blauds.
It canna file this gowden realm,
Nor Brocken-like can Calvary
Oor mountains in its mole-hill whelm! . . .

A wee kirk squats aneth the hills
Wi' Latin windas reid and blue;
It's naething but its ain inside
That's whiles begairied wi' their hue.

Ootlandish colours canna shine
Oot owre the hills that stand aboot,
And gin the congregation's dyed
They're still like Scots folk comin' oot,

And see again a michty warld
Frae silly whigmaleeries free,

And a' the skyline wipit clean
O' ony trumpery Trinity! . . .

Noo in synoptic lines
A Scot becomes a God
—A God in Murray tartan
To whom nae star's abroad.

Wha's idle fit owreturns
This stane and that to show
Asia's hotchin millions,
A mune wi' nocht below.

He looks wi' equal een
On a'thing deid and livin'
His bauchles in the Zeitgeist,
His bonnet cocked in Heaven! .

CAN I GET DEEPER DOON
THAN THIS

Can I get deeper doon than this
Amang the warld's inanities?
Oh, fegs, there's deeper faur to gang.
This wadna keep life gaen lang.
Lee go your brain and try again
It's no' sae easy as it's payin'
To be a fule like Lauder. Dod!
It's less by tryin' than gift o' God.

Gift o' God! The only road
To Paradise! Nae doot my load
O' thochts awaits a better joke
For easement tae, as stupider folk
Are eased, by puirer jokes, o' theirs,
And in the end a' Man's affairs,

Like settin' a thief to catch a thief
'll find their ain absurd relief.

Nae doot! But Man's resource o' Wit
Is faur eneuch frae that as yet.
We're a' o's pent in some belief
Or hope that lacks the right relief
To look as silly as it should
And does to minds a thocht less crude.
But gin Life in the lang rin's a'
A joke—is that a joke ava'?

I canna see't; but that's no' odd—
Owre nice for Lauder and for God,
I'm feart lest in the end I'll be
Bored to daith in Eternity,
That muckle Hippodrome Hereafter
Whaur a'thing's swallowed up in laughter,
Wi' Lauder's kilt and Chaplin's feet
Supernumerary to the Paraclete.

Let's try again. . . .

THERE'S OWRE MONY KILLYWIMPLES IN YOUR SINGIN'

There's owre mony killywimples in your singin'
It minds me o' my een
When they seek to spae the weather by the sun
And there's nocht but rainbows to be seen.

The lintie sang coonterpoint when the ouzel yelpit
But your sang's faurer frae me
Than the sun frae the earth when its rays in the grey lift
*Blinter like honesty.**

* Small flowering plant, so called from its transparent seed pouch.

[193]

MY WEALTH

He has nae treasure in his pooch
—Except a quid pro quo;
And mony a bricht Saint Andrew
That nane but he can show!

HOKUM

It isna fair to my wife and weans
It isna fair to mysel',
To persist in poverty-stricken courses
And never ring Fortune's bell.
Thoosands o' writers wi nae mair brains
In their heids than I've in my pinkie
Are rowin' in wealth while I toil for a dole,
O hoo's that accoontit for, thinkee?

Oh, it's easy, easy accoontit for, fegs.
I canna gie the folk hokum.
I can poke 'em and shock 'em and mock 'em,
But the a'e thing needfu' is hokum!
It pits a'thing else on its legs.

Losh! They'd ha' put me a brass plate up
In Langholm Academy,
And asked me to tak' the chair
At mony a London Scots spree.
They'd a' gien me my portrait in oils
By Henry Kerr, and the LL.D.,

And my wife and weans 'ud been as weel aff
As gin I'd been a dominie,

  If I'd only had hokum, hokum,
  Juist a wee thing common hokum!

A seat on the Bank o' Scotland buird,
And a public for my poetry . . .

    If I'd only had hokum, hokum,
    A modicum o' hokum!

It maitters little what line ye tak'
If you hae hokum wi't;
Butter or snash, it's a' alike,
Gar them laugh or greet.
There's naething the public winna stand
And pay for through the nose,
Barrin' the medicine that's ser'd up neat,
Whether it's bitter or whether it's sweet,
Wi' nae hokum to the dose.

But what I canna accoont for's no'
Bein' able to gie folk hokum.
I can joke 'em and sock 'em and choke 'em
But the a'e thing needfu' is hokum.
—I wish I was Neil Munro.

It isna fair to my wife and weans,
It isna fair to mysel'.
The day's lang by when Gaels gaed oot
To battle and aye fell.
I wish I was Harry Lauder,
Will Fyffe or J. J. Bell,
—Or Lauchlan Maclean Watt
For the maitter o' that!
—Dae I Hell!

Oh, it's hokum, hokum, hokum,
And this is as near't as I'll get.
The nearest I've got yet,
Losh, but it's unco like *it*,
    —That sine-qua-non,
    A soupçon
    O' precious hokum-pokum!

MARY MACLEOD *

Auld Mary Macleod in her tartan tonnag
Has drunk her whisky and snuffed her snuff,
And the Lord has put a new sang in her mooth,
 Hallelujah that's the stuff!

It alters the haill complexion o' life
And mak's a deid language o' a' we've kent.
The music the bards for thoosands o' years
 Missed is hers by an accident.

When folk say "God made the world" and think
 It took Him a' His time
And canna imagine—a' they canna imagine,
 Let them mind Mary's rhyme.

When folk say "God . . . ," but juist as the bards
 Were whummelt, the thocht o' God
Sae lang unchallenged in maist folk's heids
 Maun gang the same road.

For freedom means that a lad or lass
 In Cupar or elsewhaur yet
May alter the haill o' human thocht
 Mair than Christ's altered it.

Aye dae, the morn, for the haill o' creation
 Mair than Mary for Gaelic sang
—Or dizzens o' them in different airts
 At aince be thrang.

I never set een on a lad or a lass
 But I wonder gin he or she
Wi' a word or deed'll suddenly dae
 An impossibility.

A'e thing's certain: Christ's Second Comin'
'll no' be to Scotland whaurever it is.

* Gaelic poetess, 1569–1674.

[196]

Auld Mary Macleod in her tartan tonnag
Has finished her bottle and toomed her mull
And the sang the Lord put new in her mooth
Has turned unspeakably dull.

But no' as dull as in maist ither airts
The mind o' Scotland's aye been,
And I hope it'll be in them a' at aince
That the neist miracle's seen. . . .

THE WEAPON

Scots steel tempered wi' Irish fire
Is the weapon that I desire.

THE TWO BRUCES

There were twa Robert Bruces.
Ane edited "The Glasgow Herald."
The ither focht for Scotland
When it was *less* imperilled.

STRANGERS

Strangers are in my true love's hame.
Strangers wha hardly ken her name.
And tho' the country looks the same,
        It canna be.

Strangers are in my true love's hame.
She had to leave it when they came,
And oh! The strangers are no' to blame
        —And neither's she!

BETTER ONE GOLDEN LYRIC

Better a'e gowden lyric
Than a social problem solved
Tho' maist folk never see
The beauty that's evolved
And think a million times mair
O' their ain waugh welfare.

Better a'e gowden lyric
That nane but the poets see
Than a Messiah's praise in a day
The mob in its vain moods gies
In turn to a Prince or jockey,
A Tancy, or Jennie, Lee.

Better a'e gowden lyric
The mob'll never ken
For this in the last resort
Mak's them less apes, mair men,
And leads their leaders albeit
They're owre blin' to see it.

Better a'e gowden lyric
Than Insurance, Bankin', and Law,
Better a'e gowden lyric
Than the Castle's soarin' wa';
Better a'e gowden lyric
Than onything else ava!

TREASON

I've socht ye in and oot o' season.
Noo it's time that I learnt reason.
I'll nae langer vainly eisen
    While my youth and vigour pass.
Aiblins I'll be less displeasin'
    To some no' displeasin' lass.

Tho' you've ripened it's nae reason
Why my hert should hing to wizen
In a wind that grows mair freezin',
     And fa' rotten to the grass.
If for true love's wine I'm guisan'
     I maun try a weaker glass.

Oh there's teasin' and there's teasin'
But your cruelty shows nae easin'
And in fact it's aye increasin'
     And has come to sic a pass
That I'm contemplatin' treason
     —Equally in vain alas! . . .

NORTH OF THE TWEED

Cauld licht and tumblin' cloods. It's queer
There's never been a poet here. . . .

Shades o' the Sun-King no' yet risen
Are sleepin' in a corner on the straw.
Despair seems to touch bottom time and again
But aye Earth opens and reveals fresh depths.
The pale-wa'd warld is fu' o' locht and life
Like a glass in which water faintly stirs.
Gie owre a' this tomfoolery, and sing
The movin' spirit that nae metaphor drawn
Frae water or frae licht can dim suggest.
Leid in nae mere Longinian hypsos come
But in inhuman splendours, triumphin' wi'
"A dazzlin' disregard o' the soul."
     Nocht else'll dae.

Water nor licht nor yet the barley field
That shak's in silken sheets at ilka braith,
Its lang nap thrawin' the quick licht aboot
In sic a maze that tak's and gies at aince

[199]

As fair oot-tops the coontless ripplin' sea.
There's nae chameleon like the July fields;
Their different colours change frae day to day
While they shift instantly neath the shiftin' licht
Yet they're owre dull for this, stagnant and dull;
And even your een, beloved, and your hair
Are like the barley and the sea and Heaven
That flaw and fail and are defeated by
     The blind turns o' chance.

Thinkna' that I'm ungratefu', wi' nae mind
O' Deirdre and the fauld o' sunbeams * yet,
Or canna find on bracken slopes abune the bog
The orchis smellin' like cherry-pie;
Or that the sun's blade cuttin' straightly through
A cloudy sea fails wi' my cloudy hert,
Releasin' it frae self-disgust until I tine
A' sense o' livin' under set conditions
And live in an unconditioned space o' time
Perfect in ilka pulse and impulse, and aince mair
A seven-whistler in Kintyre, or yon broon hill
That's barren save for fower pale violets on
     A South-leanin' bank.

I've sat amang the crimson buds o' thrift
Abune the sea whaur Buachaille herds the waves;
And seen the primrose nightglow to the North
Owre Moray and the flat sea while the West
Still held a twinkle o' the morning-star,
(For in the Cairngorms simmer nicht and dawn
Come close, but canna thraw the larks' hours oot);
And hoo should I forget the Langfall
On mornings when the hines were ripe but een
Ahint the glintin' leafs were brichter still
Than sunned dew on them, lips reider than the fruit,
And I filled baith my basket and my hert
     Mony and mony a time?

* "Fold of Sunbeams"—Glendaruel.

And yet you mind, dear, on the bridal hill
Hoo yon laich loch ootshone my een in yours,
Nor wi' the heather could oor bluid compete,
Nor could the ring I gi'ed you when your hand
Lay on the crucifers compare wi' them
Save for a second when the sun seized on't.
Hair of the purple of Strathendrick Hill,
Slant e'en wi' pupils like blue-stane washed wi' rain
And the whites owre white and the hunted look
Here tak' your bairn; I've cairried it lang eneuch,
Langer than maist men wad, as weel you ken.
Noo I'll pipe insteed—what tune'll you hae?
    On Rudha nam Marbh.*

SEPARATION

    If there's a sword-like sang
    That can cut Scotland clear
    O' a' the warld beside
    Rax me the hilt o't here,

    For there's nae jewel till
    Frae the rest o' earth it's free,
    Wi' the starry separateness
    I'd fain to Scotland gie. . . .

BONNIE PRINCE CHARLIE

    A' isna gowd that glitters
    And weel I mind ane came
    And kindled in oor lyart hills
    What look't like livin' flame.

* "The Point of the Dead."

Tho' a's no' gowd that glitters
He keeps his meed o' fame.
It's easier to lo'e Prince Charlie
Than Scotland—mair's the shame! . . .

MY LOVE IS TO THE LIGHT OF LIGHTS

My love is to the light of lights
As a gold fawn to the sun
And men, wha love ocht else, to her
Their ways ha' scarce begun.

For God their God's a jealous God
And keeps her frae their sight
He hasna had her lang eneuch
Himsel' to share his delight,

And kens gin he'd been worth his saut
He'd ha' made her first, no' last,
Since but a'e glimpse, a'e thocht, o' her
Discredits a' the Past.

(A'e glimpse, a'e thocht, and men might cease
To honour his tardy pooers;
And he's no' shair she winna prove
To be no' his—but oors!)

Yet praise the Past sin' but for it
We never might ha' seen her
—And still to oor een maun temper wi't
The glory that's been gi'en her.

My love she is the hardest thocht
That ony brain can ha'e,
And there is nocht worth ha'en in life
That doesna lead her way.

My love is to a' else that is
As meaning's meaning, or the sun
Men see ahint the sunlight whiles
Like lint-white water run. . . .

From

Scots Unbound and Other Poems

1932

IOLAIR

As an eagle stirs up her nest,
  Flutters over her young,
Urges them into the void, swoops underneath,
And rests a struggler on her back for a space
  Would the songs I sung
  Might be to my race.

Alba, mother eagle, support me.
  He who sings
Struggles and cannot yet float upwards
From the high valleys among the Cairngorms like those
  Of your true brood; on the wings
  Whose movement is repose.

THE SKELETON OF THE FUTURE

Red granite and black diorite, with the blue
Of the labradorite crystals gleaming like precious stones
In the light reflected from the snow; and behind them
The eternal lightning of Lenin's bones.

A MOORLANDER LOOKS FORWARD
TO HIS BRIDE

To GORDON BOTTOMLEY

A woman's een where licht's as scarce as here?
Her nails in sic a place like stars'll glow!
Truth, it's nae vilipendin' she's to fear.
I'm used to makin' the maist o' sma' affairs.
Blith wi' a wheen heather cowes and spirts o' grass
Than ither folk wi' Earth's maist prodigal show
I mak' a world I'd swap for nane o' theirs
And twist by twist ken a' its wankishin'.
What will I no' then wi' a haill live lass?
Treasure the canna and misprize her skin?
Ken the wra moors but no' her benmaist thocht?
Wreath on my clew a' the threids that mak'
This manufacture till it looks if you please
At sun-up like a whey-drap in a cheese,
And leave sic braw material unwrocht?
—The bottle o' port that's a' the cheese can lack!

THE POINT OF HONOUR

On watching the Esk again

I would that once more I could blend her
With my own self as I did then
Vivid and impulsive in crystalline splendour
Cold and seething champagne.

(Cut water. Perfection of craft concealed
In effects of pure improvisation.
Delights of dazzle and dare revealed
In instant inscapes of fresh variation.

Exhilarating, effortless, divinely light,
In apparent freedom yet reined by unseen

[205]

And ubiquitous disciplines; darting, lint-white,
Fertile in impulse, in control—keen.

Pride of play in a flourish of eddies,
Bravura of blowballs, and silver digressions,
Ringing and glittering she swirls and steadies,
And moulds each ripple with secret suppressions.)

Once, with my boy's body little I knew
But her furious thresh on my flesh;
But now I can know her through and through
And, light like, her tide enmesh.

Then come, come, come, let her spend her
Quivering momentum where I lie here,
Wedding words to her waves, and able to tend her
Every swirl and sound with eye and ear.

No more of mere sound, the least part!
I know how it acts, connecting words, implying
A rate of movement, onomatopoeic art,
Or making a reader start trying
To interpret the mouth's actual movement
As a gesture; or acting directly
Like a tune—a mode that is different
From the rest as darkness from light to me.
These intelligible, this a mystery.
Is not consciousness of a sound an act
Of belief in it; are not movements of muscles
Transferred, apprehended, as rhythms, or fact
Of nature some other sense claims, like the tussles
You arouse of thought, hearing, touch and sight,
Variety of experience, a baffling medley
Till one wins, and I cease to know you aright
Yet dare not embezzle the dramatic insights,
The generative questionableness, knowing well
The greater risk of taking no risks,
Creating no ecstasies, changing the mights
Of old safe ecstasies to counters, discs,
Transports reduced to play-level?

[206]

The problematic, the murderous, element
Of all art eschewed; no mad leap taken
Into the symbol, driving like your stream
Through all mere images, all that may seem
Its very character; the engagement
Twixt man and being forsaken.
All stale, unprofitable, flat and thin,
No restless eager poem that speaking in
A thousand moods achieves a unity,
No wracking indispensable energy,
Only emotions forgotten in tranquillity.
Seductive solutions, genteel clarities,
What have I or you to do with these?
Am I too old to spring like a salmon
And confined to Goethean gammon?
—And yet in the summer-time you
Sometimes come down to that too.

Nay the boy's spirit its lessoning got;
Dissympathy with nature, sheer sensual force,
Lust of light and colour, the frequent note
Of free enthusiasm in its course.

What troubling flavour in this heady wine?
It hides not Dionysos' but Astarte's sting?
Mid the elemental enemies—cold, ravening brine—
The intellectual flame's survival I sing.

Malicious and unaccountable twinkle, free
Beyond human freedom from the laws of causation?
Nay, gaily, daily, over abysses more ghastly
Men cast spider-webs of creation.

(Nay, the last issue I have all but joined
But my muse still lacks—and so has missed all—
The right temper, like yours, which goes to the point
Of the terrible; the terrible crystal.

Some day I cry—and may cry my life through—
Serene and modest in self-confidence like you

[207]

I will capture the world-free illusion two
Of naught, and they one, like me and the sun's rays.

For in you and in me moves a thought
So passionate and live like a plant or beast
It has its own architecture and has brought
A new thing to Nature—mine vague, yours exprest.

If I find yours I will find my own.
What lack of integrity prevents me?
Where is the reach-point (it exists I've known long
Waiting for me) of this integrity?

Found I shall know it like a turned lock's click
But I fumble and juggle again and again.
Your every least move does the trick
But I watch your quick tumblers in vain.)

But one sweep of motion in the world to-day,
The unwearying flood of the river,
Inexplicable, alien! Water, whither away
In a flight that passes and stays forever?

Full from the rains, but the flood sediment gone;
Under the brace of the glancing current
Each pebble shines as with a life of its own,
Electric, autonymous, world-shaking-divergent.

Or comes the disturbing influence with which I tingle
Only from the shoals of fishes that seem
As though they'd be stranded there on the shingle
From the swaying waters they teem?

A wagtail flits but noiseless—by knowledge awed
Of some great unseen presence? Or food its gob in?—
Then suddenly, with expanding sweetness, a glad
Clear note rings out: Revelation!; Robin?

Stranded. I with them! Would I wish to bend her
   To me as she veers on her way again

Vivid and impulsive in crystalline splendour
   Cold and seething champagne?

No. So life leaves us. Already gleam
In the eyes of the young the flicker, the change,
The free enthusiasm that carries the stream
Suddenly out of my range.

GENETHLIACON FOR THE NEW WORLD ORDER

To Ann Orage, a Few Days Old

The world is thrilling from pole to pole
   With joy to-day
For the time is at hand from the glorious
Building of Man to knock away
The scaffolding all bestuck with names
   That has always seemed
The uglier every time that a glimpse
   Of the work behind it has streamed
Through a chink of the framework and advts.
   None of the builders now,
Least of all Jesus, can point
To his share in the finished structure, I trow
   For every individual contribution
      Is lost in the whole.
They all built better far than they knew
   And none foresaw the goal,
For the contribution of the nameless people
   Was the main thing after all.
Who could foresee an unknown flower
Having seen the leaves, the stem, and the root
—Let alone the glory of the approaching hour
Now all human history rounds to *its* fruit?
Hence the blinding star-like surprise of the work
   When the scaffolding shall fall.

The whole world is thrilling from pole to pole
    With the first clear ray
Of the starry life of the Earth that at last
    Transfigures its clay.

ETIKA PREOBRAZHENNAVO EROSA

It is easy to cry
I am one with the working classes
But no task in the world surpasses
In difficulty his who would try,
Must try since he is not, succeed or die.
Miseducated and more articulate,
Sensitised by what numbs their fate
And raised up by what keeps them down,
Only by the severest intellectual discipline
Can one of the bourgeois intelligentsia win
Up to the level of the proletariat
On this side of the grave or that
—The only goal worth aiming at.
                O remorseless spirit that guides me
                    The way seems infinite;
                What endless distance divides me
                    From the people yet!

It is next to impossible still
For me to bear any other man close—for deep
Differences surge up like a blast from Hell,
Yet I know full well
All the distinctions that divide
Man from man must be swept aside,
Sweep each other aside, cancel out,
All sources of individual pride
Are like straws on a whirling tide
Or like trees which have dried up but still sway
                In the breeze with the others
Or like men feeding on hopes drier than hay
Not knowing what they eat but always eating.

The War put an end to individuals.
They are no longer of interest—even to themselves.

A question of getting down to it, but how? Long days
I've spent in film studios considering the ways
Producers have tried to get under the skin
And far enough in but couldn't win.
Die freudlose Gasse, a simplistic city
Swimming in petty-bourgeois self-pity;
All the double tendency of the Teuton *lichtspiel*
Towards the real and away from the real;
The concoction instead of the experience;
A sketchy intellectual landscape, not the search for the truth;
Routines of literary closets, *Abwege,* richochettings
Into vortices of pseudo-psychologisings;
Not profound relationships but only exhibits,
Chic, treacherous, effete—O it's clearer yet
The only way to get is just to get,
For Christ's sake let us cease being subtile,
Abandon every specious wile.
            Fear of the maximum? Oh, oh!
                You are no way near it.
            It won't serve to take the human mind
                Just as far as it can go.
            You must take the spirit
                Further. . . .
            It is necessary to go all the way at least
                And there are no fellow-travellers.

The artist of keen nerve-ends
Can no longer yield to his periphery;
To a topography that gives neither the lie of the land
Nor its consistency, where figures of speech
Go stalking as men and women, skins drawn
Over hollow bodies, ephemera, momentarily illusive.
He must break through that aura—he must give
Intensive character-convergence, make outstand
Character-relations that do not merely spread
Like valiant steam into an ominous but compelling world,
And stop being just a bloody showman

Of guilt or innocence stuffed with straw.
Not *Lulu* but *Kameradschaft* points the way
   To something far more drastic than the law
   —Not of life or art! but theirs too—allows to-day.

That is the way—one step in a *kino*
Sluggish amid jingo lost-glory and *Bockbier* films,
Set to goosestep measures and ¾ *takt;*
One step at least on grounds of mass-reference,
Outside the land of proletarian rule at that!;
All the difference between Pabst and Pommer;
Between an artist and the ingenious composers
Of sophisticated *kino*-doggerel. Yet what
Is this and every such artistic fact
No matter how "sincere" the creative act
But a sop to Cerberus? the "cultural compulsives"
At work on "our fellow-travellers"? Rather nods from Homer
Than such kitsch. Who are Pabst
And Pommer when the *exegi monumentum aere perennius*
Is rattling on the scrap-iron heap? Let me hence,
Better luck elsewhere may cheer the roamer.
This wisdom after the event is not the life or art
   That's whitening every bourgeois heart,
            There's no time to be arch
            On the revolutionary march.

Let us look elsewhere—not to the chief turnbuckles
Holding and regulating us in the machine
Of an apparently more purposeful existence.
That's all clinkers we know though a few
Bewildered folk are still poking in the ash;
Nor where after prolonged aching priapism now
A pathological flabbiness is left pointing nowhere;
Least of all where fools are still trying to play
Each of the stops on the old-fashioned flute,
(As well read novels, or newspapers even, or Hansard;
Take Ramsay MacDonald seriously, or go to church)
            —Bunches of hams and shysters,
            With all the fat thumb business
            And a *Yiddishkeit* crutch—

In *Jew Süss, Stempanyov, Uncle Moses*
Sweetishly seductive, the poky bedroom, the symbolical red light,
Till when the curtain drops we shudder, seeing,
As if staring unblinkingly
At a "mystic photo" painted on the proscenium,
On the walls, on the faces of the audience,
              The poor lamb being tupped.
—But to Russia for a breath of fresh air!

Let us climb to where the people can be found
              Ranging in their millions
As history is climbing to world unity
—As who, when he gains a great summit
Finds he has no need to look below
To know his altitude—his eyes, his mind
Have no concern with the faithful aspect of the place,
The structure of the rocks and mountains,
Nor any tendency to exploit the scene,
To turn it to a fine "effect";
Since the world is removed from the world here.
The terror and glory of alp and glacier veil themselves;
What is communicated is feeling, but feeling of a rare kind,
The infinitely remote, the impalpable, a mingling
Of cloud and snow, a suspension of motion
Attract the surrendered spirit.
O beata solitudo! O sola beatitudo!
—All else is only the temporary wish
Of the half-wakened proletariat
    To become bourgeois themselves.

This is the music of humanity,
Here "where everything is forgiven,
And it would be impossible not to forgive";
Justification of all life in the balance of obliteration,
Mercy and stability in the ultimate release
Of the individual soul, forgiveness
In the knowledge that no individual deed
Eventually matters individually;
All the seeming divisions of life
Merely the glow upon glow in still more lucid glow

Of this outwelling of light
—A shape having no beginning or end,
    Moving upwards within itself,
    Turning backwards upon itself,
    Passing through itself, and continuing
        The process forever;
    The beat of the universal pulse
    And magic of the great *Bescherung*.
        . . . But who knows this summit, this peak moment
    As Lenin kept his beat in Russia,
    Or as one who in the circle of his *tabla taranga*
    Finds the time between two precipitating notes
To arrange a drum that has got off key by a hair's breadth?

THE SENSE OF SMELL

Smell they say is a decaying sense
    In civilised man,
And literature that pays much attention to it
    As decadent comes under the ban.

So they say who not knowing even themselves
    Think to know all else.
It's a different story of smell altogether
    That modern science tells.

Its monopoly of direct access to the cortex demands
    From disparagers of this sense
Who yet rely on cortical knowledge good grounds
    For their different preference.

Scandal to have no fit vocabulary even
    For this mighty power,
—Empyreumatic, alliaceous, hircine;
    Blind windows in a magic tower!

But reason unconcerned with what is of such
    Overwhelming concern to the mind
Is only a false face the nature of consciousness
    Continues to hide behind.

IN MEMORIAM: LIAM MAC 'ILLE IOSA

Where is the cock to the bonnet, the swing to the kilt,
The skirl of the pipes in Scotland now;
The range of the tartans outrainbowing the rainbow,
The hooching in reels that like flood-tides lilt?
Mar a tha e as the good whisky is
Everything in Scotland should be, I trow;
Aye, like the big music that within itself varies
Subtly as only a MacCrimmon knows how,
Or those shades of difference in sound that Gaelic
—Shibboleths of infinity—alone possesses
That no man of spirit can be less quick,
Less expert in, than another,
Even as there cannot be any growth
Of perfection but only growth in it.
For what mess of pottage, what Southern filth,
What lack of intricacy, fineness, impossible achievement,
Have we bartered this birthright, for what hurdy-gurdy
Exchanged this incomparable instrument?
O come, come, come, let us turn to God
And get rid of this degrading and damnable load,
So set we can give our spirits free play
And rise to the height of our form. There is no going astray,
More than there is for the rose shining full-blown,
Full to perfection with itself alone,
Come, let us obey the creative word.
God will make us flash like the blade of a sword.
Only that which aspires to a *caoin*, an edge like it
Like a melody tends to the infinite.
I am a poet; our fools ask me for logic not life.

Scotland has too much logic; but whither are all the clouds going
With which like Scotland our spirits are rife,
Before Eternity like a great wind blowing,
The race of the piled clouds after a gale
Across the world, over its cliffed edge, over the vale
Of Death till they dapple another country
As if crowding softly, softly, O God, into Thee?
O Liam, Liam, sheer white-top speeding full sail,
Lost world of Gaeldom, further and further away from me,
How can I follow, Albannach, how reachieve
The unsearchable masterpiece? You leave
No more than a swallow when the passage of its flight
So dwells in the eye one can half-believe
Its lines remain, a tracery on the light.

Am I a nightingale to remember too
What the swallow forgets—our Itys', our Alba's, death?
   While still beyond the Hebrides there in the west
   Heaven itself shines like that pheasant's breast!
Or content myself with the flight patterns you have flown through?
Meaning as an end of desire is value.
But an end of desire for Scotland? By what miracle of faith
Shall I carry that supreme song through?
Does it come to me like those forms and landscapes
Which seem to spring from a floating point of light
Our closed eyes behold just before we sleep
With endless fertility in inevitable shapes
Like Creation complete in God's sight?
   To no less a height
   My note must leap.
Ah! Thou art gone forever and have forgotten, Liam,
With the forgetfulness that one with the remembering I must know
If I, the poet, am to hold the scheme
Of both these worlds, this vast twin-theme,
   In one note—so!
   For I cannot fail
   Thinking of you so far away
To go as into the next valley and to a remote distance, yea
To the end of the world, goes the voice of the nightingale.
Ad te Domine appello; so even as Pascal against Rome

No matter what all other men think, desire, and feel
For Scotland to-day we irreconcilables carry our appeal
Completely over their heads and straight to God home.
Let them do likewise and we may meet them there
(For a moment!)—but not elsewhere.

From

Stony Limits and Other Poems

1934

STONY LIMITS

In Memoriam: Charles Doughty, 1843–1927

Under no hanging heaven-rooted tree,
Though full of mammuks' nests,
Bone of old Britain we bury thee
But heeding your unspoken hests
Naught not coeval with the Earth
And indispensable till its end
With what whom you despised may deem the dearth
Of your last resting-place dare blend.
Where nature is content with little so are you
So be it the little to which all else is due.

Nor in vain mimicry of the powers
That lifted up the mountains shall we raise
A stone less of nature's shaping than of ours
   To mark the unfrequented place.
You were not filial to all else
Save to the Dust, the mother of all men,
And where you lie no other sign needs tell
(Unless a gaunt shape resembles you again
In some momentary effect of light on rock)
But your family likeness to all her stock.

Flowers may be strewn upon the grave
   Of easy come easy go.
Fitly only some earthquake or tidal wave
O'er you its red rose or its white may throw
But naught else smaller than darkness and light
—Both here, though of no man's bringing!—

And as any past time had been in your sight
Were you now from your bed upspringing,
Now or a billion years hence, you would see
Scant difference, eyed like eternity.

Let my first offering be these few pyroxenes twinned
On the orthopinacoid and hour-glass scheme,
Fine striae, microline cross-hatchings, and this wind
Bowing plumes of vapour forever it would seem
From cone after cone diminishing sterile and grey
In the distance; dun sands in ever-changing squalls;
Crush breccias and overthrusts; and such little array
Of Geology's favourite fal-de-lals
And demolitions and entrenchments of weather
As any turn of my eye brings together.

I know how on turning to noble hills
And stark deserts happily still preserved
For men whom no gregariousness fills
With the loneliness for which they are nerved
—The lonely at-one-ment with all worth while—
I can feel as if the landscape and I
Became each other and see my smile
In the corners of the vastest contours lie
And share the gladness and peace you knew,
—The supreme human serenity that was you!

I have seen Silence lift his head
And Song, like his double, lift yours,
And know, while nearly all that seems living is dead,
You were always consubstantial with all that endures.
Would it were on Earth! Not since Ezekiel has that faw sun ringed
A worthier head; red as Adam you stood
In the desert, the horizon with vultures black-winged,
And sang and died in this still greater solitude
Where I sit by your skull whose emptiness is worth
The sum of almost all the heads now on Earth
—By your roomy skull where most men might well spend
Longer than you did in Arabia, friend!

How should we have anything to give you
    In death who had nothing in life,
Attempting in our sand-riddles to sieve you
Who were with nothing but the sheer elements rife?
Anchor of truth, facile as granite you lie,
A plug suspended in England's false dreams.
Your worth will be seen by and by,
Like God's purpose in what men deem *their* schemes,
Nothing ephemeral can seek what lies in this ground
Since nothing can be sought but the found.

The poem that would praise you must be
Like the glass of some rock, sleek brown, crowded
With dark incipient crystal growths, we see;
Or a glimpse of Petavius may have endowed it
With the tubular and dumb-bell-shaped inclusions surrounded
    By the broad reaction rims it needs.
I have seen it in dreams and know how it abounded
—Ah! would I could find in me like seeds!—
As the north-easterly garden in the lunation grows,
A spectacle not one man in ten millions knows.

I belong to a different country than yours
And none of my travels have been in the same lands
Save where Arzachel or Langrenus allures
Such spirits as ours, and the Straight Wall stands,
But crossing shear planes extruded in long lines of ridges
Torsion cylinders, crater rings, and circular seas
And ultra-basic xenoliths that make men look midges
Belong to my quarter as well, and with ease
I too can work in bright green and all the curious interference
Colours that under crossed nicols have a mottled appearance.

FROM "ON A RAISED BEACH"

—Each of these stones on this raised beach,
  Every stone in the world,
Covers infinite death, beyond the reach
Of the dead it hides; and cannot be hurled
Aside yet to let any of them come forth, as love
  Once made a stone move
  (Though I do not depend on that
  My case to prove).
So let us beware of death; the stones will have
Their revenge; we have lost all approach to them,
But soon we shall become as those we have betrayed,
And they will seal us as fast in our graves
As our indifference and ignorance seals them;
  But let us not be afraid to die.
No heavier and colder and quieter then,
No more motionless, do stones lie
  In death than in life to all men.
It is no more difficult in death than here
—Though slow as the stones the powers develop
To rise from the grave—to get a life worth having;
And in death—unlike life—we lose nothing that is truly ours.

Diallage of the world's debate, end of the long auxesis,
Although no ebrillade of Pegasus can here avail,
I prefer your enchorial characters—the futhore of the future—
To the hieroglyphics of all the other forms of Nature.
Song, your apprentice encrinite, seems to sweep
The Heavens with a last entrochal movement;
And, with the same word that began it, closes
Earth's vast epanadiplosis.

PLACENTA PREVIA,
or THE CASE OF GLASGOW

It'll be no easy matter to keep the dirt in its place
And get the Future out alive in *this* case!

FIRST LOVE

I have been in this garden of unripe fruit
    All the long day,
Where cold and clear from the hard green apples
    The light fell away.

I was wandering here with my own true love,
    But as I bent o'er,
She dwindled back to her childhood again
    And I saw her no more.

A wind sprang up and a hail of buds
    About me rolled,
Then this fog I knew before I was born
    But now—cold, cold!

THE POT HAT,
or BALLAD OF THE HOLY GRAIL

He's broken the ceremonial pot
    O, it's broken forever.
Into a thousand orts
    He's gane and gar'd it shiver.

It sat at the feet o' the witches
    Mair lurid than the nails on the toes

O' yon nether maimers squat in their mess
   When he dirled it frae under their nose.

Gloomy under the skinklan' gauds,
   Grumblin' wi' their skins still awash
Wi' the ale, they lout on the hearth-stane
   Beaten, lamentin' the smash.

Huddlin' like thunder cloods they heard him
   Like the lichtnin' laugh
—"Sorrow on the day we've seen
   This bright blinkin' calf."

The meet wishin'-bowl o' the carlines
   Is shingle to his wud tide;
The auld mind-can is broken and strewn
   In shards on ilka side.

Frae the beginnin' o' time that moody kettle,
   That roomy-brewin' ewer, was the deep o' rest,
Feasted they did wha got to that lucky well,
   Wham the wily wimmen had as their guest.

Fu' o' hugs they had been for him tae
   And cried him to sit under the ewer
But he hugged ill-will and felt feedin' in him
   The bowl-brakin' poo'er.

Warder o' the seed-spell abode, he'd come hame
   Frae the far hunt when the day was din
Joggin' into the cellar gloomy and icy
   Amang the shaggy kin o' the Inn.

The huggin' Goths were thrang inside
   And the cry gaed up:
"The son o' man has come into the cellar,
   Beware for the magic cup."

But ane o' the wimmen replied
   In the throes o' her spite and malice:

"Rammin' strong men tho' you are
    Even you canna brak oor chalice.

"There's nane to match it; the mightiest o' Kings
    Canna get its marrow onywhere;
The wale o' truce-cups; the essence
    O' a' Easter's foresight is there."

Then he seized the broth-stane *glari* *
    And slogged it against a pillar,
But it was borne back haill yont her skirts
    And lood was the jeer intill'r.

Syne a voice frae naewhere kennin' that harlot,
    The Eden-seether, the wisdom o' the adder,
Cried: "Clour it on her heid—for that's harder
    Than ony cauldron on Earth." Sae he had her.

Risin' frae the knees he brocht the dish doon
    Wi' the haill o' his wecht on the heid
O' yon churlish enchantress and at aince
    The muckle beaker was dung abreid.

"Ochone, my treasure is gane frae me,
    There's nae mendin' this a'e thing sae choice,
Oot through my ain fury gangs the ale-keel o' my hoose."
    In endless lamentation she's lifted her voice.

He's taen nae notice; stridin' owre the flair
    He's lifted the entire ring o' the hull
O' yon ewer o' the Earth-ruiner and worn it
    As a holy trophy enringin' his skull.

---

* *Glari*—Icelandic for glass or glazed ware.

SHETLAND LYRICS

To "A. T. Cunninghame"

- I -
With the Herring Fishers

"I see herrin'."—I hear the glad cry
And 'gainst the moon see ilka blue jowl
In turn as the fishermen haul on the nets
And sing: "Come, shove in your heids and growl."

"Soom on, bonnie herrin', soom on," they shout,
Or "Come in, O come in, and see me"
"Come gie the auld man something to dae.
It'll be a braw change frae the sea."

O it's ane o' the bonniest sichts in the warld
To watch the herrin' come walkin' on board
In the wee sma' 'oors o' a simmer's mornin'
As if o' their ain accord.

For this is the way that God sees life,
The haill jing-bang o's appearin'
Up owre frae the edge o' naethingness
—It's his happy cries I'm hearin'.

"Left, right—O come in and see me,"
Reid and yellow and black and white
Toddlin' up into Heaven thegither
At peep o' day frae the endless night.

"I see herrin'," I hear his glad cry,
And 'gainst the moon see his muckle blue jowl,
As he handles buoy-tow and bush-raip
Singin': "Come, shove in your heids and growl!"

- II -
Deep-Sea Fishing

I suddenly saw I was wrang when I felt
That the gapin' mooths and gogglin' een

O' the fish were no' what we should expect
Frae a sea sae infinite and serene.

I kent I'd be equally wrang if I wished
My nice concern wi' its beauty to be
Shared by the fishermen wha's coarser lives
Seemed proof to a' that appealed to me.

Aye, and I kent their animal forms
And primitive minds, like fish frae the sea,
Cam' faur mair naturally oot o' the bland
Omnipotence o' God than a fribble like me.

- III -
Colla Firth in Winter

Nae mair wi' a bricht kerchief rowed her heid
Bonnie lass by bonnie lass eidently bends
Owre the lang row o' farlins doon the quayside
Wi' piles o' glitterin' herrin' at her quick finger ends.

There's a press o' craft roond the pierheid nae mair,
Sailin' boats, motor boats, drifters and a'
Wi' cran baskets swingin' and trollies kept ga'en
A' the 'oors o' the mornin' as hard's they can ca'.

I dodge oot and in o' the shadowy voes
Wi' nae fishermen to crack wi', nae lassies to tease.
There's naething to hear and naething to see
Save whiles a ferlie my ain spirit gi'es.

Why am *I* still here while a' else is awa'?
Why has time ta'en the lave and spared naething but me?
Is it freendship or juist the whim o' a foe?
Naething else can I miss wi' this riddle to ree!

- IV -
A Daughter of the Sea

A wumman cam' up frae the blae depths o' the sea
And "I'm Jeannie MacQueen," she said, lauchin', to me.

But it's "gi way wi' your oyster-shine, lassie, gi way"
—For she'd a different colour in the nail o' each tae.

- V -
Gruney

You say there's naething here
   But a bank o' snaw?
But the sin whiles shows in't
   Gleg een ana'.

I'll be like these white birds
   Sittin' facin' the ocean
Wi' here and there in their stillness
   Vigil's pin-point motion.

- VI -
The Bonxie *

I'll be the Bonxie, that noble scua,
That infects a' ither birds wi' its qualms.
In its presence even the eagle
Forbears to pounce on the lambs.

For it fechts wi' nocht less than itsel'
And prefers to encounter great odds.
Guid-bye to mankind. Henceforth I'll engage
Only angels, archangels, devils and gods.

- VII -
To a Sea Eagle

I used to walk on solid gr'und
Till it fell awa' frae my feet
And, left in the void, I'd instantly
To get accustomed wi't.

Watchin' your prood flight noo I feel
As a man may dae wi' a bairn,

* The Great Scua.

For withoot ony show at a'
In deeper abysses I'm farin'.

Aye, withoot ony show at a',
Save whiles a sang I may sing
Gets in resonance wi' the sun
And ootshines't like a turnin' wing.

De Profundis

I delight in this naethingness
Mair than ever I did
In the creation it yielded
And has aince mair hid.

Sae an ardent spirit
Should submerge a' it's learned
And enjoy to the full
Whatna leisure it's earned.

For what is the end
O' a' labour but this?
—Earth's fruits to the flesh;
To the soul the Abyss.

- IX -
Mirror Fugue

Whiles I've seen a wheen gulls
Seem to equal the croods
O' the white waves by joinin'
Hands wi' the cloods,
Till atween them they've made
  A complete and clear
Heavenly facsimile
O' the hydrosphere

[228]

—Till the shapes in the lift
And the seas' wild smother
Seemed baith to mak'
And to mirror each other.

But my thochts that gang questin'
    Abune the haill earth
Whiles fly where there's naething
    To eke oot their dearth.
They are to the laigh then
Like the stars or the sun
Where ony reflection's
Confined to the one
    —They are to the Earth
    Like licht, or its lack,
    Earth maun tak' as it gets
    And no' answer back.

And they are to the heich
—Wha can tell what they are?
Or chart the diplomacy
    O' star upon star?
For the Earth is a star
As weel as the neist
Tho' few are alive
To the fact in the least
    —And for a' I can ken
    My fremt notions may be
    Hand in glove wi' a' else
    In ways kittle to see.

Ostentatiously tho' the gulls
Wi' the cloods dado up
I'm content to establish
A mair gingerly grup.
As wi' flash upon flash
O' sheet-lichtnin' in space
The relation atween them
Is whiles ill to trace.

Sae wi' thocht upon thocht
There's a structure nae doot,
But I'm blithe in the meantime
Juist to hae them glint oot.

Aye, wi' thocht upon thocht,
Like the wild-fire playin'
My richt hand needna ken
What my left hand's da'en.
Tho' the seas' wud marble
In a mackerel lift's glassed
Through the hollow globe flaughts
Frae ootside it are cast
    Flames fickler to partner
    Than the gulls and the cirrus.
    But the cutchack can wait
    While the gleids still bewhirr us.

For the queerest sensation
Intriguin' the air
A' agog for the former
Is there—and no' there.
The queerest sensation
Intriguin' the air
Kyths kir as a rabbit.
And whuds through a gair.

Glory on the water and grace in the welkin
But how sall I follow this flicker away,
Why follow, how fail, this fey flicker there,
                    This faint flicker where,
Wi' my wingbeats biddin' good-bye to the gulls,
To the sea, and the sun, and a' the laigh?

TOWARDS A NEW SCOTLAND

- I -

In these lane voes whaur the airms o' bare land
Lie on the grey waters like shadows oor boat
Seems to haud a' the life that there is—there's nae need
To rin a line oot; there's nae fish to be got
　　—Yet aye there's a cry, "I see white in the lum"
　　And up on the line coontless ferlies come.

Toom tho' the waters may look, useless oor quest,
We find on ilka hook a yield 'yont a' hope
—A scallop, a hoo, a sea-sponge, and syne
A halibut big as a table-top
　　Never say die; tho' auld Scotland seems bare
　　Oot wi' your line; there's prodigies there.

- II -

As the hills o' Morven were hills afore
The Himalayas or Alps were born
And established through a' geological time,
Can look at sic muckle ephemera wi' scorn

Sayin': "We saw you come and we'll see you gang
Nae maitter hoo you may too'er the day,"
Sae a' the giantisms o' England and Empire
Auld Scotland can dismiss in the self-same way.

- III -

Was it for little Belgium's sake
Sae mony thoosand Scotsmen dee'd?
And never ane for Scotland fegs
Wi' twenty thoosand times mair need!

- IV -

I wad dae onything for you, Scotland, save
—Even tho' your true line should be wi' such—
Become like ninety per cent o' Scots;
That 'ud be askin' faur owre much!

[231]

Ah, Scotland, you ken best. Why should I complain
That my poo'ers tae canna redound to you,
But micht hae been jewels elsewhere if I'd foreseen
   An' been to you a kennin' mair untrue?

Why should I complain when for centuries back
You've cast sae muckle aside that maist men deem
The best you bred—maist fit to serve and honour you,
   And elsewhere these worthless glories gleam?

Why should I complain wha least o' a' men rate
What you rejected as foreigners and renegades rate,
But at whatever cost approve your barrenness
   Faur abune a' their meretricious state?

The time isna ripe yet and in vain I hae tried
To separate the base elements you ne'er could accept
Frae sic faint forerinners o' your comin' dawn
   As whiles I thocht within me leapt.

Ah, Scotland, you ken best. I've been hailly wrang,
Mista'en bog-fires for your true licht at last.
Yet gladly I rejected ither literatures for yours,
   Nor covet them noo you've ootcast!

And sae my failure suddenly reveals itsel'
A pairt—a strengthenen'—o' your reserved intent;
Harder the task, greater the triumph; I'm prood to be
   Failin' the latter wi' the former blent.

Ah, Scotland, you ken best. Why should I complain
That my poo'ers tae canna redound to you;
They couldna been jewels elsewhere; I couldna been
   To you ony mair—or less—untrue!

My dreams for you, Scotland, no' till I heard
Them repeated on ither folks' lips did I ken

Their utter inadequacy to your need
And rejoice in your steadfast sterility again.

My dreams for you, Scotland, they flamed in me
To a monstrous height while I dreamed them alane;
I kent they were better than ocht that opposed
Save you—and you hadna spoken to me then.

My dreams for you, Scotland, as soon as I heard
Ithers cry I was right and repeat what I'd said
I kent I was hopelessly wrang and was glad
O' the light sic fools inadvertently shed!

- VII -
Let nae man think he can serve you, Scotland,
Withoot muckle trial and trouble to himsel'.
The slightest service to you compares
Wi' fetchin' a bit o' Heaven doon into Hell.

Let wha wad serve you reflect for a minute
On a' the thoosands that seemed to and failed to
—Ony service demands heich qualities then
These coontless thoosands ne'er scaled to.

And even at the best hoo mony folk coont
O' the least consequence to you since Time began.
Lightly to fancy he's o' the favoured few
Nearly aye disposes o' the claims o' a man.

Nay, fegs, it's wi' you as wi' a lion-cub
A man may fetch hame and can play wi' at first,
But if he has it lang, it grows up and syne
—Suddenly his fool's paradise is burst!

- VIII -
Surely the weediest of all the sons of Mars,
   The final shakings of his poke,
A pimply-faced Cockney soldier in Edinburgh Castle
   I saw, and thus he spoke.

Looking down upon the heaving city there
    As o'er the precipice he spat:
"Gor-blimey, we've made Scotland wot she is;
    Wot would she be wivaht?"

FROM "THE WAR WITH ENGLAND"

The social scene could be little
    But confusion and loss to me,
And Scotland, better than all your towns
    Was a bed of moss to me.
I had to lie on the hills and watch
The founts that to keep their tryst
Had found their way through the wards of the rock
Slower than the second coming of Christ
    To know how my task was priced.

I was better with the sounds of the sea
    Than with the voices of men
And in desolate and desert places
    I found myself again.
For the whole of the world came from these
And he who returns to the source
May gauge the worth of the outcome
And approve and perhaps reinforce
Or disapprove and perhaps change its course.

Now I deal with the hills at their roots
    And the streams at their springs
And am to the land that I love
    As he who brings
His bride home, and they know each other
Not as erst, like their friends, they have done,
But carnally, casually, knowing that only
By life nigh undone can life be begun,
    And accept and are one.
—*When was anything born in Scotland last,*
Risks taken and triumphs won?

HYMN TO SOPHIA: THE WISDOM OF GOD

See "La Russie et l'Eglise Universelle"
by Vladimir Solovyov

Our broken cries of shame dispute
   Death's pitiless and impious law
As the whole Earth with straining hearts
   Towards thee we draw.

Conscious that still in sexes split
   And generations without end,
We cannot to the emprise yet
   A due strength bend.

And the rose knows us not and wastes
   Its precious power; and in the stone
Obliviously sleeps a strength
   Beyond our own.

Yet will creation turn to thee
   When, love being perfect, naught can die,
And clod and plant and animal
   And star and sky,

Thy form immortal and complete,
   Matter and spirit one, acquire,
—*Ceaseless till then, O Sacred Shame,*
   Our wills inspire!

THE PROGRESS OF POETRY

A few moments ago I would fain have thought
Of the movements that from age to age produced
The great crustal arches and downfolds and thus wrought
Vast changes of land and sea.
Now I am loosed.

There seems a vaster change in me.
Unthinkable for a moment as if they were not
Those fragments of which I had hoped to think
In Skye and the Ord of Caithness, with all my beloved lot
Of cornbrash, and coral rag, and forest marble sink
Below my speculative power—yet not from my spirit's sight
But each as when a film unexpectedly stops running
And dynamic significance is lost and one sees instead
A sharp static beauty and feels after all it is sometimes grand
To look long and intently at one thing at a time,
So, dissociated from my stream of consciousness, these
Familiar objects of my thought are separated
From all their usual aspects and stand
In a strangeness fools might deem sublime
Like that appearance of a new earth and heaven
    To an airman given
When he first sees a cloud's upper surface below
Him carved dazzlingly like a field of mountainous snow.
This has been a test perhaps to see if I
Would even yet to mere fancy fall
Or be, as beneath a Mediterranean sky
Content to turn subject into object withal,
To that outwardness of which the limestone relief in that clear light
Is both encouragement and model—though the power
Of concentrating on the object of passionate thought until
It seems to come to life and exist of its own right
Has not tempted me in this trying hour
As fully as it might perhaps—I have not felt the awe,
I have not seen in these bright stationary forms
That flow begin which is the law
Of all creative work, until they rise
To the full height of the imaginative act
That wins to the reality in the fact,
And child of our incalculable Scottish storms
Suddenly I see with ecstasy
(My life resuming its normal course
And all my beloved stones
And other old interests—and none as if by force—
Taking their place in it as easily
As in that clear still scene, but with very different tones,

Colours and appearances—now dark, tumultuous, and to my heart)
Elpeodigra eard, and know I must go there,
Not in a swift ship over the blue Aegean sea,
Or fishing boat leaping to the flash
Of red oars in the early sunlight
In Phaleron Bay, but over cold knotted hacking waters where
Nap Nihtscua, and no presentness, greets art.
Far, far, and nigh impossible is this journey
Abandoned by almost all men else, and rash
Would any man be of mere whim to venture so,
But the *gana* rises in me and I go
(Walking off with Villon who found out for himself
What all subsequent French poetry consists of forgetting,
And on that ever darker and more difficult course,
The progress of poetry to the present day,
That leads from the proud adventures of the Theban eagle
"With a voice for the intelligent," full of shafts
From the current politics of Athens, Thebes, Aegina, and the gossip
Of the Court of Heiro and the famous fancy
Of the shrill whetstone on the tongue which drew him on
Gratifying the superior senses, to Meredith's
"Death is the word of a bovine day"
And all his acrobatic figurations, and so
To the marvellous obscurity of Rilke
Where what begin as metaphors all turn
To autonomous imaginative realities all pursuing
Their infinitely complicated ways on ampler pinions
Than sailed yon azure deep. Poetry has suffered no decline
In leaving gold shining like a blazing fire at night
Above all other lordly wealth to come thus far
To "the crooked trouble-laden Embryo
That holds, as though it feared some frightfulness,
Its hands before its half-completed eyes
And on whose high domed forehead sits the fear
Of all those things which it has never suffered." . . .)
And already, see, in the dark forms as never in the clear,
The vague cavernous shade in which the common people move,
The spirit rises, and all my friends are here,
Every myrionous human Calvary of modern life,
And I bid farewell to the melancholy, the disillusion,

The ideal heavenly virgins, the moon, the hate of our kind,
Vanished youth, and all juvenile enthusiasms, . . .
Hail, Gogol, we are of like mind!
I seek to plumb no deeper yet awhile,
My engine's taken up the depth I dropped again
Through the great overfall and's in the famous plume,
Prodigious jet of rushing winds that fling
A barrage of ice for miles to leeward of the peak
Over whose summit now I find the slip-stream
Strangely bereft of its accustomed force.

CATTLE SHOW

I shall go among red faces and virile voices,
See stylish sheep, with fine heads and well-wooled,
And great bulls mellow to the touch,
Brood mares of marvellous approach, and geldings
With sharp and flinty bones and silken hair.

And through th' enclosure draped in red and gold
I shall pass on to spheres more vivid yet
Where countesses' coque feathers gleam and glow
And, swathed in silks, the painted ladies are
Whose laughter plays like summer lightning there.

BALEFIRE LOCH *

O never heed the earnin'-grass,
    The foolstanes and the carmele,
Be edgie if you're to come wi' me.
    The artation's wi' yersel'.

* It seems advisable to gloss a few words in this poem (which, like passages in my "Water Music" and "Scots Unbound," is primarily an exercise of delight in the Scots sense of colour), viz: earnin'-grass, butterwort; foolstanes, orchis morio, and

It's a cauld coal to blaw at,
 Ilka step'll be to your clift
Owre cobblie grun' for switchbells even
 To the middle o' the lift.

To the bezel, collet, cabochon
 O' the ring that hauds the jewel,
The chine o' the bottomless barrel o' Hell,
 The hob o' the quenchless fuel.

Up, up, into the dullyeart heights
 O' this duchas o' my dreams!
The swallow bigs in the cot-hoose wa';
 The phoenix there it seems.

Nae fish can live but the cardui there,
 The bonniest o' them a',
Wi' its dark olive back and bright reid belly,
 And underfins crimson and snaw.

And nocht else save whiles a cheliderect
 'Neath the butter-clocks shoots green-sloke,
Or a cheirotherium still lays a hand
 On a dour unprintable rock.

Haul yersel' up by the blasted birns
 And lower on the doudlar syne
Till you turn an arress whaur the sun
 Inalow you seems to shine.

On grufe, and stop your groozin' syne,
 Like a top the waters spin.
Blehand and cannel their colours flee,
 Bawd's-bree to baudequin.

---

mascula (Linnaeus); carmele, heath-pease (Gaelic, cairmeal); clift, crotch; duchas (guttural), ancestral home or hereditary provenance; cheliderect, a kind of serpent; cheirotherium, labyrinthodont; green-sloke, oyster-green; blehand, a brownish colour inclining to purple or violet; cannel, cinnamon; bawd's bree (the colour of), hare soup; baudequin, tissue de fil d'or; arress, stone-edge; bedene, in sequence; on grufe, lie flat on your belly; bank, ruff or roll.

As if to twice its erstwhile size,
    Deil's addle at its root,
Fusin' a' darkness and a' light
    The sun had floo'ered oot.

Pitmirk and noon in ane combined,
    But stained wi' richer dyes
Than either had that blout by blout
    These deeps bedene devise.

While owre us muckle lintwhite cloods
    Like the bare doups o' pious Jews,
Gang up on catsteps as it were
    Frae this sacred pool they use.

The bandless gas beats mony a bank
    Amang yon glairy alga yet,
Bide whaur ye are! There's time eneuch
    To plumb and scale the infinite.

SCOTLAND'S PRIDE

Let us have no more talk of the service they gave,
Tell us no more as you have told us so long
That these were noble or clever or brave,
And deserve their place your great sons among;
Take a hundred years and let the facts decide.
Put all the conventional tributes aside,
And who's done aught for you, Scotland? Who's tried?

Have we fewer starving, fewer in want
In Scotland during the period in review?
Have we fewer slums despite all the cant,
Or thousands of homes yet that would make swine spew?
Is there less land under cultivation or more?
Aren't we worse off on every score?
Then what the Hell are they famous for?

All your nobility can be stroked off first,
Titles they may have—but none to respect.
No country in the world has ever been cursed
With such a gang of hyaenas as have somehow annexed
All your dukedoms and earldoms and historic estates,
No man of them heeds save in as much as he gets
Wealth to waste in London who would else starve on his wits.

Your divines come next. They may have served God,
But they have certainly rendered no service to man;
The prestige you give them is undoubtedly odd,
Since great though they be not even you can
Once they are dead say who the Devil they were,
But in ninety-nine cases in a hundred prefer
To forget them completely and in that do not err.

As for your politicians, not a man of them's been
Other than a servant of your deadliest foe.
Look round the whole country to-day and it's seen
Not one of them has aught to his credit to show.
Notable statesmen no doubt—but for whose good but their own?
Come, let any use they've accomplished be shown,
Your affairs all to rack and to ruin have gone.

You've had your usual supply of so-called great sons
In the period in question, but their filial regard
Wouldn't do credit, it seems, to a skunk's ones,
And if you still think that this verdict's too hard,
To problems a damned sight harder you're tied,
And the only men who have really tried
To solve them are a few on the rebel side,
Despised, rejected, hounded down and decried
By the fools on whom like a fool you've relied.

JOHN MacLEAN (1879–1923)

All the buildings in Glasgow are grey
With cruelty and meanness of spirit,
But once in a while one greyer than the rest
      A song shall merit
Since a miracle of true courage is seen
For a moment its walls between.

Look at it, you fools, with unseeing eyes
And deny it with lying lips!
But your craven bowels well know what it is
      And hasten to eclipse
In a cell, as black as the shut boards of the Book
You lie by, the light no coward can brook.

It is not the blue of heaven that colours
The blue jowls of your thugs of police,
And "justice" may well do its filthy work
      Behind walls as filthy as these
And congratulate itself blindly and never know
The prisoner takes the light with him as he goes below.

Stand close, stand close, and block out the light
As long as you can, you ministers and lawyers,
Hulking brutes of police, fat bourgeoisie,
Sleek derma for congested guts—its fires
Will leap through yet; already it is clear
Of all MacLean's foes not one was his peer.

As Pilate and the Roman soldiers to Christ
Were Law and Order to the finest Scot of his day,
One of the few true men in our sordid breed,
A flash of sun in a country all prison-grey.
Speak to others of Christian charity; I cry again
For vengeance on the murderers of John MacLean.
Let the light of truth in on the base pretence
Of Justice that sentenced him behind these grey walls.
All law is the contemptible fraud he declared it.
Like a lightning-bolt at last the workers' wrath falls

On all such castles of cowards whether they be
Uniformed in ermine, or blue, or khaki.

Royal honours for murderers and fools! The "fount of honour"
Is poisoned and spreads its corruption all through,
But Scotland will think yet of the broken body
And unbreakable spirit, MacLean, of you,
And know you were indeed the true tower of its strength,
As your prison of its foul stupidity, at length.

FROM "ODE TO ALL REBELS"

*"Deluded men despise me when I have taken
human form."*
BHAGAVAD-GITA, IX. 11. CF. JOHN I. 10.

As the heavy earth is the same below
Though insubstantialised in the sunshine
I see a man's slack mouth and goggling eyes
Behind this glory and know them for mine
Nor if I could would I lose for a moment
Divine in human or human in divine.
O double vision fighting in the glass!
Now light blots out this last distinction of class.
   O Magical change, O miracle
   I am suddenly beyond myself.
     Red, white, and square,
   Tearing the soul to rags!

Folk recognise—with regret it may be—
Man's kinship with the most loathsome brute
Joggling his protruding sternum there
And letting his animal nosies out,
   All they can have patience with,
   All they can pity,
All they can hide in their madhouses,
   In their gaols and hospital wards,

All that's diseased, misshapen, obscene,
    Mankind accepts and guards;
But when an angel appears, a man
Infinitely superior to man, as here,
From a man no better than other men,
An idiot like them, they howl with fear,
Or perjure their sight, and gibe and jeer
And deny that the like can ever appear,
    Let alone be one with the other.

"*L'extrême esprit est accusé de folie*
    Comme l'extrême défaut.
Rien que la médiocrité est bon.
    C'est sortir de l'humanité
Que de sortir du milieu."

"*Und wir, die an steigendes Glück*
denken, empganden die Rührung,
die uns beinah bestürzt,
wenn ein Glückliches fällt."

It's against all sense and what's the use
Of decency, worship, a shepherded soul,
If a creature like this can suddenly emerge—
Regardless of all most men can thole,
Yet visibly dowered with the light of lights,
The glory of God he shows yet denies,
When even if they tried like vices themselves,
Instead of the wisdom and virtues they prize,
None of them, not even the most reverend and upright,
Would ever be transfigured in similar wise?
God should consult with the Government or Church
Or get the medical profession to advise,
Not act in such an irrational way
In deciding on who He glorifies,
And not—as too often—let scallywags,
Lechers and topers, win such a prize.
With due respect we'll not follow His lead.
Mankind at least must always keep its head.
The wise are confounded, calculations upset.

Law set at naught, and order contemned—
O the Angel of Death is covered with eyes
But I stand in a guise still more terrible gemmed.—
   I think you are right.
   Culture's leading to the extinction of Man.
   What? Stop the culture?
      That's not my plan.
I am Ishmael, the only man
Who's the friend of all men.
(And who has ever known certitude
Must here recognise its voice again!)
   I tell you all else is vain.

—Every man who havers about honest toil
And believes in rewards and punishments,
In a God like Public Opinion
Or conformable to human reason,
And the sanctity of the financial system,
All that appeal to the Past or the Future,
Or think that two and two make four,
Or that they can judge 'twixt virtue and vice,
Health and disease, sanity and insanity,
Or that thought can be its own judge;
Who cannot believe in something for nothing
(Not stopping to ask whence their lives come);
Every man who is afraid of leisure,
Every man who with needless toil shuts out
The free, abundant, intolerable light;
All the men of science, the enemies of truth;
All imposers and accepters of any taboos;
All taskmasters and their bondagers,
Every man who says we must hold together,
Dependent on each other—not just on God;
That we are members of one another
And cannot stand alone—not wholly alone—
Or escape from the old apron-strings and cry
"Woman, what have you to do with me?"
All who are afraid of becoming too clever
And prefer a decent stupidity;
All who cry: "Hold—that's going too far.

We don't know where—if at all—it'll stop;"
All who believe we should be of one mind
Or at least agreed upon certain things,
Obey the same laws, honour the same God,
Subscribe to some "common humanity";
Deny that the wind always blows where it lists
And isn't in the habit of answering prayer;
Say that God prefers the just to the unjust,
That differences are only evolved to be
Resumed into undifferentiated oneness again;
All who trust any external authority,
All short circuiters of consciousness,
Believers in any State or system or creed,
All who expect clear explanations,
Fixed standards, and reasonable methods,
All the rulers and all the ruled,
    And everybody else,
These are the devils, the impious ideas;
Rebels, all cries of "Hold—have a care!"
    Tell us where our enemies are.
Our task is to destroy them all and return
Victorious to the spirit that in us should burn,
Our sole concern, that all but all men spurn,
And that spurns all men—all men, even us;
And can make nothing of the word victorious.

HARRY SEMEN

I ken these islands each inhabited
Forever by a single man
Livin' in his separate world as only
In dreams yet maist folk can.

Mine's like the moonwhite belly o' a hoo
Seen in the water as a fisher draws in his line.
I canna land it nor can it ever brak awa'.
It never moves, yet seems a' movement in the brine;

A movin' picture o' the spasm frae which I was born,
It writhes again, and back to it I'm willy-nilly torn.
A' men are similarly fixt; and the difference 'twixt
    The sae-ca'd sane and insane
Is that the latter whiles ha'e glimpses o't
    And the former nane.

Particle frae particle'll brak asunder,
Ilk ane o' them mair livid than the neist.
A separate life?—incredible war o' equal lichts,
Nane o' them wi' ocht in common in the least.
Nae threid o' a' the fabric o' my thocht
Is left alangside anither; a pack
O' leprous scuts o' weasels riddlin' a plaid
    Sic thrums could never mak'.
Hoo mony shades o' white gaed curvin' owre
To yon blae centre o' her belly's flower?
Milk-white, and dove-grey, we' harebell veins.
Ae scar in fair hair like the sun in sunlicht lay,
And pelvic experience in a thin shadow line;
Thocht canna mairry thocht as sic saft shadows dae.
Grey ghastly commentaries on my puir life,
A' the sperm that's gane for naething rises up to damn
In sick-white onanism the single seed
Frae which in sheer irrelevance I cam.
What were the odds against me? Let me coont.
What worth am I to a' that micht ha'e been?
To a' the wasted slime I'm capable o'
Appeals this lurid emission, whirlin' lint-white and green.
Am I alane richt, solidified to life,
Disjoined frae a' this searin' like a white-het knife,
And vauntin' my alien accretions here,
Boastin' sanctions, purpose, sense the endless tide
I cam frae lacks—the tide I still sae often feed?
O bitter glitter; wet sheet and flowin' sea—and what beside?

Sae the bealin' continents lie upon the seas,
    Sprawlin' in shapeless shapes a' airts,
Like ony splash that ony man can mak'
    Frae his nose or throat or ither pairts,

Fantastic as ink through blottin'-paper rins.
But this is white, white like a flooerin' gean,
Passin' frae white to purer shades o' white,
Ivory, crystal, diamond, till nae difference is seen
Between its fairest blossoms and the stars
Or the clear sun they melt into,
And the wind mixes them amang each ither
Forever, hue upon still mair dazzlin' hue.

Sae Joseph may ha'e pondered; sae a snawstorm
Comes whirlin' in grey sheets frae the shadowy sky
And only in a sma' circle are the separate flakes seen.
White, whiter, they cross and recross as capricious they fly,
Mak' patterns on the grund and weave into wreaths,
Load the bare boughs, and find lodgements in corners frae
The scourin' wind that sends a snawstorm up frae the earth
To meet that frae the sky, till which is which nae man can say.
They melt in the waters. They fill the valleys. They scale the peaks.
There's a tinkle o' icicles. The topmaist summit shines oot.
Sae Joseph may ha'e pondered on the coiled fire in his seed,
The transformation in Mary, and seen Jesus tak' root.

THE LITTLE WHITE ROSE

The rose of all the world is not for me.
I want for my part
Only the little white rose of Scotland
That smells sharp and sweet—and breaks the heart.

LAMENT FOR THE GREAT MUSIC

Fold of value in the world west from Greece
Over whom it has been our duty to keep guard
Have we slept on our watch; have death and dishonour

Reached you through our neglect and left you in lasting sleep?
That we see you no longer and are as body without soul,
Nidh inmheadhonach idir bheith ann agus gan bheith ann! *

Vain as Christ's cry upon the cross the sense
Of God's desertion or that endless exile
To which God does not matter since it springs
From the incommensurableness of men's desires and goods,
Each man, like the angels of St. Thomas, a separate species
Tending to a unique perfection so that even God
Cannot redeem the exile. Vain as Christ's cry
If that indeed were vain, as in vain we ask!
To remember the great music and to look
At Scotland and the world to-day is to hear
An Barr Buadh † again where there are none to answer
And to feel like Oisin *d' eis na Feine* ‡ or like Christ
   In that least homoousian hour.
Vain as Christ's cry in Scotland to-day,
Vain as the early Christians' superstitious expectation
(As when the cumulus clouds proper to thunder
In addition to their own conjunction of high light and deep shadow
Take on the wildly prophetic colours of snow)
Which those who call themselves Christians now
(Reconciled to an indefinite postponement of the blessed occasion)
Say was happily mistaken, since from that disappointment
—One of the first great purifications of the Christian faith—
The Christianity which they have inherited has grown,
—"Yellow with God"! § *Ionmolta malairt bhisigh,* ‖
So doubtless we are truer Scots, truer men,
Despite mere appearances than you old masters of the
     Ceol Mor.
And, besides, as *The Scotsman* says, it is likely enough

* "A somewhat in a state between existence and non-existence."
† The horn with which Fionn summoned his battalions; also the name Padraic Pearse gave it when he founded a little Gaelic paper wherewith to arouse national idealism.
‡ A withered babbling old man, "Oisin after the Fiana" (i.e., when his love for Ireland made him return to it from Tir na n-og), in that immortal phrase which has in it more than Virgilian tears.
§ One of Sean O' Neachtain's comical instances of the blunders of would-be speakers of English, as when the clown says "yellow with God" or *buidhe le Dia.*
‖ Eochy O'Hosey's pungent, "A Change for the Better Deserves Praise!"

The great music has had a real if imponderable influence
On subsequent piping after all—like Christ on the Kirk!
      —My God, can you not read history and see
      They have never had what you are fain to save?

Who would wish to undo nineteen hundred years
Of world-history and Christian experience, let alone
Scotland's vast progress in the last century or so?
There's no knowing what greater purifications are to come.
I feel them in my bones. Even we, we Christians and Scots
Will soon seem as primitive and impure—*as na cianaibh*— *
As the earliest Christians or you do to us.

Are we, looking at all the accumulated wealth
Of Scotland to-day, to be as foolish as Fearghall
And for the sake of a few pibroch—for *Scarcity of Fish,
Lament for the Children,* and *The Pretty Dirk*— †
Cry like him: "In that bright land of shining fields
I received not the Lord's Body . . . I was deceived . . .
Though I owned all Alba, better were one mass!"
Or prize a cruit ‡ of Irish wood above all our forests?

Is it any argument to say that the Pope of Rome
And England's Primate and Scotland's Moderator
And their countless underlings would not recognise
Christ if he appeared among them, or at least
Not immediately, especially if he appeared
(Not privily to each one of them, when the rest
Would all the more disbelieve—but to all)
In a Byzantine guise—in the unfamiliar,
Somewhat familiarly unfamiliar, guise not of the Canon
But of the uncanonical writings and made them feel
A sense of spiritual reversion? Surely it would be
Against the spirit of the religion whose fundamental charter

* From strange lands.
† "Scarcity of Fish," "Lament for the Children," "The Pretty Dirk"—names of great
pibroch.
‡ Hand-harp; a famous story in bardic history when Gilbride came to Scotland to
recover Domhnull's *cruit* and received the answer that its own possessor prized it
above all Scotland's forests, although it was only a bit of an Irish tree.

Is that "God so loved the world," for a figure
So mysterious, and tremendous, and above all forbidding
As would denounce all the practical necessities of life
And know nothing of the growth of Immanentism,
The revelation of unity in the widest differences,
And the steady elimination from religion
Of the sheer arbitrariness that during its history
Friend and foe alike so often attributed to it
(And not even speak in the *beurla* * at that
But in an uncouth jargon almost as bad as Scots)
To emerge at this juncture—like a bull in a china shop?

> *Cibe eaglais leanas siad*
> *ni thainig riamh romba fein*
> *ma si sin an eaglais fhior*
> *cionnas diaorfaid Criost ar bhreig* †

It is equally absurd to say that most of those
Keenest on pipe-music only know its degenerate forms,
And that these are the foes of the great music
Not knowing the difference between studying you and knowing
        you.
It is equally absurd to say that lovers of music
The world over have neglected you to their loss,
That you showed the way to far greater heights
Than all the other courses music has followed.
Is the whole of modern music to be dismissed
With derision and scorn as when Grainne
Having lost a romantic husband decided to settle down
With a rich and important one, and married Fionn,
And Oisin cried, while she bowed her head with shame,
"Dar linne, a Fhinn, coimheudfair fein Grainne go maith an so
        suas! ‡
But if there be any in the world susceptible
Of loyalty to the great music yet, such words of mine

* The English language.
† "Whatsoever Church they *follow* it never was in being *before* themselves; if that
then be the true Church how will they exonerate Christ from lying?"
‡ "It is likely, Fionn, that you will take good care of Grainne henceforward!"

Will be no *Ard-fostadha-na-feinne*.*
No matter how contemptuously I dismiss the plea
That an intelligence other than human, even if capable
Of understanding our concepts, would probably see no reason
For interpreting the universe as we must, your music
As I hear it is not as you did and may well be
Unrecognisable to you. You were good Catholics
—Watching me narrowly now from the *dachaidh bhuan* †
And your attitude to the course of history
And to your contemporary duties was similar to theirs
And indeed you islanders knew and I cannot deny
That the shells of molluscs generally have a dextral screw
Since a right-twisted shell lies apt for the waves
Breaking upon it to press it more closely to the rock;
And there are ingenious ways of accounting
For occasional left-twisted shells! All this
Only shows how far from the great music I am.
Gabhlanach an rud an sceamhuidheacht.‡
If I cannot reach any satisfactory solution
Of the problem of God's relation to time
Your art is more inexplicable in terms of your beliefs
Than men's lack of it to-day in terms of theirs.
Meaning regarded as an end of desire is value
And unifies succession in time. Like Christianity
Your art is *sui generis* and since it refuses
Any explanation in terms of the ordinary forces
Laws and standards of the world, we must seek
An interpretation of these in terms of it
Or find something analogous to the fact that the God
Of Christianity may appear adequate
If not as an explanation at least as a solution
Of the world we know; and quarrel no more
With the cry that history had to happen
    And is its own justification.

* The Height of the arrestation of the Fiana, where under the influence of a cozen-ing fair-woman's mischief Fionn lost his head and hurled venomous reproaches at his chieftains till they all deserted him, but Caoilte ran after them and prevailed on them to return.
† The everlasting home.
‡ "Romances are involved in affairs."

These things will pass. "The world will come to an end
But love and music will last for ever."
Sumeria is buried in the desert sands,
Atlantis in the ocean waves—happier these
Than Scotland, for all is gone, no travesty
Of their ancient glories lives
On the lips of degenerate sons as here.
That is what is hard to bear; the decivilised have every grace
As the antecedent of their vulgarities,
Every distinction as the precedent of their mediocrities,
No silly tune but has the excuse
That the feint was suggested, made easy,
By some once living sweetness.
Pride they have bartered for a lowly mind.
Since forgetfulness has befallen these sons of Scotland
If they suppose it suffices to claim Scotland
In virtue of shooting the grouse or as the price
Of drinking whisky—a vulgar doggerel
Concocted plainly, without excess of involution,
Prospers best now! Praise no man nor any satirise!
     An mhaith do bhi na bi dhi
     An mhaith ata', tar tairse. . . .*
We wear our laurels with a difference,
Seeing a regiment leaving for the front
A light of destiny used to play about them.
Nothing would ever be the same again. Already
We caught a glimpse of the glory of history,
The halo of honour. But now we go our ways
With no such illumination round our heads
And no sense of inferiority to those
Who had it. We too are playing our parts
In greater battles that have no romance;
Glory and genius belong to the past
When people still thought in terms of individuals.
Now only weaklings do, seeking for strength
In lives more tangled and desperate than their own.
We who are strong think only in terms

* "The good that hath been, meddle not with; the good that now is dwell on that"
(writ sarcastic).

Of classes and masses, in terms of mankind.
We have no use for the great music.
All we need is a few good-going tunes.

Behind these voices there are others crying
The entire race is on the wrong track. It is impossible
To continue this search for unattainable ends.
It is a matter of finding one's way
From romantic dreams to honest recognition of truth,
To substitute reality for ideas, and find the harmony
Between desire, ability, and will in man.

It is in vain to cry to either of these
"In the individual Scot as in his country
All fineness of living, all vitality, all art
Is necessarily lost. There is nothing but ruins;
    Ground for the unconscionable alien,"
Or to murmer in hopeful explanation
    "God must still be creating—still sinking himself
Irrecognisably in lower and lower forms of life."
Others will tell you that men of the Isles charged
At Bannockburn to the skirl of the pipes,
That the sound of the pibroch rose loud and shrill
Where the fire was hottest at Waterloo;
At Alma its notes made the blood
Surge in the veins of the Forty-second;
To the fainting men and women in the residency at Lucknow
The far-off strains heralded miraculous deliverance.
At Dargai the pibroch sent the Gordons
Storming up the heights—and so the story goes on.
And they will tell you how when Scotland brought home
The greatest of her heroes dead—the routineer Haig,
Whose lack of imagination carried him through;
But at what loss!—it was only when the piper came down the nave
Pouring forth the lament which enshrines the heroes of Flodden
And all the dead in all the Floddens of History
Only then did the eyes grow dim with tears,
The sob rise in the throat, and sorrow for him
Who called the nation to put their backs to the wall
Find fit expression—for the world can change beyond expression

But the heart of man changes not
(Like the God each side invokes in every war)
And yesterday, and to-day, and forever
The bagpipes commit to the winds of Heaven
The deepest emotions of the Scotsman's heart
In joy and sorrow, in war and peace.
What is a mere question of the relative merit
Of pibrochs in one period as against another
In comparison with that? Are the heights of Dargai
Not more important than the heights of art?
What does it matter what we are fighting for
So long as the good fight goes on and the same excuses serve?
A living dog is better than a dead lion
And to pretend that they are the self-same beast
    Does no harm to the latter!
*Cha till, cha till, cha till mi tuill . . .**
    I do not wonder at it.

Your occasions were trumpery as theirs and far from my liking,
Welcomes to Royalty, Salutes to Chiefs; and I marvel
At the music that towered into Eternity from them
—From the kiss of a king's hand † I would have given nothing for
And the like. But so it is in the world of the spirit.
The difference not only of degree but of kind
Between the germinal idea and its consummation
Can beggar description. So the humble endeavour
To convince mankind of invincible ignorance
Led to Platonic intellectualism, and Spinoza's quest
For the good life for man reached final expression
In the starkest affirmations of the metaphysical categories
With which the armoury of thought is equipped.

* The lament composed by Donald Ban MacCrimmon on the eve of setting out with his chief in 1745; Sir Walter Scott's translation reads:

"Return, return, return shall I never
Though MacLeod should return, not alive shall MacCrimmon,
In war nor in peace, ne'er return will MacCrimmon."

† "I gave a kiss to the King's hand"—this tune was played extempore by Patrick Mor MacCrimmon when, in May 1657, the King's army was lying before Stirling and there was a competition among the pipers (eighty of whom were present); the King (King Charles the Second) noticing that Patrick Mor MacCrimmon received special respect from the others called him to his side and gave him his hand to kiss.

—A fig for most of your pretexts! But my soul for the results
—A little later when it is mine to give! Only one occasion
Would I have loved to witness—after Inverurie *
When Lord Louis Gordon's pipers kept silence
Since Duncan Ban MacCrimmon was his prisoner.
No Scottish Army or English, no army in the world,
Would do that to-day—nor ever again—
For they do not know and there is no means of telling them
That Kings and Generals are only shadows of time
But time has no dominion over genius.

Yet the waves will not wash the feet
Of MacLeod's Maidens † for ever, and all modern Science
May vanish from human memory as the great days
Of Assyria and Egypt and Rome when they seemed
Indestructible as Europe and America now
In their triumphs of aeroplanes, wireless, and submarines.
The State has its root in time. It will culminate in time.
Greater things than this will fall. All religion will fall.
Neither moral principles nor artistic forms
Have any eternity ahead of them. How much
Are we at bottom obliged to hold fast to?
Who can guarantee that two and two
    Are not five on Jupiter?
*Thou language where language ends; thou time
Standing upright for ever on the path of vanishing hearts;
Thou feeling to whom, Oh thou change of feeling into what?
Heartspace growing out of us; innermost part of us rising over us,
Surging out in holy farewell! Thou Inner standing round us
As experienced distance, as the other side of air,
Pure, towering, uninhabitable—once inhabited here!*

You remind me now of a sunset by the Urr and the Peaks of Screel
When the tide-forsaken river was a winding ribbon of ebony
Faintly washed with silver. With the passing of the splendour from
    the heights
The middle distance and foreground were suddenly lit up

---

* At the battle of Inverurie, 1745; "the silent bagpipes of Lord Louis Gordon on the
morning after the battle of Inverurie was the greatest tribute ever paid to genius."
† MacLeod's Maidens—the rocks that stand sentinel in the Minch.

With a light (like that in which shingle lies under the sea-tide's
    forefoot)
Bursting from some hidden spring of the afterglow. All else
Was darker save the quickened feeling—like the sense of a man
Who returns from foreign scenes to the country of his blood and
    birth.
The light melted from the water: mist curtained the hills,
But, breaking from the mist, the peaks again took shape.
Dark and mysterious, yet clear and vivid, under the kindling con-
    stellations.
Even as you look to me away beyond Scotland now
In the night of our national degradation.
The line of the river was lost but out of the distance pressed
The swelling murmur of the hunting tide of the Solway.
The estuary would soon be a sea and a mirror for the stars.

Is not the rich fruit of the Arbor Vitae
Which is all antiquity and no decay
Rejected because of its rough concealing rind
By the forest pigs, though it contains meat
Of heart-succouring savour and drink of brain-renewing power?
Beside it, Tartar-like, sits the times' civility
And eats its dead dog off a golden dish.
The abomination of desolation is always in the holy places.

Is Scotland not that small unsightly root,
That leaf darkest and with prickles on it
That in another country bears a peerless flower
But not in this soil? Or did it bloom here once
And can it bloom no more? Or is the secret
Of Uamh an Oir still spiritually accessible
To such of the sons of men as worthily undertake the search?
Or are we seeming people but the disfigured fairies in Glen Brittle,
The dead leaves necessary to the coming flowering?
After having found the supreme and wonderfully retarded
Flower of culture man grieves at not being able
To make the general public understand it. He is ready
To renounce the pride of never being satisfied
In favour of that other pride
Of being intelligible to all—In vain!

[257]

But I know the root I am gripping in the darkness here
Is the unstruck note that gives all the others scope,
That deepest root from which even Freedom can unfold.
I too who have never become eingeburgert elsewhere
Feel changed in Scotland, grown strange to myself,
And waken to its realities as baffled Samson woke
Shorn and tethered. My native land should be to me
As a root to a tree. If a man's labour fills no want there
His deeds are doomed and his music mute.
This Scotland is not Scotland. How can I think of you
In these cities you never saw, a different world altogether,
Swollen huge with thoughts not thought that should have been
    thought,
Watchwords not proclaimed, songs not sung,
Tears unshed for ever and deeds undone beyond achievement now?
These denationalised Scots have killed the soul
Which is universally human; they are men without souls;
All the more heavily the judgment falls upon them
Since it is a universal law of life they have sinned against.
To try to relate your art to this is like insisting
That the man in the moon come to terms with the man in the street.
If I were on one of the islands on a sunny day
Reverse of the Brocken spectre, every flash I saw
Of wing or wave, look of an eye, curve of a lip,
Swing of a kilt, would surely magnify itself
Into the land of light you inhabit. Nay, I feel
I know your music best when as it were an island pool
Away here I hold a glass of water between me and the sun
And can only tell the one from the other by the lint-white quiver,
The trembling life of the water—like a man bending his head
As from outside, as a man can, to look at his whole mind
As if it did not belong to him though he knows
It is yet that by which he knows all that he knows.
It is that marvel of all marvels, the perfect knowledge
Of knowing that what is known is perfect
Yet distinct and vital from the perfection with which that is known
—The *peripeteia* that not only follows but forepoints and forelays
The course of the spirit which blows where it lists.
It is the realisation of the light upon which
Not only life but the very existence of the universe depends;

[258]

Not only animal life but earth, water, air.
If it faded it would mean the end of "everything."
It does not fade. Our spirit is of a being indestructible.
Its activity continues from eternity to eternity.
It is like the sun which seems to set to our earthly eyes
But in reality shines on unceasingly.
It is the movement which the mind invents
For its own expression not otherwise than the stars.

As every faculty, with every minutest organ of our nature,
Owes its whole reality and comprehensibility
To an existence incomprehensible and groundless
Because the ground of all comprehension, not without the union
Of all that is essential in all the functions of our spirit,
Not without an emotion tranquil from its very intensity,
Shall we worthily contemplate in the magnitude
And integrity of the world that life-ebullient stream.
It is not lawful to inquire from whence it springs,
As if it were a thing subject to space and time.
It neither approaches hither nor again departs from hence elsewhere.
But it either appears to us or it does not appear.
So we ought not to pursue it with a view to detecting
Its secret source, but watch in quiet till it suddenly shines upon us;
Preparing ourselves for the blessed spectacle as the eye
Waits patiently for the rising sun. The mind creates only to destroy;
Amid the desolation language rises, and towers
Above the ruins; and with language, music;
Its apprehension an activity of concentrated repose
So still that in it time and space cease to be
And its relations are with itself, not with anything external.

It is the supreme reality (not the Deity of personal theism)
Standing free of all historical events in past or future,
Knowable—but visible to the mind alone;
Wherefore the Church for its own purposes borrowed
The method you carried to perfection, and in plain-song
Found the musical voice of a dividuality
Which has no communal link with mankind
Though, having the mystic association of primitive music,
It still has the power to work on human superstition.

Yet the neuma, the song which hangs on to the end of a word
Without a word—uaill-ghuth an Aoibhnis—*
Avails it little now—the parrot-like contrivance
Of the jubilant sound signifying that the heart conceives
What it is unable to express. It is not in the Church
That men now find, when they must, some similar means
Of indicating a rapt and mysterious
Communion with the spiritual world.
But the Ceol Mor is only yours in your own perfect form
(The gracing that brings the notes of the melody from the flat to the
          round
Are only melisma between notes in India and Araby,
To smooth the transitions between the notes like the movements
Of the dancers who do not disclose the physical means
Of their passing from pose to pose.)
It is world-wide, ageless. It is the *Sufi Nida* and *Saut;*
It is the Indian *Ragas,* and melodies of the old *slokas* and *ghazals,*
Deliberately cast in a non-rhythmic mould because the composers
          knew
That rhythm is an animal function, whereas poetry and music,
Involving no bodily activity of the artist in their making,
Can exist in a purely psychological relation to society
And would be equally "true" in a world of disembodied spirits;
And, as Plato knew, it is futile for artists
To discuss subtle distinctions, nuances of the scale,
And listen as though they sought to discover secrets,
While all of them in the practice of their art neglect
The theories of the mind and follow nothing but the law of their own
          ears.
The supreme reality is visible to the mind alone.
Let these impious imitators and charlatans all go then
As Alasdair MacMhaighstir Alasdair would have sent every red-coat
Ad bhileach dhubh us cocard innt'
     Sgoiltear i mar chal mu 'n cluais! †

Seeing your music so, I am filled with lightness and exaltation
As though by some miracle exempt from the rule of life,
From time, consequence, and price—an illusion

* "The exultant note of joy" (the title of O'Heffernan's passionate song).
† "His black hat, bordered and cockaded, split like a cabbage round his ears."

Proceeding from within me as music from an instrument,
—But no sooner do I begin to recognise
This aerial independence of circumstance
As the illusion of love itself and to whisper: This is love,
Than the illusion is dissipated, fleeing as Eros fled
Before Psyche's lamp and I see that I am naked
And am ashamed and glad when the shadows cover me.
—Do lights cast shadows? Have all the lights that streamed
From wings and waves and eyes and lips into your radiance
Made me their antipodes: or grey and bare
And well-nigh lifeless as your islands actually are.
Ah, it is necessary to see the islands to know you,
As one only half-understands Homer till one has seen
The Greek islands really dancing in chorus
From the high blue shoulder of a toppling wave,
But no longer in the Hebrides is there only
Water and fire as of yore; the grey rocks
Are gaining ground and the seas are black with their shadows.

I am as lonely and unfrequented as your music is.
I have had to get rid of all my friends.
All those to whom I had to accommodate myself.
If one's capital consists in a calling
And a mission in life one cannot afford to keep friends.
I could not stand undivided and true amongst them.
Only in the solitude of my thought can I be myself
Or remember you clearly. It is like hearing a dipper's song.
Most of our songbirds are heard without accompaniment
But the dipper seldom except among rushing waters
Which obscure the music, diminish its volume, and rob it
Of much of its sweetness. I heard one once by a stream run low
After a long drought and took him for a mavis at first.
No doubt a large flat rock behind him was a sounding-board
Enhancing the beauty and volume of the melody;
Even so it was wonderfully rich. We allow too little
As a rule for the babbling stream or the cascade's roar.
Ah, happy they who no less lonely
Are companioned by a future—who foresee
The struggle of a nation into consciousness of being,
The significance of that being, and the necessity

Of the forms taken by the struggle towards it
And sing accordingly
—Subtle, intangible, a distant music
Heard only in the lull of the gusty wind;
They are animated and restrained in the soul
Not by that instinctive love of a native land
To which all can respond but by a mystical sense
Of the high destiny of a nation—swallowed up
Neither in the delights of living nor in the torment
Of the problem of individual existence.
But I am companioned by an irrecoverable past,
By a mystical sense of such a destiny foregone . . .
Time out of mind . . . Oh, Alba, my son, my son!

And yet this darkness is related to your light.
Only such a light could make one see
So great a darkness. So those who have had to dwell
In solitude, at the furthest remove from their fellows,
Serve the community too. Their loneliness
Is only because they belong to a wider community
Than that of their immediate environment,
Not to one county or race, but to humanity,
Not to this age but to all time,
As your pibrochs that reached to Eternity
—Your pibrochs that are like the glimpses
Of reality transcending all reason
Every supreme thinker has, and spends the rest of his life
Trying to express in terms of reason.
Your pibrochs that in the grey life of these islands
Are like the metaphysic of light in the style of Plotinus,
The great one-word metaphors of the Enneads,
Gleaming Godlike in the dry and formal diction,
The light that *has* been on sea and land;
Or as I have seen before the East had begun to brighten
On a hill at the point where the fir forests give way
To moorland while below me was tumbled scree
—At which hour and altitude the silence is absolute;
No sound of bird or beast, no breath of wind,
A stillness so oppressive that one caught one's ears
Straining in vain for any small sound to rise from the glen—

Suddenly from the stillness and the shadows of the night
The day came, a thing created, a great majestic presence
Taking possession from sky to range and range to sea
And instantly the silence was broken by a shower
Of silvery notes floating down across the morning
And looking up I saw a skurry of jackdaws
Diving headlong for the screes—as they fell
They caught the first sunbeams and twinkled like stars.
But it was their sharp clear notes, softened by the distance,
Which arrested the senses as a greeting to the day,
Like a peal of bells which glittered as they rang,
But the shadows of the hillside closed upon the salute,
The silence came again, and in a minute or two the dawn was gone.

I am horrified by the triviality of life, by its corruption and help-
    lessness,
No prospect of eternal life, no fullness of existence, no love without
    betrayal,
No passion without satiety. Yet life could be beautiful even now.
But all is soiled under philistine rule. What untouched spiritual
    powers
Are hidden in the dark and cold, under the suffocating atmosphere
Of philistine life, waiting for a better time when the first ray of light
And breath of fresh air will call them to life and let them unfold?
Civilisation has hitherto consisted in the diffusion and dilution
Of habits arising in privileged centres. It has not sprung from the
    people.
It has arisen in their midst by a variation from them
And it has afterwards imposed itself on them from above
A state composed exclusively of such workers and peasants
As make up most modern nations would be utterly barbarous.
Every liberal tradition would perish in it. The national and historic
Essence of patriotism itself would be lost, though the emotion no
    doubt
Would endure, for it is not generosity that the people lack.
They possess every impulse; it is experience they cannot gather,
For in gathering it they would be constituting the higher organs
That make up an aristocratic society. Day, the surrounding world,
    the life of men
Is entangled and meaningless; society is the endless human triviality;

The judgment of the world pulls at the roots of the best plants of
　　life.
Man himself, aside from historic aggregations, is only
The shadow of a passing cloud, his very existence hardly more than
　　an illusion.
His thought resembles the ray of a fountain; it rises, sparkles,
Reaches a certain height and falls and begins the process again.
—Would it were even beginning again in Scotland to-day!
There is no tyranny so hateful as a vulgar anonymous tyranny like
　　ours.
It is all permeating, all thwarting; it blasts every budding novelty
And sprig of genius with its omnipresent and fierce stupidity.

Yet there is no great problem in the world to-day
Except disease and death men cannot end
If no man tries to dominate another.
The struggle for material existence is over. It has been won.
The need for repressions and disciplines has passed.
The struggle for truth and that indescribable necessity,
Beauty, begins now, hampered by none of the lower needs.
No one now needs live less or be less than his utmost.
And in the slow and devious development that has brought men to
　　this stage
Scottish genius has played a foremost role. Yet I turn to you,
For unselfish intellect rises like a perfume
Above the faults and follies of the world of will.
But for the excellence of the typical swift life no nation
Deserves to be remembered more than the sands of the sea.

I am only that Job in feathers, a heron myself,
Gaunt and unsubstantial—yet immune to the vicissitudes
Other birds accept as a matter of course; impervious to the effects
Of even the wildest weather, no mean consideration in a country
　　like this;
And my appetite is not restricted to any particular fare.
Hence I am encountered in places far removed from one another
And widely different in an intimately topographical sense
—Spearing a rat at the mouth of a culvert at midnight
And bolting an eel on the seashore in the halflight of dawn—

Communal dweller yet lone hunter, lumbering yet swift and sus-
    tained flier,
The usual steely expression of my eyes does not flatter me;
Few birds perhaps have so successfully solved
The problem of existence as my grey lanky self
That in light or darkness, wet or shine, subsists
By a combination of alertness, patience, and passivity.
A kind of Caolite mac Ronain * too; but it takes
    All my wits in Scotland to-day.

This is the darkness where you have been; and have left
I think forever. It is the darkness from which nothing is cast out,
No loss, no wanton pain, no disease, no insanity,
None of the unripe intelligence of so-called dead nature,
Abortive attempts of nature to reflect itself.
All the unintelligible burden that alone leads to the height
Where it seems that extremes meet and I could reach you
i bh-fogus do dhul ar neamh-nidh,† with a *leim eanamhail.* ‡
In this depth that I dare not leave
I who am no dilettante of chaos and find
No bitter gratification in the contemplation of ultimate Incoherence
Know that the world is at any given moment anything it may be
    called
And even more difficult to group round any central character,
Yet it is out of this aimless dispersion, all these zig-zagging efforts,
All this disorderly growth, that the ideal of an epoch ends
By disentangling itself. Myriads of human activities
Are scattered in all directions by the indifferent forces
Of self-interest, passion, crime, madness—but out of their number
Some few of these activities are endowed with a little constancy
By the pure in heart, for reasons which seem to respond
To the most elementary designs of the spirit.
Civilisation, culture, all the good in the world
Depends ultimately on the existence of a few men of good will.

* "The grey spare swift runner, he who saved Fionn once by that wonderful feat of
gathering couples of all the wild beasts and birds of Ireland (a ram and a crimson
sheep from Inis, two water-birds from the Erne, two cormorants from the Cliath,
two foxes from Slieve Gullion, and the rest)."
† "On the confines of vanishing."
‡ "Bird-like leap."

The perspective will converge upon them yet.
I dare not leave this dark and distracted scene.
I believe in the necessary and unavoidable responsibility of man
And in the ineluctable certainty of the resurrection
And know that the mind of man creates no ideas
Though it is ideas alone that create.
Mind is the organ through which the Universe reaches
Such consciousness of itself as is possible now, and I must not brood
On the intermittence of genius, the way consciousness varies
Or declines, as in Scotland here, till it seems
Heaven itself may be only the best that is feasible
For most people, but a sad declension from music like yours.
Yes, I am prepared to see the Heavens open
And find the celestial music poor by comparison.
Yet my duty is here. It is now the duty of the Scottish genius
Which has provided the economic freedom for it
To lead in the abandonment of creeds and moral compromises
Of every sort and to commence to express the unity of life
By confounding the curse of short-circuited thought
Circumscribing consciousness, for that is the thought
Of compromise, the medium of the time-server.
This must be done to lead men to cosmic consciousness
And as it cannot be quick, except on occasion
And *that* the creative instant, the moment of divine realisation,
When the self is lit up by its own inner light
Caused in the self by its intensity of thought
Possibly over a long period, it must be thought of as a craft
In which the consummation of the idea, not in analysis but in syn-
     thesis,
Must be the subject of the object—life.
Wherefore I cannot take the bird-like leap to you
Though well I know that: "He that can endure
To follow with allegiance a fallen lord
Does conquer him that did his master conquer."

I dare not leap to you now. But after all since I cannot believe
You will ever be really for everyone or even for many
And are likely to pursue in the hereafter
A separate destiny from theirs—or simply because
I long to hear the great pipers play their great music themselves.

And they all dead (save one) centuries before I was born,
And have one glimpse of my beloved Scotland yet
As the land I have dreamt of where the supreme values
Which the people recognise are states of mind
Their ruling passion the attainment of higher consciousness,
And their actual rulers those in whom they find,
Or think they do, the requisite knowledge for such attainments
And where one is not required to believe anything
But even warned of the dangers of doing so
Except with infinite qualifications and care,
My duty done, I will try to follow you on the last day of the world,
And pray I may see you all standing shoulder to shoulder
With Patrick Mor MacCrimmon and Duncan Ban MacCrimmon
        in the centre
In the hollow * at Boreraig or in front of Dunvegan Castle
Or on the lip of the broken graves in Kilmuir Kirkyard †
While, the living stricken ghastly in the eternal light
And the rest of the dead all risen blue-faced from their graves
(Though, the pipes to your hand, you will be once more
Perfectly at ease, and as you were in your prime)
All ever born crowd the islands and the West Coast of Scotland
Which has standing room for them all, and the air curdled with
        angels,
And everywhere that feeling seldom felt on the earth before
Save in the hearts of parents or in youth untouched by tragedy
That in its very search for personal experience often found
A like impersonality and self-forgetfulness,
And you playing: "Farewell to Scotland, and the rest of the Earth,"
The only fit music there can be for that day
—And I will leap then and hide behind one of you,
Us Caismeachd phiob-mora bras shroiceadh am puirt. ‡

Look! Is that only the setting sun again?
Or a piper coming from far away?

* I.e., the pipers' hollow where the students at the college of the MacCrimmons
(1500–1800) practised. Ten generations of MacCrimmons were the hereditary pipers
of MacLeod of MacLeod, whose seat is at Dunvegan Castle in the Isle of Skye.
Boreraig was where the MacCrimmons lived.
† Near Dunvegan.
‡ "While the notes of the great pipes shrilly sound out their cries" (from Alasdair
MacMhaighstir Alasdair).

SKALD'S DEATH

I have known all the storms that roll.
I have been a singer after the fashion
Of my people—a poet of passion.
    All that is past.
Quiet has come into my soul.
Life's tempest is done.
    I lie at last
A bird cliff under the midnight sun.

THE BACK O' BEYOND

Bend doon, the sunsmite oot o' your een,
To this lanely pool and see
A'e shadow gantin' 'mang shadows there
And mind since mair wi' me
Hoo months afore they were born
Mony a fine simmer's day
'S come doon through their mither's joy
To where men lay.

Stand up; and at midday yet
What a glunsh we get!

MILK-WORT AND BOG-COTTON

To Seumas O'Sullivan

Cwa' een like milk-wort and bog-cotton hair!
I love you, earth, in this mood best o' a'
When the shy spirit like a laich wind moves
And frae the lift nae shadow can fa'
Since there's nocht left to thraw a shadow there
Owre een like milk-wort and milk-white cotton hair.

Wad that nae leaf upon anither wheeled
A shadow either and nae root need dern
In sacrifice to let sic beauty be!
But deep surroondin' darkness I discern
Is aye the price o' licht. Wad licht revealed
Naething but you, and nicht nocht else concealed.

AN APPRENTICE ANGEL

To L. M. W.

- I -

Try on your wings; I ken vera weel
It wadna look seemly if ony ane saw
A Glasgow Divine ga'en flutherin' aboot
In his study like a drunk craw.

But it 'ud look waur if you'd to bide
In an awkward squad for a month or mair
Learnin' to flee afore you could join
Heaven's air gymnkhana aince you get there.

Try on your wings, and gi'e a bit flap,
Pot belly and a', what does it maitter?
Seriously prepare for your future state
—Tho' that's never been in your natur'!

- II -

As the dragonfly's hideous larva creeps
Oot o' the ditch whaur it was spawned
And straight is turned to the splendid fly,
Nae doot by Death's belated hand
You'll be changed in a similar way,
But as frae that livin' flash o' licht
The cruel features and crawlin' legs
O' its former state never vanish quite
I fancy your Presbyterian Heaven
'll be haunted tae wi' a hellish leaven.

[269]

WATER MUSIC

To William and Flora Johnstone

Wheesht, wheesht, Joyce, and let me hear
  Nae Anna Livvy's lilt,
But Wauchope, Esk, and Ewes again,
  Each wi' its ain rhythms till't.

- I -

Archin' here and arrachin there,
  Allevolie or allemand,
Whiles appliable, whiles areird,
  The polysemous poem's planned.

Lively, louch, atweesh, atween,
  Auchimuty or aspate,
Threidin' through the averins
  Or bightsom in the aftergait.

Or barmybrained or barritchfu',
  Or rinnin' like an attercap,
Or shinin' like an Atchison,
  Wi' a blare or wi' a blawp.

They ken a' that opens and steeks,
  Frae Fiddleton Bar to Callister Ha',
And roon aboot for twenty miles,
  They bead and bell and swaw.

Brent on or boutgate or beschact,
  Bellwaverin' or borneheid,
They mimp and primp, or bick and birr,
  Dilly-dally or show speed.

Brade-up or sclafferin', rouchled, sleek,
  Abstraklous or austerne,
In belths below the brae-hags
  And bebbles in the fern.

[270]

Bracken, blaeberries, and heather
  Kèn their amplefeysts and toves,
Here gangs ane wi' aiglets jinglin',
  Through a gowl anither goves.

Lint in the bell whiles hardly vies
  Wi' ane the wind amows,
While blithely doon abradit linns
  Wi' gowd begane anither jows.

Cougher, blocher, boich and croichle,
  Fraise in ane anither's witters,
Wi' backthraws, births, by-rinnin's,
  Beggar's broon or blae—the critters!

Ir burnet, holine, watchet, chauve,
  Or wi' a' the colours dyed
O' the lift abune and plants and trees
  That grow on either side.

Or coinyelled wi' the midges,
  Or swallows a' aboot,
The shadow o' an eagle,
  The aiker o' a troot.

Toukin' ootrageous face
  The turn-gree o' your mood,
I've climmed until I'm lost
  Like the sun ahint a clood.

But a tow-gun frae the boon-tree,
A whistle frae the elm,
A spout-gun frae the hemlock,
And, back in this auld realm,
Dry leafs o' dishielogie
To smoke in a "partan's tae!"

And you've me in your creel again,
  Brim or shallow, bauch or bricht,

Singin' in the mornin',
  Corrieneuchin' a' the nicht.

- II -
Lappin' on the shirrel,
  Or breengin' doon the cleuch,
Slide-thrift for stars and shadows,
  Or sun-"couped owre the heuch."

Wi' the slughorn o' a folk,
  Sightsmen for a thoosand years,
In fluther or at shire
  O' the Border burns' careers,

Let them popple, let them pirl,
  Plish-plash and plunk and plop and ploot,
In quakin' quaw or fish-currie
  I ken a' they're aboot.

And 'twixt the pavvy o' the Wauchope,
  And the paspey o' the Ewes,
And the pavane o' Esk itsel',
  It's no' for me to choose.

Be they querty, be they quiet,
  Flow like railya or lamoo,
Only turn a rashmill or
  Gar a' the country tew,

As it's froggin' in the hills,
  Or poors pipestapples and auld wives,
Sae Waich Water glents and scrows,
  Reels and ratches and rives.

Some day they say the Bigly Burn
  'll loup oot frae its scrabs and thistles,
And ding the bonnie birken shaw
  A' to pigs and whistles.

[272]

And there's yon beck—I winna name't—
   That hauds the fish that aince was hookit
A century syne—the fisher saw't,
   And flew, and a' his graith forsookit.

And as for Unthank Water,
   That seeps through miles o' reeds and seggs,
It's aye at pilliewinkie syne
   Wi' the gowdnie's eggs.

Nae mair than you could stroan yoursel'
   The biggest o' them you may say,
Yet lood and still I see them stoan
   To oceans and the heaven's sway.

Fleetin' owre the meadows,
   Or cleitchin' in the glaur,
The haill world answers to them,
   And they rein the faurest star.

Humboldt, Howard, Maury,
   Hildebrandsson, Hahn, and Symons,
A digest o' a' their work's
   In these dour draps or diamonds.

And weel I ken the air's wild rush
   As it comes owre the seas,
Clims up and whistles 'twixt the hills,
   Wi' a' the weather gie's,

O' snaw and rain and thunder,
   Is a single circle spun
By the sun's bricht heat and guided by
   Earth's spin and the shapes o' the grun'.

Lappin' on the shirrel,
   Or breengin' doon the cleuch,
I can listen to the waters
   Lang—and no' lang—eneuch.

[273]

Wheesht, wheesht, Joyce, and let me hear
No' Anna Livvy's lilt,
But Wauchope, Esk, and Ewes again,
Each wi' its ain rhythms till't.

TARRAS

This Bolshevik bog! Suits me doon to the grun'!
For by fyke and finnick the world's no' run.
Let fools set store by a simperin' face,
Ithers seek to keep the purale in place
Or grue at vermin—but by heck
The purpose o' life needs them—if us.
Little the bog and the masses reck
O' some dainty-davie or fike-ma-fuss.
Ho for the mother of usk and adder
Spelderin' here in her coal and madder
Faur frae Society's bells and bladder.

The fog-wa' splits and a gair is set
O' corbie oats and corcolet
And drulie water like sheepeik seeps
Through the duffie peats, and cranglin' creeps,
Crowdles like a crab, syne cowds awa',
Couthless eneuch, yet cuttedly tae,
Tho' here and there in a sudden swaw
Corky-heidit as if in a playsome way,
But its lichtest kinks are a cowzie sport,
That nocht can cuddum—nocht can sort
For't, endless torsion, riddlin' port.

Ah, woman-fondlin'! What is that to this?
Saft hair to birssy heather, warm kiss
        To cauld black waters' suction.
        Nae ardent breists' erection
But the stark hills'! In what dry-gair-flow
Can I pillow my lowin' cheek here

Wi' nae paps' howe below?
What laithsome parodies appear
O' my body's secrets in this oorie growth
Wi' its peerieweeries a' radgie for scouth
And the haill ratch and rive o' a world uncouth?

Her cautelles! On cods o' crammasy sundew
Or wi' antrin sprigs o' butterwort blue,
Here in a punk-hole, there in a burn,
She gecks to storm and shine in turn,
Trysts wi' this wind and neist wi' that,
Now wi' thunder and syne wi' snaw,
Bare to the banes or wi' birds in her hat,
                    —And has bairns by them a',
                                        ——Bairns!

Bycomes o' bogs and gets o' cairns,
Ultimate flow of her flosh and ferns . . .
The doup of the world is under you here
And, fast in her shochles, she'll find ye,
When you're drawn to where wind and water shear,
Shuttles o' glaur, and shot-heuch, to wind ye,
Till you peugle and hoast in the shug-bog there,
While she lies jirblin' wide to the air
And now and then lets a scannachin flare.

Come pledge her in a horse-punckin then!
Loons to a byssim, pock-shaikin's o' men,
Needna come vauntin' their poustures to her.
Their paramuddle is whey to her heather.
To gang through her mill they maun pay
Ootsucken multure to the auld vulture,
Nor wi' their flauchter-spades ettle to play,
Withoot thick paikies to gaird their cul-ture!
What's ony schaftmon to this shud moss?
Or pooky-hair to her matted boss?
—Pledge her wha's mou' can relish her floss!

WHY I BECAME A SCOTTISH NATIONALIST

Gi'e me Scots-room in life and love
And set me then my smeddum to prove
In scenes like these. Like Pushkin I
My time for flichty conquests by,
Valuing nae mair some quick-fire cratur'
Wha hurries up the ways o' natur',
Am happy, when after lang and sair
Pursuit you yield yoursel' to me,
But wi' nae raptur, cauldly there,
Open but glowerin' callously,
Yet slow but surely heat until
You catch my flame against your will
And the mureburn tak's the hill.

CHEVILLE

For Kaikhosru Sorabji

Who remembers the Great Flood? The scope
Of the waters and their deafening din
Towering like God over the spirits of men,
Flocks, forests, and villages cast to the deep,
Who can sustain the menace of Nature
And praise forces to which life is straw
—Or glimpse them without seeming to outgrow
His mortality in huge recognition?
Tiger-cub torrent, shall I watch you and try
To think of all water is to the world?—
Seeing, and sorry for, all drowned things, sorry
Yet with, *cheville,* a sense of God's glory.

DYTISCUS

The problem in the pool is plain.
Must men to higher things ascend
For air like the Dytiscus there,
Breathe through their spiracles, and turn
To diving bells and seek their share
Of sustenance in the slime again
Till they clear life, as he his pool
To starve in purity, the fool,
Their finished faculties mirrored, fegs,
Foiled-fierce as his three pairs of legs?
Praise be Dytiscus-men are rare.
Life's pool still foul and full of fare.
Long till to suicidal success attain
We water-beetles of the brain!

THE OON OLYMPIAN

Come a' nit-wits, knaves and fools,
Conventional folk, and celebrate
Goethe's centenary, and cry again
Hoo noble he was, serene, and great.

You're likely judges to pronounce
On sicna qualities nane can doot
And least o' a' yoursel's, wha ha'e
The big battalions to boot.

Is there a humble soul who lacks
A' lear, yet's no' a specialist
On the beautifu', and good, and true
And o' creation feels the gist?
Things hidden frae the wise are yours,
The brain-prood err this way and that,
Thank God the general mind o' Man,
Securely ignorant, stands pat.

Great Goethe represented this;
Your ain kind *in excelsis* his,
And a successfu' business man
Even Faust, at last, we see.

Yet no' because he's ane o' you
Owre you fork his colossal legs,
—*Or aiblins gang up parallel;*
Wi' sic a giant it's ill to tell.
Maist o' you dinna ken or care
That or ocht else aboot him, fegs,
—*Tak'n his genius juist forgrantit,*
As he took a'thing else he wantit.
The haill thing's sham—evasion o' thocht
By hook or crook; and empty fame.
As Goethe in his time was blin'
To a' worth while, sae in his name,

To creative force you turn blin' een,
Dodgin like him a' mental strife,
Intent to win by cowardice
And life-denial Eternal Life.

Order?—o' weaklin's wha require
Safe-gairdit lives and daurna trust
Their inner sel's; and Form?—that fears
Further developments o' Dust.

Ersatz antiquity that turns
Poetry to nocht but a preserve
For educatit folk, wha find
The present owre muckle for their nerve.

A moderate literature that tak's
Ready-made conventions o' the real,
Misses a Hölderlin, and hates
A Jean Paul like the deil,

Ignores brute facts and a' the deep
Fissures o' life and pays nae heed

To dialectic logic workin' at aince
In coontless coonter ways insteed

O' the cosh continuity
A stabilisation fool
Like Goethe, false to his ain age,
Mak's his privy dookin' pool.

Owre nice to look Daith in the face,
Or tak' cognisance o' decay
Nae man worth ca'in a man can thole
Sic thowless things as you the day.

Lang while a sheer anachronism
A life devoted to the muse?
—Oor impotence as poets in this
We'll aiblins plausibly excuse.

Or cry that you reflectit weel
The coorse that history 'bood tak'
—And ca' it genius to be swept
On willy-nilly wi' the pack?

But a' the wisdom o' the past,
A' the glozin', trimmin', truth,
Since beauty against beauty wars,
Life'll aye thraw off wi' little ruth.

Consciousness springs frae unplumbed deeps
And maist o' men mak' haste
To kep odd draps in shallow thoughts
  And let the rest rin waste.
Quickly forgettin' ocht they catch
  Depends upon the kittle coorse
O' a wilder fount than they daur watch
Free-springin' in its native force
Against the darkness o' its source.
Wha fear the cataract and like
  Some spigot's drip insteed,
Wha prate o' laws and turn blin' een,

On the anarchy that's gied,
Owreshadowed wi' its chaos still,
Even sic puir arbitrary forms
May weel haud to—they need them ill—
Thoughts faur frae elementary storms
Tricklin' through thin domestic pipes
To their wee ta'en-forgrantit types.

Auld Goethe never wet his feet
*   But had the water laid on*
Baith H. and C., nor kent nor cared
*   The deeps his pipes made raid on,*
A michty expert on H_2O
Almaist hailly in terms o' taps
Plus a shoo'er o' rain, a river's flow,
Even a keek at the sea perhaps
—But Oh! that the Heavens had opened and let
A second Flood on this plumbers' pet!

Hoist them like ba's, ye fountains, yet
*   Upon your loupin' jets,*
O' wha's irregular ups and doons
Nae metronome the measure gets,
The fools wha think that they can pose
*   As authorities on thought*
Yet daurna look whence it arose
Nor faddom the conditionin' o't
—And let the bobbin' craturs think
It's them that gars you rise and sink!

Poet wha *ootgrew* Poetry
Weel may Philistia approve
Your cute prolepsis and the sheer
Opportunism o' your move,

Deny a' human values and applaud
Man's vegetative side, pleased wi'
Your *Gelegenheitsgedicht,* like Keats'
Poetry that comes like leafs to a tree.

This isna poetry? Sing
Some simple silly sang
O' willows or o' mimulus
A river's banks alang.

Aboot the metamorphosis
O' plant and beast a poet may
Sing but o' the struggle for't
In man and cosmos—nay!

The intricacies o' the mind
For poetry arena suited.
Be like a daisy and you'll be
A poet—wha can doot it?

Keep clear communication lines
Whatever else you keep,
For poets' bood to follow
Each ither aye like sheep.

Nor speir hoo faur you paved the way
For Poetry's relegation or
Juist kent what public you could ha'e
'Ud gang that airt—and ran before.

Nae ivory too'er! Poets mauna seek
To jouk the common needfu' jobs
And general interest o' mankind.
That o' a' use their verses robs.

Goethe was richt; the "Farbenlehre"
Was his best work; and he did richt
In turnin' Faust to drainage schemes
And fashin' nae mair wi' verbal sleight.

And I am richt in ga'en back
In like wise to the Muckle Toon;
And dungarees are better wear
For a man than a scarlet goon.

Nae poet can be nocht but that;
But man, freend, citizen, as weel.
Let him tak' tent he disna tine
Sicht o' a' that in poet's zeal.

Nae ivory too'er! Goethe was richt
In thus growin' oot o' poesy
—Wad Christ'd ootgrown religion tae
And gane back to the carpentry!

Auld banes be oors! Let poets dee young
Sic foolishness is no' for us
While a "Times Literary Supplement"
Promotes oor donnart hobbies thus.

Wha fund in Poetry a *cul-de-sac*
Wi' poetic justice to anither
Blin' alley turned, and witless missed
The times' trend a'thegither,

And drag on noo i' the least alive
To the vital in life and letters.
Your fifty years' funeral in Weimar
Still the "rinnin' concern" o' your debtors.

Hach! Bein' nae bourgeois perquisite
The *Fortwirkende* in mankind
Has ta'en a coorse restrictin' you
To a meaner role than you divined.

Pragmatic test? What do you think
You mean to the world's *workers* noo?
"Continually operative"—no' in them
If still in a dispensable few.

If still in a dispensable few
A whilie langer—and then
Life's saltatory way'll mak' them
Deid ends, as you to me or apes to men.

Ridiculous optimist, maintain
Your proofless unity o' the real.
There's pluralisms abroad at last
Ha'e a' sic follies in a creel.

The quantum theory's dung to blauds
The classic picture o' the world.
Nae shameless syncretism ser's
Sic humpty-dumpties aince doonhurled

A' the King's horses, a' his men
Can never cock them up again
—But there's eneuch Aunt Sallies left
To shy at still, nae mind what's gane.

Ah! weel micht Goethe cry that Daith
Is Nature's plan for life t' abound.
For Life *and Daith!* And the same need
For supersession in culture's found.

It's time you had it. There can be
Nae revolutions worth the name
Wha's leaders still in spiritual things
Uphaud auld fetishes o' Fame.

Let Lunatscharskies blether on
O' "divine monuments o' ancient thought"
The psyche's richt to revolution tae
—And canna ha'e owre muckle o't.

Ideas by the company they keep
Are kent, and henceforth nane worth ha'en
—And or lang nane ava'—'ll be seen
Wi' ony o' yours, oon Olympian.

Come a' you nitwits, knaves and fools
O' the educatit classes,
The name o' Goethe isna kent
—And never will be—to the masses.

ANTENORA

The stream is frozen hard. Going by
This wintry spectacle I descry
How even Edinburgh folk may be
In Scotland, not Antenora, yet,
Not traitors to their land, condemned
To a frore fate in Cocytus' pit,
But seasonably Scottish in their way,
And thaw, though hellish slow, some day!

OF JOHN DAVIDSON *

I remember one death in my boyhood
That next to my father's, and darker, endures;
Not Queen Victoria's, but Davidson, yours,
And something in me has always stood
Since then looking down the sandslope
On your small black shape by the edge of the sea,
—A bullet-hole through a great scene's beauty,
God through the wrong end of a telescope.

* Scottish poet who committed suicide in 1909.

First Hymn to Lenin and Other Poems

1931

FIRST HYMN TO LENIN

To Prince D. S. Mirsky

Few even o' the criminals, cravens, and fools
Wha's voices vilify a man they ken
They've cause to fear and are unfit to judge
As they're to stem his influence again
But in the hollows where their herts should be
    Foresee your victory.

Churchills, Locker-Lampsons, Beaverbrooks'll be
In history's perspective less to you
(And them!) than the Centurions to Christ
Of whom, as you, at least this muckle's true
—"Tho' pairtly wrang he cam' to richt amang's
    Faur greater wrangs."

Christ's cited no' by chance or juist because
You mark the greatest turnin'-point since him
But that your main redress has lain where he's
Least use—fulfillin' his sayin' lang kept dim
That whasae followed him things o' like natur'
    'Ud dae—and greater!

Certes nae ither, if no' you's dune this.
It maitters little. What you've dune's the thing,
No' hoo't compares, corrects, or complements
The work of Christ that's taen owre lang to bring
Sic a successor to keep the reference back
    Natural to mak'.

Great things ha'e aye ta'en great men in the past
In some proportion to the work they did,
But you alane to what you've dune are nocht
Even as the poo'ers to greater ends are hid
In what's ca'd God, or in the common man,
    Withoot your plan.

Descendant o' the unkent Bards wha made
Sangs peerless through a' post-anonymous days
I glimpse again in you that mightier poo'er
Than fashes wi' the laurels and the bays
But kens that it is shared by ilka man
    Since time began.

Great things, great men—but at faur greater's cost!
If first things first had had their richtfu' sway
Life and Thocht's misused poo'er might ha' been ane
For a' men's benefit—as still they may
Noo that through you this mair than elemental force
    Has f'und a clearer course.

Christ said: "Save ye become as bairns again."
Bairnly eneuch the feck o' us ha' been!
Your work needs men; and its worst foes are juist
The traitors wha through a' history ha' gi'en
The dope that's gar'd the mass o' folk pay heed
    And bide bairns indeed.

As necessary, and insignificant, as death
Wi' a' its agonies in the cosmos still
The Cheka's horrors are in their degree;
And'll end suner! What maitters 't wha we kill
To lessen that foulest murder that deprives
    Maist men o' real lives?

For now in the flower and iron of the truth
To you we turn; and turn in vain nae mair,
Ilka fool has folly eneuch for sadness
But at last we are wise and wi' laughter tear

The veil of being, and are face to face
　　Wi’ the human race.

Here lies your secret, O Lenin,—yours and oors,
No’ in the majority will that accepts the result
But in the real will that bides its time and kens
The benmaist resolve is the poo’er in which we exult
Since naebody’s willingly deprived o’ the good;
　　And, least o’ a’, the crood!

CHARISMA AND MY RELATIVES

To William McElroy

No’ here the beloved group; I’ve gane sae faur
(Like Christ) yon’t faither, mither, brither, kin
I micht as weel try dogs or cats as seek
In sic relationships again to fin’
The epopteia I maun ha’e—and feel
　　(Frae elsewhere) owre me steal.

But naewhere has the love-religion had
A harder struggle than in Scotland here
Which means we’ve been untrue as fechters even
To oor essential genius—Scots, yet sweer
To fecht in, or owre blin’ to see where lay,
　　The hert o’ the fray.

We’ve focht in a’ the sham fechts o’ the world.
But I’m a Borderer and at last in me
The spirit o’ my people’s no’ content
Wi’ ony but the greatest enemy,
And naer mair plays at sodgers but has won
　　To a live battle-grun’.

A fiercer struggle than joukin it’s involved.
Oorsels oor greatest foes. Yet, even yet,

I haud to "I" and "Scot" and "Borderer"
And fence the wondrous fire that in me's lit
Wi' sicna barriers roond as hide frae'ts licht
Near a'body's sicht.

And cry as weel try dogs or cats as seek
In sic relationships again to fin'
The epopteia that, yet f'und, like rain
'Ud quickly to the roots o' a' thing rin
Even as the circles frae a stane that's hurled
    In water ring the world.

Sae to my bosom yet a' beasts maun come,
Or I to theirs,—baudrons, wi' sides like harps,
Lookin' like the feel o' olives in the mooth,
Yon scabby cur at whom the gutter carps,
Nose-double o' the taste o' beer-and-gin,
    And a' my kin.

And yet—there's some folk lice'll no' live on,
I'm ane o' them I doot. But what a thocht!
What speculations maun a man sae shunned
No' ha'e until at last the reason's brocht
To view acceptable, as the fact may be
    On different grun's to them and me.

BEYOND EXILE

Salonika, 1916.

Praise God that still my feet can find
In distant lands the old hill-road,
And tread always no alien clay
But their familiar sod.

And all the ocean's broad estate
Be but a gleaming band to me

That slips between the bending fields
To find no foreign sea.

No stranger's roof-tree covers me,
Albeit I travel far and wide,
And sundering leagues but closer bind
Me to my darling's side.

And if I pass the utmost bourne
Why, then, I shall be home again—
The quick step at the quiet door,
The gay eyes at the panel.

AT MY FATHER'S GRAVE

The sunlicht still on me, you row'd in clood,

We look upon each ither noo like hills

Across a valley. I'm nae mair your son.

It is my mind, nae son o' yours, that looks,

And the great darkness o' your death comes up

And equals it across the way.

A livin' man upon a deid man thinks

And ony sma'er thocht's impossible.

THE SEAMLESS GARMENT

*"Whene'er the mist which stands 'twixt God and thee
Defecates to a pure transparency"*
                                        COLERIDGE

You are a cousin of mine
    Here in the mill.
It's queer that born in the Langholm
    It's no' until
Juist noo I see what it means
To work in the mill like my freen's.

I was tryin' to say something
    In a recent poem
Aboot Lenin. You've read a guid lot
    In the news—but ken the less o'm?
Look, Wullie, here is his secret noo
In a way I can share it wi' you.

His secret and the secret o' a'
That's worth ocht.
The shuttles fleein' owre quick for my een
    Prompt the thocht,
And the coordination atween
    Weaver and machine.

The haill shop's dumfoonderin'
    To a stranger like me.
Second nature to you; you're perfectly able
    To think, speak and see
Apairt frae the looms, tho' to some
That doesna sae easily come.

Lenin was like that wi' workin' class life,
    At hame wi't a'.
His fause movements couldna been fewer,
    The best weaver Earth ever saw.
A' *he'd* to dae wi' moved intact
    Clean, clear, and exact.

A poet like Rilke did the same
  In a different sphere,
Made a single reality—a' a'e 'oo'—
  O' his love and pity and fear;
A seamless garment o' music and thought
But you're owre thrang wi' puirer to tak' tent o't.

What's life or God or what you may ca't
  But something at ane like this?
Can you divide yoursel' frae your breath
  Or—if you say yes—
Frae your mind that as in the case
O' the loom keeps that in its place?

Empty vessels mak' the maist noise
  As weel you ken.
Still waters rin deep, owre fu' for soond.
  It's the same wi' men.
Belts fleein', wheels birlin'—a river in flood,
Fu' flow and tension o' poo'er and blood.

Are you equal to life as to the loom?
  Turnin' oot shoddy or what?
Claith better than man? D'ye live to the full,
  Your poo'er's a' deliverly taught?
Or scamp a'thing else? Border claith's famous.
Shall things o' mair consequence shame us?

Lenin and Rilke baith gied still mair skill,
  Coopers o' Stobo, to a greater concern
Than you devote to claith in the mill.
  Wad it be ill to learn
To keep a bit eye on *their* looms as weel
And no' be hailly ta'en up wi' your 'tweel'?

The womenfolk ken what I mean.
  Things maun fit like a glove,
Come clean off the spoon—and syne
  There's time for life and love.
The mair we mak' natural as breathin' the mair

Energy for ither things we'll can spare,
    But as lang as we bide like this
Neist to naething we ha'e, or miss.

Want to gang back to the handloom days?
    Nae fear!
Or paintin' oor hides? Hoo d'ye think we've got
    Frae there to here?
We'd get a million times faurer still
If maist folk change profits didna leav't till
A wheen here and there to bring it aboot
—Aye, and hindered no' helped to boot.

Are you helpin'? Machinery's improved, but folk?
    Is't no' high time
We were tryin' to come into line a' roon?
    (I canna think o' a rhyme).
Machinery in a week mak's greater advances
Than Man's nature twixt Adam and this.

Hundreds to the inch the threids lie in,
    Like the men in a communist cell.
There's a play o' licht frae the factory windas.
    Could you no' mak' mair yoursel'?
Mony a loom mair alive than the weaver seems
For the sun's still nearer than Rilke's dreams.

Ailie Bally's tongue's keepin' time
    To the vibration a' richt.
Clear through the maze your een signal to Jean
    What's for naebody else's sicht
Short skirts, silk stockin's—fegs, hoo the auld
Emmle-deugs o' the past are curjute and devauld!

And as for me in my fricative work
    I ken fu' weel
Sic an integrity's what I maun ha'e,
Indivisible, real,
Woven owre close for the point o' a pin
    Onywhere to win in.

WATER OF LIFE

What looks on water and's no' affected yet
By memories o' the Flood, and, faurer back,
O' that first flux in which a' life began,
And won sae slowly oot that ony lack
O' poo'er's a shrewd reminder o' the time
   We ploutered in the slime?

It's seldom in my active senses tho'
That water brings sic auld sensations as that
(Gin it's no' mixed wi' something even yet
A wee taet stronger); but in lookin' at
A woman at ony time I mind oor source
   And possible return of course.

Happy wha feels there's solid ground beneath
His feet at ony time—if ony does.
Happy? That's aiblins ga'en a bit owre faur.
I only mean he differs frae me thus
Tho' I'm whiles glad when a less shoogly sea
   Than ithers cradles me.

And if I'm no' aye glad o't it's because
I was sae used to waters as a loon
That I'm amphibious still. A perfect maze
O' waters is aboot the Muckle Toon,
Apairt frae't often seemin' through the weather
   That sea and sky swap places a'thegither.

Ah, vivid recollection o' trudgin' that
Crab-like again upon the ocean-flair!—
Juist as in lyin' wi' a woman still
I feel a sudden cant and sweesh aince mair
Frae Sodom or Gomorrah wi' yon Eastern whore
   T'oor watery grave o' yore.

She clung to me mair tightly at the end
Than ane expects or wants in sic a case,
Whether frae love or no' I needna say,

A waste o' guid material—her face
Fastened on mine as on a flag a sooker
   And naething shook her.

Although my passion was sair diluted then
I mind the cratur' still frae tip to tae
Better than ony that I've troked si' syne
—The gowden pendants frae her lugs, her skin
Sae clear that in her cheeks the glints 'ud play
As whiles wi' bits o' looking-glass as loons
   We'd gar the sun loup roon's.

Nae doot the sudden predicament we shared
Has fixed her in my mind abune the lave,
A kind o' compensation for the way
She was sae tashed and lightlied by the wave
Oot o' my recognition and slarried by
   The infernal sly.

A man never faced wi' death kens nocht o' life.
But a' men are? But micht as weel no' be!
The ancient memory is alive to few
And fewer when it is ken what they see,
But them that dae fear neither life nor death,
   Mindin' them baith.

Nae man can jouk and let the jaw gang by.
To seem to's often to dodge a silly squirt
While bein' whummled in an unseen spate
Lodgin' us securely in faur deeper dirt
Or carryin' us to heichts we canna see
   For th'earth in oor e'e.

Nae gulfs that open 'neath oor feet'll find
Us hailly at a loss if we juist keep
The perspective the deluge should ha' gien's
And if we dinna, or if they're mair deep
Than even that is muckle guidance in,
   It's there altho' we're blin'.

Whatever is to be, what's been has been;
Even if it's hailly undune that deed'll bear
A sense o' sequence forever in itsel',
Implyin', and dependent on, what erst was there,
Tho' it's no' conscious o't—less conscious o't
   Than men o' their historic lot.

Hoo I got oot o' yon I dinna ken,
But I am ready noo at ony time
To be hurled back or forrit to ony stage
O' ocht we've ever been twixt sun and slime
Or can become, trustin' what's brocht aboot
   A' th'ither sequels to the water-shute.

Shall wellspring and shower, ebb-tide and neap,
Refuse their separate pairts cryin' let's be ane,
In function as natur', appearance as fact?
Foul here, fair there, to sea and sky again
The river keeps its course and ranges
   Unchanged through a' its changes.

Wha speak o' vice and innocence, peace and war,
Culture and ignorance, humility and pride,
Describe the Fairy Loup, the thunder-plump,
The moss-boil on the moor, the white-topped tide;
And the ane as sune as the tither'll be
   Brocht doon to uniformity.

Ah, weel I ken that ony ane o' them,
Nae maitter hoo vividly I ca't to mind,
Kennin' the world to men's as light to water,
Has endless beauties to which my een are blind,
My ears deaf—aye, and ilka drap a world
   Bigger than a' Mankind has yet unfurled.

EXCELSIOR

Sae worked the instinct in the seas
And jungles we were born in
But sicna cares are useless noo
Tho' aiblins no' for scornin'.

Sae worked the kindnesses we got
Frae shadows gane ayont recall.
Sae work whatever relationships
May haud us still in thrall.

Still on we fare and tine oor need
O' modern mither's as monkey's care,
Syne wives, bairns, freens, and in the end
Oorsels we well can spare.

And aye the force that's brocht life up
Frae chaos to the present stage
Creates new states as ill for us
As oors for eels to gauge.

The promise that there'll be nae second Flood
I tak' wi' a' the salt I've saved since then.
Extinction? What's that but to return
To juist anither Muckle Toon again?
—A salutary process bringin' values oot
   Ocht less 'ud leave in doot.

It teach't me mony lessons I've ne'er forgot—
That it's no' easy to thraw cauld water on life;
The changes a man can safely undergang
And bide essentially unchanged; the strife
To tak' new forms and in it no' forget
   We've never managed yet.

The Factory Gullets and the Skipper's Pool
Are different as Dr. Jekyll and Mr. Hyde
But the quick changes o' the Esk that joins
These twa afore it meets the Solway Tide

'Ud faur ootrin the divers thochts o' Man
  Sin' Time began.

And yet, tho' hospitable to them a',
The Esk is drawn on like a knotless threid
Juist owre lang for's to see the end o't yet,
Tho' noo and then I tak' it in my heid
That the pirn in the hills it's birlin' frae
  Maun near ha' ser'd its day.

Or else I feel like payin' oot line
Forever to an unimaginable take,
And ken that in the Buck and Croon Hotels
They'd lauch my tale to scorn, altho' gudesake,
They credit mony hardly less faur-fetched.
  Heaven kens if mine is stretched!

The Buck and Croon Hotels—guid judges baith
O' credibility I've cause to ken;
A wee hauf wi' the emphasis on the wee,
And day and daily d'they no' see again
A miracle clean-flypit, in the maitter
  O' wine turn't back to water?

Weel the Waterside folk kent what I mean;
They were like figures seen on fountains whiles.
The river made sae free wi' them—poored in and oot
O' their een and ears (no' mooths) in a' its styles,
Till it clean scooped the insides o' their skulls
  O' a' but a wheen thochts like gulls.

Their queer stane faces and hoo green they got!
Juist like Rebecca in her shawl o' sly.
I'd never faur to gang to see doon there
A wreathéd Triton blaw his horn or try,
While at his feet a clump o' mimulus shone
  Like a dog's een wi' a' the world a bone.

From

Second Hymn to Lenin and Other Poems

1935

SECOND HYMN TO LENIN

Ah, Lenin, you were richt. But I'm a poet
(And you c'ud mak allowances for that!)
Aimin' at mair than you aimed at
Tho' yours comes first, I know it.

An unexamined life is no' worth ha'in'.
Yet Burke was richt; owre muckle concern
Wi' Life's foundations is a sure
Sign o' decay; tho' Joyce in turn

Is richt, and the principal question
Aboot a work o' art is frae hoo deep
A life it springs—and syne hoo faur
Up frae't it has the poo'er to leap.

And hoo muckle it lifts up wi' it
Into the sunlicht like a saumon there,
Universal Spring! For Morand's richt—
It s'ud be like licht in the air—

Are my poems spoken in the factories and fields,
In the streets o' the toon?
Gin they're no', then I'm failin' to dae
What I ocht to ha' dune.

Gin I canna win through to the man in the street,
The wife by the hearth,
A' the cleverness on earth'll no' mak' up
For the damnable dearth.

[298]

"Haud on haud on; what poet's dune that?
   Is Shakespeare read,
Or Dante or Milton or Goethe or Burns?"
   —You heard what I said.

—A means o' world locomotion,
The maist perfected and aerial o' a'.
Lenin's name's gane owre the haill earth,
But the names o' the ithers?—Ha!

What hidie-hole o' the vineyard d'they scart
Wi' minds like the look on a hen's face,
Morand, Joyce, Burke, and the rest
That e'er wrote; me noo in like case?

Great poets hardly onybody kens o'?
Geniuses like a man talkin' t'm sel'?
Nonsense! They're nocht o' the sort
Their character's easy to tell.

They're nocht but romantic rebels
Strikin' dilletante poses;
Trotsky—Christ, no' wi' a croon o' thorns
But a wreath o' paper roses.

A' that's great is free and expansive.
What ha' they expanded tae?
They've affected nocht but a fringe
O' mankind in ony way.

Barbarian saviour o' civilization
Hoo weel ye kent (we're owre dull witted)
Naething is dune save as we ha'e
Means to en's transparently fitted.

Poetry like politics maun cut
The cackle and pursue real ends,
Unerringly as Lenin, and to that
Its nature better tends.

[299]

Wi' Lenin's vision equal poet's gift
And what unparalleled force was there!
Nocht in a' literature wi' that
Begins to compare.

Nae simple rhymes for silly folk
But the haill art, as Lenin gied
Nae Marx-without-tears to workin' men
But the fu' course instead.

Organic constructional work,
Practicality, and work by degrees;
First things first; and poetry in turn
'll be built by these.

You saw it faur off when you thocht
O' mass-education yet.
Hoo lang till they rise to Pushkin?
And that's but a fit!

Oh, it's nonsense, nonsense, nonsense,
Nonsense at this time o' day
That breid-and-butter problems
S'ud be in ony man's way.

They s'ud be like the tails we tint
On leavin' the monkey stage;
A' maist folk fash aboot's alike
Primaeval to oor age.

We're grown-ups that haena yet
Put bairnly things aside
—A' that's material and moral—
And oor new state descried.

Sport, love, and parentage,
Trade, politics, and law
S'ud be nae mair to us than braith
We hardly ken we draw.

Freein' oor poo'ers for greater things,
And fegs there's plenty o' them,
Tho' wha's still trammelt in alow
Canna be tenty o' them—

In the meantime Montéhus' sangs—
But as you were ready to tine
The Russian Revolution to the German
Gin that ser'd better syne,

Or foresaw that Russia maun lead
The workers' cause, and then
Pass the lead elsewhere, and aiblins
Fa' faur backward again,

Sae here, twixt poetry and politics,
There's nae doot in the en'.
Poetry includes that and s'ud be
The greatest poo'er amang men.

—It's the greatest, *in posse* at least,
That men ha'e discovered yet
Tho' nae doot they're unconscious still
O' ithers faur greater than it.

You confined yoursel' to your work
—A step at a time;
But, as the loon is in the man,
That'll be ta'en up i' the rhyme,

Ta'en up like a pool in the sands
Aince the tide rows in,
When life opens its hert and sings
Withoot scrupe or sin.

Your knowledge in your ain sphere
Was exact and complete
But your sphere's elementary and sune by
As a poet maun see't.

For a poet maun see in a'thing,
Ev'n what looks trumpery or horrid,
A subject equal to ony
—A star for the forehead!

A poet has nae choice left
Betwixt Beaverbrook, say, and God.
Jimmy Thomas or you,
A cat, carnation, or clod.

He daurna turn awa' frae ocht
For a single act o' neglect
And straucht he may fa' frae grace
And be void o' effect.

Disinterestedness,
Oor profoundest word yet,
But how far yont even that
The sense o' onything's set!

The inward necessity yont
Ony laws o' cause
The intellect conceives
That a'thing has!

Freend, foe; past, present, future;
Success, failure; joy, fear;
Life, Death; and a'thing else,
For us, are equal here.

Male, female; quick or deid,
Let us fike nae mair;
The deep line o'cleavage
Disna lie there.

Black in the pit the miner is,
The shepherd reid on the hill,
And I'm wi' them baith until
The end of mankind, I wis.

Whatever their jobs a' men are ane
In life, and syne in daith
(Tho' it's sma' patience I can ha'e
Wi' life's ideas o' that by the way)
And he's nae poet but kens it, faith,
And ony job but the hardest's ta'en.

The sailor gangs owre the curve o' the sea,
The hoosewife's thrang in the wash-tub,
And whatna rhyme can I find but hub,
And what else can poetry be?

The core o' a' activity,
Changin't in accordance wi'
Its inward necessity
And mede o' integrity.

Unremittin', relentless,
Organized to the last degree,
Ah, Lenin, politics is bairns' play
To what this maun be!

ON THE OCEAN FLOOR

Now more and more on my concern with the lifted
        waves of genius gaining
I am aware of the lightless depths that beneath them lie;
And as one who hears their tiny shells incessantly raining
On the ocean floor as the foraminifera die.

A DOG'S LIFE *

"Tell me," I asked a cripple who goes on all fours
Like a dog, pads on his hands, "Don't poor souls like you
Feel the need to believe in something beyond this world
Far more than we others do?"

"No. Not with a life like mine," he replied.
"It's not we who need God. He could tell us no more
If he does exist than we understand already
And are thankful for."

AT THE CENOTAPH

Are the living so much use
That we need to mourn the dead?
Or would it yield better results
To reverse their roles instead?
The millions slain in the War—
Untimely, the best of our seed?—
Would the world be any the better
If they were still living indeed?
The achievements of such as are
To the notion lend no support;
The whole history of life and death
Yields no scrap of evidence for't.—
Keep going to your wars, you fools, as of yore;
I'm the civilisation you're fighting for.

O EASE MY SPIRIT

"And as for their appearances, they four had one likeness, as
if a wheel had been in the midst of a wheel."
                    Ezekiel

O ease my spirit increasingly of the load
Of my personal limitations and the riddling differences

* With acknowledgements to Pär Lagerkvist.

[304]

Between man and man with a more constant insight
Into the fundamental similarity of all activities.

And quicken me to the gloriously and terribly illuminating
Integration of the physical and the spiritual till I feel how easily
I could put my hand gently on the whole round world
As on my sweetheart's head and draw it to me.

KNOWLEDGE OF GOD

To an Oxford Grouper

I know all you can say and understand too well
Your determination to credit Christ too
With the sort of mysticism, that's sufficed so many
From Paul, who began it, down to you.

But hold! In future with me just remember
That Christ at any rate had the sense,
With probably as close personal knowledge of God,
Never to speak of His religious experience.

BIRTH OF A GENIUS AMONG MEN

The night folded itself about me like a woman's hair.
Thousands of dispersed forces drawn as by a magnet
Streamed through the open windows—millions of stars
        poured through;
What destiny were they seeking in us, what outlet?

An immense vigour awoke in my body.
My breast expanded and overflowed into the night.

I was one with Scotland out there and with all the world
And thoughts of your beauty shone in me like starlight.

You were all female, ripe as a rose for the plucking,
I was all male and no longer resisted my need.
The earth obeyed the rhythm of our panting.
The mountains sighed with us. Infinity was emptied.

To both of us it seemed as if we had never loved before.
A miracle was abroad and I knew that not merely I
Had accomplished the act of love but the whole universe
    through me,
A great design was fulfilled, another genius nigh.

Yet I lay awake and as the daylight broke
I heard the faint voices of the Ideas discuss
The way in which they could only express themselves yet
In fragmentary and fallacious forms through us.

AT THE GRAVESIDE

There is no stupid soul who neither knows
The rudiments of human history
Nor seeks to solve the problems of this life
But still must give his witless testimony
On huge conundrums. —Faithless in small things,
Let all such cease their fond imaginings.
The eyes of fools are on the ends of God.
I postpone all such thoughts beneath this sod.

BEHIND THE SYMBOLS

Let the hearts of my people be lifted up
Once more with the daily sight
Of an eagle wheeling on majestic vans
    That is our Scottish birthright.

Fill their lives again with the noblest form
    At liberty in Europe still—
The red stag pausing with lifted hoof
    On the sun-assailing hill.

For these are among Earth's glorious symbols
To souls of men needing symbols yet
And a man must be well nourished on these
    To embrace the Infinite.

But the supreme spirit enters into all
    As an otter into its watery home
As if without dividing its flow
    And making no ripple, bubble, or foam.

Even so in the course of time I hope
My people will open their hearts until
They are like the lochs the hill-streams feed
    Forever—but cannot overspill.

THE IMPOSSIBLE SONG

The only song for which I care
Is one other men may hear
But cannot understand
Save as a man may "share"
But cannot really bear
    Another's pain.

It's neither here nor there
Whether or not men listen.
What they think's of no account,
That is their own affair,
For which who sings can spare
    No time or thought.

It's such a song as all men sing
Tho' few ever hear themselves,

Or could believe it if they did;
As utterly unreasonable a thing
As would be some constant mourning
    That couldn't get used to death.

As one dog barking may set
Another off till all the dogs
Are howling together at the moon
Is what may happen to mankind yet
If such a song should ever get
    Free tongue—as I desire.

But, of course, that cannot be,
Most men are naturally unable
To hear a song like that at all
And those who can at once agree
That it's some sweeter melody
    And at once it is—to them.

And soon there's nobody left, you see,
To hear it as it really is,
For Reason with good reason
Must always pack its jury
And none can question its decree
    In the nature of the case.

All men die, and, of course, men say
We must accept the fact
Whether we like it or not.
There's no use carrying on that way.
What can we hope to gain by it, pray?
    My song's like that.

It's such a song that if another
Is heard to sing it raises
The very devil in all men's hearts
And makes them quick to smother
Such a source of endless bother—
    Lest they're heard at it too!

[308]

Many a voice they've buried alive
In conspiracies of silence,
Many a voice still sings unheard
Behind thick walls no sound can drive
A way through, nay, might easier rive
    The gaolers' hearts.

Just so hears the nightingale
Cries: "Beautiful must be
The land you learned your song in"
And hears without avail
The lying bird reply: "Words fail
    To tell its ugliness."
So reason grounds on groundlessness.

And do I seek to speak again
Even in such a form as this
The impossible words? —Of course, I don't,
I only say—and say in vain—
There's nothing else for which I'm fain
    Or care a damn about.

Let all men laugh as at a child
Crying broken-hearted for the moon—
Fit cause for manly laughter!
God Himself would needs have smiled
If He had ever heard such wild
    Nonsense from Nazareth—if not Calvary!

The child is right and must not be
Consoled until the world ends
Nor eat nor sleep but night and day
Cry on unceasingly.
In any other child I see
    A monstrous brat of death, not life.

As far as mankind is concerned
Plotinus, Pascal, and the rest
Who said them never really said

Such things; all men long since discerned
They cannot be said and so they've learned
    To treat them as unspoken.

Yet the infamous alliance
Of Aristotle and Plato
With the murderers of Socrates
Is nothing to the reliance
To meet any such defiance
    Most men have in each other.

For, of course, they punish us too
Tho' the crime we're guilty of
Is impossible and undone—
As viciously as they can do
And all wise men to the godless crew
    Play Anytus and Meletus—
All wise men condemn the true
    As Pontius Pilate did.

Your song, O God, that none dare hear
Save the insane and such as I
Apostates from humanity
Sings out in me with no more fear
Than one who thinks he has the world's ear
    From his padded cell—
Insane enough, with you so near,
To want, like you, the world as well!

THANKSGIVING

O well may timid and grasping folk
Rejoice that once according to Holy Writ
An innocent man was tortured to death
For their benefit; and be content—now they have it!

IN THE CHILDREN'S HOSPITAL

"Does it matter? Losing your legs?"
SIEGFRIED SASSOON

Now let the legless boy show the great lady
How well he can manage his crutches.
It doesn't matter though the Sister objects,
"He's not used to them yet," when such is
The will of the Princess. Come, Tommy,
Try a few desperate steps through the ward.
Then the hand of Royalty will pat your head
And life suddenly cease to be hard.
For a couple of legs are surely no miss
When the loss leads to such an honour as this!
One knows, when one sees how jealous the rest
Of the children are, it's been all for the best!—
But would the sound of your sticks on the floor
Thundered in her skull for evermore!

LO! A CHILD IS BORN

I thought of a house where the stones seemed suddenly changed
And became instinct with hope, hope as solid as themselves,
And the atmosphere warm with that lovely heat,
The warmth of tenderness and longing souls, the smiling anxiety
That rules a home where a child is about to be born.
The walls were full of ears. All voices were lowered.
Only the mother had the right to groan or complain.
Then I thought of the whole world. Who cares for its travail
And seeks to encompass it in like lovingkindness and peace?
There is a monstrous din of the sterile who contribute nothing
To the great end in view, and the future fumbles,
A bad birth, not like the child in that gracious home
Heard in the quietness turning in its mother's womb,
A strategic mind already, seeking the best way
To present himself to life, and at last, resolved,

Springing into history quivering like a fish,
Dropping into the world like a ripe fruit in due time—
But where is the Past to which Time, smiling through her tears
At her new-born son, can turn crying: "I love you"?

THINK NOT THAT I FORGET

Think not that I forget a single pang
Of all that folk have tholed,
Agonies and abominations beyond all telling,
Sights to daunt the most bold.

There are buildings in every town where daily
Unthinkable horrors take place.
I am the woman in cancer's toils,
    The man without a face.

I am all cruelty and lust and filth,
    Corruption and law-made crime—
The helpless prisoners badgered in their cells
    In every land and clime,

All "gallant soldiers" murdering for pay
    (Plus "little Belgium" or like affair)
And heroic airmen blithe to give
    Poor tribes Death from the air,

And all the hidden but no less hideous deeds
    Sound citizens are always privily at—
Only in the mean natures and vicious looks
    Of their children, themselves, or their underlings caught.

Oh, there's as much of it in Great Britain here
    As in Sing-Sing or in Cayenne—
Differently disguised, of course, and hiding
    In the most "decent and God-fearing" men.

There is no horror history's ever known
  Mob passion or greedy fear wouldn't soon
Make them do over again—slovens and cowards
  Moving pig-eyed in their daily round.

They face nothing—their whole lives depend
  On ignorance and base contempt
For all that's worth-while in the powers of Man
  From any share in it exempt.

In the midst of plenty in poverty,—
  To Art no better than apes—
Think not that I am unaware
  Of one of their loathsome shapes.

Aristocratic sentiments?—Yes! But remember
These Yahoos belong to no single class.
You'll find far more in proportion to numbers
  In palaces and west-end clubs than in the mass.

ANOTHER EPITAPH ON AN ARMY
OF MERCENARIES *

It is a God-damned lie to say that these
Saved, or knew, anything worth any man's pride.
They were professional murderers and they took
Their blood money and impious risks and died.
In spite of all their kind some elements of worth
With difficulty persist here and there on earth.

* In reply to A. E. Housman's.

THE SALMON LEAP

I saw one shadow shoot up and over
While ten failed to make it again and again,
But most of the salmon without an effort
In the bottom of the pool all day had lain.

Suddenly, effortlessly, like a flight of birds,
Up and over I saw them all slip.
The secret, I think, was the melted snow
Coming down and flicking them like a whip.

The majority of people make no attempt
In life to explore the infinite,
But who can tell what Death's cold touch
May prompt the lazy louts to yet?

THE TWO PARENTS

I love my little son, and yet when he was ill
I could not confine myself to his bedside.
I was impatient of his squalid little needs,
His laboured breathing and the fretful way he cried
And longed for my wide range of interests again,
Whereas his mother sank without another care
To that dread level of nothing but life itself
And stayed day and night, till he was better, there.

Women may pretend, yet they always dismiss
Everything but mere being just like this.

IF THERE ARE BOUNDS TO ANY
MAN

If there are bounds to any man
Save those himself has set
To far horizons they're postponed
And none have reached them yet.

And if most men are close curtailed
And keep a petty groove
'Tis their own sloth that is to blame,
Their powers they will not prove.

Preferring ease to energy,
Soft lives to steel-like wills,
And mole-heaps of morality
To the eternal hills.

All Earth's high peaks are naked stone
And so must men forego
All they can shed—and that's all else!—
Proportionate heights to show.

REFLECTIONS IN AN IRONWORKS

Would you resembled the metal you work with,
Would the iron entered into your souls,
Would you became like steel on your own behalf!
You are still only putty that tyranny rolls
Between its fingers! You makers of bayonets and guns
For your own destruction! No wonder that those
Weapons you make turn on you and mangle and murder—
You fools who equip your otherwise helpless foes!

IF I WAS NOT A SOLDIER

If I wasn't a soldier, a soldier said,
What would I be? —I wouldn't be,
It's hardly likely it seems to me,
A money lord or armament maker,
Territorial magnate or business chief.
I'd probably be just a working man,
    The slave of a licensed thief,—
One of the criminals I'm shielding now!

If I wasn't a soldier, a soldier said,
I'd be down and out as likely as not
And suffering the horrible starving lot
Of hundreds of thousands of my kind,
And that would make me a Red as well
Till I rose with the rest and was batoned or shot
By some cowardly brute—such as I am now!

THE CHANGEFUL WORLD

Earth has gone through many great changes.
    Why should it now cease changing?
Would a world all machines be as strange as
    That in which the saurians went ranging?

I don't care although I never see again
    A bird, a beast, a flower, a tree,
Or any of the other features
    Of Earth's traditional scenery,
Nor can I understand why most folk cling
    To these so passionately,
And yet believe that they are bound
    When this brief life is done
For a land where none of these can be found
    Any more than in yonder sun.

But who from sperm to maturity
   Has come need have no fear
To leave his further course to whatever
   Arranged that incredible career!

AFTER TWO THOUSAND YEARS

The Christians have had two thousand years
   And what have they done?—
Made the bloodiest and beastliest world ever seen
   Under the sun.

No Christian refuses to profit himself
   From his brother's misfortune.
The devil who would sup with our Christian banks
   Must sup with a hellish long spoon.

The Christian Churches are all built up
   In utter defiance of all Christ taught.
Co-religionists war at home and abroad,
   Each side supported by the self-same God.

And blandly the Bishops bestow their blessings
   On any murderer or fraud with the wit
To pay them, lip-serve the Cross, and keep
   The working-classes carrying it.

IN THE SLUMS OF GLASGOW

I have caught a glimpse of the seamless garment
And am blind to all else for evermore.
The immaculate vesture, the innermost shift,
   Of high and low, of rich and poor,

[317]

The glorious raiment of bridegroom and bride,
   Whoremonger and whore,
I have caught a glimpse of the seamless garment
And have eyes for aught else no more.

Deep under the γνῶθι σεαυτόν of Thales I've seen
The Hindu Atmānam ātmanā pāsya, and far deeper still
In every man, woman, and child in Scotland even
The inseparable inherent cause, the inalienable thrill
The subtle movement, the gleam, the hidden well-water,
All the lin-gāni of their souls, God's holy will.
As a shining light needs no other light to be seen
The soul is only known by the soul or knows anything still.

It was easier to do this in the slums, as who prefers
A white-faced lass—because the eyes show better, so.
Life is more naked there, more distinct from mind,
Material goods and all the other extraneous things that grow
Hardening over and hiding the sheer life. Behind speech, mind and
      will
Behind sensation, reflection, knowledge, and power—lo!
Life, to which all these are attached as the spokes of a wheel to the
      nave;
The immensity abiding in its own glory of which I have caught the
      glow.

The same earth produces diamonds, rock-crystal, and vermilion,
The same sun produces all sorts of plants, the same food
Is converted into hair, nails and many other forms.
These dogmas are not as I once thought true nor as afterwards false
But each the empty shadow of an intimate personal mood.
I am indifferent to shadows, possessing the substance now.
I too look on the world and behold it is good.

I am deluded by appearances no more—I have seen
The goodness, passion, and darkness from which all things spring,
Identical and abundant in the slums as everywhere else
Taking other forms—to which changing and meaningless names
      cling,—

But cancelling out at last, dissolving, vanishing,
   Like the stars before the rising sun.
Foam, waves, billows and bubbles are not different from the sea,
But riding the bright heavens or to the dark roots of earth sinking
Water is multiform, indivisible and one,
Not to be confused with any of the shapes it is taking.

I have not gained a single definite belief that can be put
In a scientific formula or hardened into a religious creed.
A conversion is not, as mostly thought, a turning towards a belief,
It is rather a turning round, a revolution indeed.
It has no primary reference to any external object.
It took place in me at last with lightning speed.
I suddenly walk in light, my feet are barely touching the ground,
I am free of a million words and forms I no longer need.

In becoming one with itself my spirit is one with the world.
The dull, aching tension is gone, all hostility and dread.
All opposing psychic tendencies are resolved in sweet song
My eyes discard all idle shows and dwell instead
In my intercourse with every man and woman I know
On the openings and shuttings of eyes, the motions of mind, and,
    especially, life, and are led
Beyond colour, savour, odour, tangibility, numbers, extensions,
Individuality, conjunction, disjunction, priority,
Posteriority—like an arrow sped,
And sheer through intellection, volition, desire, aversion,
Pleasure, pain, merit and demerit—to the fountain-head,
To the unproduced, unproducing, solitary, motionless soul
By which alone they can be known, by which alone we are not mis-
    led.

I have seen this abhyasa most clearly in the folk of these slums,
Even as I have known the selfless indefatigable love of a mother
Concerned only for the highest possible vitality of her children,
Leaving their lives free to them, not seeking to smother
Any jet of their spirits in her own preconceptions or wishes—
Would such were the love of every one of us for each other!

I have seen this abhyasa most clearly in the folk of these slums
Even as I know how every one of the women there,

Irrespective of all questions of intelligence, good looks, fortune's
    favour,
Can give some buck-navvy or sneak-thief the joy beyond compare—
Naked, open as to destitution and death, to the unprudential
Guideless life-in-death of the ecstasy they share—
Eternity, as Boethius defined it,—though few lovers give it his
    terms—
"To hold and possess the whole fulness of life anywhere
In a moment; here and now, past, present and to come."—
The bliss of God glorifying every squalid lair.

The sin against the Holy Ghost is to fetter or clog
The free impulse of life—to weaken or cloud
The glad wells of being—to apply other tests,
To say that these pure founts must be hampered, controlled,
Denied, adulterated, diluted, cowed,
The wave of omnipotence made recede, and all these lives, these
    lovers,
Lapse into cannon-fodder, sub-humanity, the despised slum-crowd.

I am filled forever with a glorious awareness
Of the inner radiance, the mystery of the hidden light in these dens,
I see it glimmering like a great white-sailed ship
Bearing into Scotland from Eternity's immense,
Or like a wild swan resting a moment in mid-flood.
It has the air of a winged victory, in suspense
By its own volition in its imperious way.
As if the heavens opened I gather its stupendous sense.
For here too, Philosophy has a royal and ancient seat,
And, holding an eternal citadel of light and immortality,
With Study her only comrade, sets her victorious foot
On the withering flower of the fast-ageing world. —Let all men see.

Now the babel of Glasgow dies away in our ears,
The great heart of Glasgow is sinking to rest,
Na nonanunno nunnono nana nananana nanu,
Nunno nunnonanunneno nanena nunnanunnanut.
We lie cheek to cheek in a quiet trance, the moon itself no more
    still.
There is no movement but your eyelashes fluttering against me,

And the fading sound of the work-a-day world,
Dadadoduddadaddadi dadadodudadidadoh,
Duddadam dadade dudde dadadadadadodadah.

THE STORM-COCK'S SONG

My song today is the storm-cock's song.
When the cold winds blow and the driving snow
Hides the tree-tops, only his song rings out
In the lulls in the storm. So let mine go!

On the topmost twig of a leafless ash
He sits bolt upright against the sky
Surveying the white fields and the leafless woods
And distant red in the East with his buoyant eye.

Surely he has little enough cause to sing
When even the hedgerow berries are already pulped by the frost
Or eaten by other birds—yet alone and aloft
To another hungry day his greeting is tossed.

Blessed are those who have songs to sing
When others are silent; poor song though it be,
Just a message to the silence that someone is still
Alive and glad, though on a naked tree.

What if it is only a few churning notes
Flung out in a loud and artless way?
His "Will I do it? Do it I will!" is worth a lot
When the rest have nothing at all to say.

From

The Islands of Scotland

1939

PERFECT

On the Western Seaboard of South Uist
Los muertos abren los ojos a los que viven

I found a pigeon's skull on the machair,
All the bones pure white and dry, and chalky,
But perfect,
Without a crack or a flaw anywhere.

At the back, rising out of the beak,
Were domes like bubbles of thin bone,
Almost transparent, where the brain had been
That fixed the tilt of the wings.

IN THE SHETLAND ISLANDS

I am no further from the "centre of things"
In the Shetlands here than in London, New York, or Tokio,
No further from "the great warm heart of humanity,"
Or the "general good," no less "central to human destiny,"
Sitting alone here enjoying life's greatest good,
The pleasure of my own company,
Than if I were one with the crowds in the streets
In any of the great centres of population,
Or in a mile-long cinema queue, or a unit
In a two-hundred-thousand spectatorate
At Twickenham or Murrayfield or Ibrox

Or reading a selection of today's newspapers
Rather than Keller's *Probleme der englischen Sprache und Kultur,*
Or Heuser's *Die Kildare-Gedichte: die ältesten
mittel-englischen Denkmäler in anglo-irischer Überlieferung,*
Or Exposito's articles in Hermathena
On the Latin writers of mediaeval Ireland,
Or Curtis on *The Spoken Languages
Of Mediaeval Ireland,* or Heuser on the peculiar dialect
Of English spoken less than a hundred years ago
—Direct descendant of the language of the Kildare poems—
In the baronies of Forth and Bargy in County Wexford
And often (wrongly) described as a mainly Flemish speech.

The newspaper critic was talking rubbish, as usual,
When he made the shallow gibe, the fool reproach,
That in resuming his work in the Castle of Muzot
Rilke with all his insistence on *Bejahung*
"Could only praise life when protected from it."

If personal participation were to be demanded,
Privacy forbidden, and any abstention
From any show of "life"—from any activity
Most people indulge in—construed
As a flight from reality, an insulation from Life,
All but the most rudimentary forms of life,
All but the "life" of the stupidest people,
Would speedily become impossible.
Rilke at Muzot or Duino was no more
"Protected from life" than any fool
At a street corner or in the House of Commons
Or in the columns of *The Scotsman.*
To be exclusively concerned with the highest forms of life
Is not to be less alive than "normal" people.

ISLAND FUNERAL

The procession winds like a little snake
Between the walls of irregular grey stones
Piled carelessly on one another.
Sometimes, on this winding track,
The leaders are doubled back
Quite near to us.

It is a grey world, sea and sky
Are colourless as the grey stones,
And the small fields are hidden by the walls
That fence them on every side.

Seen in perspective, the walls
Overlap each other
As far as the skyline on the hill,
Hiding every blade of grass between them,
So that all the island appears
One jumble of grey boulders.
The last grey wall outlined on the sky
Has the traceried effect
Of a hedge of thorns in winter.

The men in the stiff material
Of their homespun clothes
Look like figures cut from cardboard,
But shod in their rawhide rivelins
They walk with the springing step of mountaineers.
The women wear black shawls,
And black or crimson skirts.

A line of tawny seaweed fringes the bay
Between high-water mark and low.
It is luminous between the grey of rocky shore
And the grey of sullen water.

We can now and then look over a wall
Into some tiny field. Many of these

Are nothing but grey slabs of limestone,
Smooth as any pavement,
With a few blades of grass
Struggling up through the fissures,
And the grey surface of that rock
Catches and holds the light
As if it was water lying there.

At last the long line halts and breaks up,
And, like a stream flowing into a loch,
The crowd pours from the narrow lane
Into the cemetery where on an unfenced sandhill
The grey memorial stones of the island
Have no distinction from the country.
The coffin lies tilted a little sideways
On the dark grey sand flung up from the grave.

A little priest arrives; he has a long body and short legs
And wears bicycle clips on his trousers.
He stands at the head of the grave
And casts a narrow purple ribbon round his neck
And begins without delay to read the Latin prayers
As if they were a string of beads.
Twice the dead woman's son hands him a bottle
And twice he sprinkles the coffin and the grave
With holy water. In all the faces gathered round
There is a strange remoteness.
They are weather-beaten people with eyes grown clear,
Like the eyes of travellers and seamen,
From always watching far horizons.
But there is another legend written on these faces,
A shadow—or a light—of spiritual vision
That will seldom find full play
On the features of country folk
Or men of strenuous action.
Among these mourners are believers and unbelievers,
And many of them steer a middle course,
Being now priest-ridden by convention
And pagan by conviction,

But not one of them betrays a sign
Of facile and self-lulling piety,
Nor can one see on any face
"A sure and certain hope
Of the Resurrection to eternal life."
This burial is just an act of nature,
A reassertion of the islanders' inborn certainty
That "in the midst of life we are in death."
It is unlike the appointed funerals of the mainland
With their bitter pageantry
And the ramp of undertakers and insurance companies
That makes death seem incredible and cruel.
There are no loafing onlookers.
Everyone is immediately concerned
In what is taking place.
All through their lives death has been very close to them,
And this funeral of one who had been "a grand woman"
Seems to be but a reminder
Of the close comradeship between living and dying.

Down in the bay there is a row of curraghs
Drawn up on the sand. They lie keel upwards,
Each one shining black and smooth
Like some great monster of the sea,
Symbols to the island folk of their age-long
Battle with the waves, a battle where in daily life
The men face death and the women widowhood.

Four men fill in the grave with dark grey sand,
Then they cover the sand
With green sods and rough-hewn boulders,
And finally an old man with a yellow beard
Helps the four young gravediggers
In levering a great slab of stone
Until it lies flat upon the grave,
And the people watch all this in silence.
Then the crowd scatters east and west
And, last, the four gravediggers,
All of them laughing now
With the merriment of clowns.

There are few and fewer people
On the island nowadays,
And there are more ruins of old cottages
Than occupied homes.
I love to go into these little houses
And see and touch the pieces of furniture.
I know all there is to know
About their traditional plenishing
And native arts and crafts,
And can speak with authority
About tongue-and-groove cleats,
The lipped drawer, and the diameters of finials.
But I know them also in their origin
Which is the Gaelic way of life
And can speak with equal authority
About a people one of whose proverbs
Is the remarkable sentence:
"Every force evolves a form."
While this thing lasted
It was pure and very strong.
In an old island room the sense is still strong
Of being above and beyond the familiar,
The world as we know it,
In an atmosphere purified,
As it were, from the non-essentials of living
—An intangible feeling,
Difficult to describe,
But easy to recall to anyone
Who has stood in such a room
And been disturbed by the certainty
That those who once inhabited it
Were sure of every thought they had.

To enter almost any of the island rooms even today
Is to be profoundly conscious of this emanation,
At once so soothing and so strangely agitating.
Fifty years ago a visitor wrote: "They are there to stay,
And that fact accounts for a great deal.
It is partial explanation of the contentment
On the faces of the island women.

It is a reason for the repose and settledness
Which pervade an island village
—That indefinable something,
So altogether unlike the life of ordinary villages,
And which you feel in the air,
And are conscious of by some instinct, as men claim
To be aware of the presence of spirits.
There is no restlessness,
Or fret of business,
Or anxiety about anything.
It is as if the work was done,
And it was one eternal afternoon."
But they have not, in fact, stayed,
Foully forced out by their inferiors—
Red-faced, merely physical people
Whose only thought looking over
These incomparable landscapes
Is what sport they will yield
—How many deer and grouse.
The old stock are few and ever fewer now.
But they expected to stay,
And they deserved to stay,
Just as they expected there would always be
Thousands of them to work incessantly and serenely
At the making of objects which said:
"There is great beauty in harmony."
They lived as much like one another as possible,
And they kept as free as they could of the world at large.
It is not their creed as such, however,
That explains them and the beauty of their work.

It is rather the happiness with which they held it,
The light-heartedness with which they enslaved themselves
To the various rituals it demanded,
And also the circumstance that they were all
Poor people—whose notions of form
Were both ancient and basic.
They began with the barest patterns, the purest beginnings
Of design, in their minds, and then
Something converted them into artists

With an exalted lyric gift.
What that something was
No one can claim perfectly to know.
Some of them were reported as believing
In assistance from the angels.
Whatever the source, the result was some
Of the most beautiful work the world has ever seen.

And even now, in Edinburgh or Glasgow or London,
I often move my ear up close
The better to distinguish in the raucous mixture
The sound of the cornet I want to hear,
And you may see my face light up
With recognition and appreciation at various points,
And hear me comment, "The greatest of them all."
The term is justified—this island note,
This clear old Gaelic sound,
In the chaos of the modern world,
Is like a phrase from Beiderbecke's cornet,
As beautiful as any phrase can be.
It is, in its loveliness and perfection,
Unique, as a phrase should be;
And it is ultimately indescribable.

Panassié speaks of it as "full and powerful,"
But also as "so fine
As to be almost transparent,"
And there is in fact
This extraordinary delicacy in strength.
He speaks of phrases that soar;
And this, too, is in fact
A remarkable and distinguishing quality.
Otis Ferguson speaks of "the clear line
Of that music," of "every phrase
As fresh and glistening as creation itself,"
And there is in fact
This radiance, and simple joyousness.
These terms tell a great deal, but there remains
Much that eludes words completely
And can only be heard.

And though one can account for the music
Up to a certain point by the quality of the person
—The "candour, force, personal soundness, good humour"—
There have been other people—and still are, no doubt—
With candour, force, personal soundness and good humour
And one has still to explain, as always,
How these qualities translated themselves
In this instance into such musical phrases.
In the din of our modern world
The Gaelic spirit plays merely
As an unfeatured member of well-known bands
—Which means that one hears it sometimes—very rarely!—
For a full chorus, sometimes merely for a phrase,
Sometimes only in the background with the rest of the brass.
But even the phrase detaches itself from its surroundings
As something exquisite and perfect; and even playing
Along with the others in the background
It stands out from them,
Not through any aggressiveness but solely
Through the distinctive quality of its style.
"The greatest of them all"—but
There is little life left on the island now,
And soon the last funeral
Will take place there,
And in the rowdy chaos of the world
The sound of this cornet will be heard no more
—One will listen and one's face will never
Light up with recognition and appreciation again.

Yet if the nature of the mind is determined
By that of the body, as I believe,
It follows that every type of human mind
Has existed an infinite number of times
And will do so. Materialism promises something
Hardly to be distinguished from eternal life.
Minds or souls with the properties I love
—The minds or souls of these old islanders—
Have existed during an eternal time in the past
And will exist for an eternal time in the future.
A time broken up of course

By enormous intervals of non-existence,
But an infinite time.
If one regards these personalities
As possessing some value
There is a certain satisfaction
In the thought that in eternity
They will be able to develop
In all possible environments
And to express themselves
In all the ways possible to them
—A logical deduction from thoroughgoing Materialism
And independent of the precise type
Of materialism developed.
It is quite unimportant whether we call
Our ultimate reality matter, electric charge,
Ψ-waves, mind-stuff, neural stuff, or what not,
Provided it obeys laws which can, in principle,
Be formulated mathematically.

The cornet solo of our Gaelic islands
Will sound out every now and again
Through all eternity.

I have heard it and am content for ever.

ON BEING BACK IN MANCHESTER

After a Holiday in the Shetland Islands

There is nothing you can let yourself look at here,
Except now and then to get the full sensation
(An unmentionable one!) to remind you
It really *is* going on. And after the Shetlands
Where the opposite holds and you want to stretch your eyes
And not miss anything—the islands' sharp clear changing looks
That gain by not being a separate fact—
(But these and all the other impressions—

Like the contrariety or mutual exclusiveness
Of sea and sky, that, if they were painted,
English critics would denounce as unnatural and impossible,
Or the stereoscopic effect of the light
That brings the gutters on the far hillside
Up as close and clear as the lines on one's hand,—
Become clear and far-off by being talked of,
And I want them to be still clear
But close-to as my feeling is)
It is painful and unpleasant all the time.
With all the clearness of the other air
In mind and even in habit, I find
I am straining to see properly
As if I were in the half-dark here,
And getting a headache from it too.

THE KIND OF POETRY I WANT

A poetry the quality of which
Is a stand made against intellectual apathy,
Its material founded, like Gray's, on difficult knowledge,
And its metres those of a poet
Who has studied Pindar and Welsh poetry,
But, more than that, its words coming from a mind
Which has experienced the sifted layers on layers
Of human lives—aware of the innumerable dead
And the innumerable to-be-born,
The voice of the centuries, of Shakespeare's history plays
Concentrated and deepened,
"The breath and finer spirit of all knowledge,
The impassioned expression
Which is in the countenance of all science."

A speech, a poetry, to bring to bear upon life
The concentrated strength of all our being
(Eloquent of victory in the stern struggle for self-conquest
—Real freedom; life free, unhampered, unalloyed;
A deep religious impulse moving us, not that
Interpreted by others through systems of belief and practice,
But the craving for the perfect synthesis of thought and action
Which alone can satisfy our test
Of ultimate truth, and conception of life's purpose.)
And not like only the 8 per cent of the fuel
That does useful work in the motor-car—the bare 2 per cent
The best incandescent lamp converts of the energy received
Into radiation visible to the human eye
—Against the glow-worm's 96 per cent efficiency.

Is not this what we require?—
Coleridge's esemplasy and coadunation
Multeity in unity—not the Unity resulting
But the mode of the conspiration
(Schelling's *In-eins-bildung-kraft*)
Of the manifold to the one,
For, as Rilke says, the poet must know everything,
Be μινδεδνεσς * (a phrase which I have borrowed
From a Greek monk, who applies it
To a Patriarch of Constantinople),
Or, as the Bhagavad-Gita puts it, *visvato-mukha*.†
A poetry full of erudition, expertize, and ecstasy
—The acrobatics and the faceted fly-like vision,
The transparency choke-full of hair-pin bends,
"Jacinth work of subtlest jewellry," poetry *à quatre épingles*—
('Till above every line we might imagine
A tensely flexible and complex curve
Representing the modulation,
Emphasis, and changing tone and tempo
Of the voice in reading;
The curve varying from line to line
And the lines playing subtly against one another
—A fineness and profundity of organization
Which is the condition of a variety great enough
To express all the world's,
As subtle and complete and tight
As the integration of the thousands of brush strokes
In a Cézanne canvas),
Alive as a bout of all-in wrestling,
With countless illustrations like my photograph of a Mourning
    Dove
Taken at a speed of 1/75,000 of a second.
A poetry that speaks "of trees,
From the cedar tree that is in Lebanon
Even unto the hyssop that springeth out of the wall,"
And speaks also "of beasts and of fowl,
And of creeping things and of fishes,"
And needs, like Marya Sklodowska on her laboratory table,

* I.e., myriad-minded.
† *Visvato-mukha*—facing in all directions.

[334]

For its open-eyed wonderment at the varied marvels of life,
Its insatiable curiosity about the mainspring,
Its appetite for the solution of problems,
Black fragments of pitch-blende from Saxony and Bohemia,
Greenish-blue chalcolite from Portugal and Tonkin,
Siskin-green uranium mica from France,
Canary-yellow veined carnotite from Utah,
Greenish-grey tjujamunite from Turkestan,
Pinkish-grey fergusonite from Norway,
Gold-tinted Australian monazite sand,
Greenish-black betafite from Madagascar,
And emerald-green tobernite from Indo-China.
And like my knowledge of, say, interlocking directorships,
Which goes far beyond such earlier landmarks
As the Pujo Committee's report
Or Louis Stanley's "Spider Chart";
And everywhere without fear of Chestov's "suddenly,"
Never afraid to leap, and with the unanticipatedly
Limber florescence of fireworks as they expand
Into trees or bouquets with the abandon of "unbroke horses."
Or like a Beethovian semitonal modulation to a wildly remote key,
As in the Allegretto where that happens with a sudden jump of
    seven sharps,
And feels like the sunrise gilding the peak of the Dent Blanche
While the Arolla valley is still in cloud.
And constantly with the sort of grey-eyed gaiety
So many people feel exalted by being allowed to hear
But are unable to laugh at—as in the case of the don
Who, lecturing on the first Epistle to the Corinthians,
In a note on the uses of αλλα mentioned αλλα *precantis,*
Which an undergraduate took down as *Allah precantis!*

In photographic language, "wide-angle" poems
Taking in the whole which explains the part,
Scientifically accurate, fully realized in all their details,
As Prudentius's picture of the gradually deputrifying Lazarus,
Or Baudelaire's of the naked mulatto woman,
Or Pope's most accurate particularities
In the Epistle to Lord Bathurst,
Or like a magic of grammar, a syntactical magic,

Of the relations of thought with thought whereby
By means of the syntax a whole world of ideas
Is miraculously concentrated into what is almost a point.
No mere passive hyperaesthesia to external impressions
Or exclusive absorption in a single sense,
But a many-sided active delight in the wholeness of things
And, therefore, paradoxically perhaps,
A poetry like an operating theatre,
Sparkling with a swift, deft energy,
Energy quiet and contained and fearfully alert,
In which the poet exists only as a nurse during an operation,
Who only exists to have a sponge ready when called for,
Wads of sterilized cotton wool—nothing else
Having the smallest meaning for her.

A poetry not for those who do not love a gaping pig,
Or those made mad if they behold a cat,
And least, those who, when the bagpipe sings i' the nose,
Cannot contain their urine.

The poetry of one the Russians call "a broad nature"
And the Japanese call "flower heart,"
And we, in Scottish Gaeldom, *"ionraic."*
The poetry of one who practises his art
Not like a man who works that he may live
But as one who is bent on doing nothing but work
Confident that he who lives does not work,
That one must die to life in order to be
Utterly a creator—refusing to sanction
The irresponsible lyricism in which sense impressions
Are employed to substitute ecstasy for information,
Knowing that feeling, warm heart-felt feeling,
Is always banal and futile.
Only the irrations and icy ecstasies
Of the artist's corrupted nervous system
Are artistic—the very gift of style, of form and expression,
Is nothing else than this cool and fastidious attitude
Towards humanity. The artist is happiest
With an idea which can become
All emotion, and an emotion all idea.

A poetry that takes its polish from a conflict
Between discipline at its most strenuous
And feeling at its highest—wherein abrasive surfaces
Are turned upon one another like millstones,
And instead of generating chaos
Refine the grist of experience between them.
The terrific and sustained impact
Of intellect upon passion and passion upon intellect,
Of art as a vital principle in the process
Of devising forms to contain itself,
Of germinal forces directed,
Not upon a void or an ego,
But upon living materials, in a way
That becomes physically oppressive
To almost everybody,
Recalling the figure of Aschenbach, "whose greatest works
Were heaped up to greatness in layer after layer,
In long days of work, out of hundreds
And hundreds of single inspirations."

A poetry throwing light on the problems of value,
—Deriving its stimulating quality, its seminal efficacy,
Not from the discovery, as old as the Greeks,
That moral codes are relative to social factors,
But from the nice and detailed study of the mechanisms
Through which society
Determines attitudes in its members
By opening to them certain possibilities
By induction into objectively recognized statuses
While closing quite effectively other possibilities
—A poetry, not offering a compromise between naive atomism,
Giving an utterly unrelated picture of social phenomena,
And the unrealistic conception of a mystical social *Gestalt,*
The defining quality of which is intuited by transcendental means
(That growing danger, as a reaction from the bankruptcy
Of the atomistic approach, of a mystical
Organismic approach instinct with anti-rationalistic obscurantism),
But seeking to do justice to the discrete
As well as to the organically integrated aspects of society,
To the disruptive as well as to the cohesive forces

[337]

—A poetry that men weary of the unscientific wrangling
Of contemporary social and political dogmatists
Will find a liberating experience
—Rich in its discoveries of new problems,
Important questions so far unsuspected,
For which field research does not yet apply
The data necessary to answer them.

A poetry that is—to use the terms of Red Dog *—
High, low, jack and the goddamn game.

   And, constantly, I seek
A poetry of facts. Even as
The profound kinship of all living substance
Is made clear by the chemical route.
Without some chemistry one is bound to remain
Forever a dumbfounded savage
In the face of vital reactions.
The beautiful relations
Shown only by biochemistry
Replace a stupefied sense of wonder
With something more wonderful
Because natural and understandable.
Nature is more wonderful
When it is at least partly understood.
Such an understanding dawns
On the lay reader when he becomes
Acquainted with the biochemistry of the glands
In their relation to diseases such as goitre
And in their effects on growth, sex, and reproduction.
He will begin to comprehend a little
The subtlety and beauty of the action
Of enzymes, viruses, and bacteriophages,
Those substances which are on the borderland
Between the living and the non-living.
He will understand why the biochemist
Can speculate on the possibility
Of the synthesis of life without feeling
That thereby he is shallow or blasphemous.

* Red Dog—American pastime.

He will understand that, on the contrary,
He finds all the more
Because he seeks for the endless
—"Even our deepest emotions
May be conditioned by traces
Of a derivative of phenanthrene!"

A poetry in which the images
Work up on each other's shoulders like Zouave acrobats,
Or strange and fascinating as the Javanese dancer,
Retna Mohini, or profound and complicated
Like all the work of Ram Gopal and his company.

Or, again, like Sohan Lal's "Hunter's Dance" in Kathakali style,
Overwhelming in its concentrated force and vertiginous rhythm,
Showing the astounding acrobatic technique
Formerly practised in Malabar by the Nayar warrior-caste
Now the chief practitioners of the Kathakali dance-drama.

Poetry of such an integration as cannot be effected
Until a new and conscious organisation of society
Generates a new view
Of the world as a whole
As the integration of all the rich parts
Uncovered by the separate disciplines.
That is the poetry that I want.

A poetry abstruse as hedge-laying
And full as the countryside in which
I have watched the practice of that great old art,
—Full of the stumbling boom of bees,
Cuckoos contradicting nightingales all through a summer day,
Pheasants travelling on fast, dark wings,
—Or like a village garden I know well
Where the pear-trees bloom with a bravery of buds,
The cydonia blossoms gloriously against its wall,
And roses abound through April, May and June,
—And always with a surprising self-sufficiency
Like that of almost any descriptive passage of Mary Webb's *

* The novelist, Mary Webb, was a friend of the author.

[339]

—The fact that she was not wholly herself in all she wrote
Creating a sort of finality and completeness
In each part of any given whole,
The integrity of her experience revealing itself in many ways,
In the fulfilment of rare powers of observation,
In the kind of inward perception which recognised
"The story of any flower" is "not one of stillness,
But of faint gradations of movement that we cannot see,"
The outer magic and the inward mystery imaginatively reconciled,
Her deep kinship, her intuitive sympathy with leaf and flower
Extending without a break into the human kingdom,
And flowering there in an exquisite appreciation
Of the humours of single characters,
And a rare power to make them live and speak
In their own right and idiom.

There are few writers who can so capture
The elusive spirit of a countryside.
Alive and deeply felt in the mind
It dies on the pen,
Slain by the cold winds of propaganda,
The mists of exaggeration,
The warm fog of sentimentality.
The very desire to pin it down is in itself
Almost sufficient to ensure its doom.
It dies, and its corpse,
Pinned to each page by the unwitting writer,
Becomes overwhelmingly offensive to the sensitive reader.
To capture it alive and undamaged,
To display it with unfaded colours,
Is a miracle—only to be achieved
By humility, simplicity,
A sharp sense of humour,
And a practical working knowledge,
Subtly concealed, of country matters,
With decoration that clarifies,
And raises to heights of imagination,
The bare facts—literary graces concealing
No poverty of context, lack of virility, emptiness of thought,
But, held in perfect control,

Contributing the substance of poetry
To subjects "with quietness on them like a veil,"
A manifold of fast-vanishing speech,
Customs and delights
—Cussomes, wivetts, short and long bachelors,
Short and long hag-hatters,
Rogue-why-winkest-thou,
And Jenny-why-gettest-thou . . .*

A poetry, since I am writing of the country,
That like a wrestling bout on a village green
Divides the people and wins only those
Who are honest, strong, and true
—Those who admire the man
Who has the faster mind,
The faster, suppler, better-governed body—
For there is not only a class war
But a war in the working-class itself
Between decency and self-respect on the one hand
And a truckling spirit, seeking self-gain, on the other.

A poetry fully alive to all the implications
Of the fact that one of the great triumphs
Of poetic insight was the way in which
It prepared the minds of many
For the conception of evolution,
—The degree to which the popular mind
Was sensitized by it to the appeal of Nature,
And thus how poetry has progressed
Until, for example, flowers
Can never be thought of again
In a generalised way.
Chaucer's "floures white and rede"
Gave way in Spenser's April eclogue
To pinks, columbines, gillyflowers,
Coronations, sops-in-wine, cowslips,
Paunce and chevisaunce.
Bacon's "Of Gardens" is as much a formal plan

* These unfamiliar terms are references to old English rural customs and dialect expressions.

As a Loggan print of a Jacobean Great House;
Conceived as a whole, the garden is thought of
As a generalised form of beauty.
It is the whole that matters, not the parts.
And where they were considered separately
The parts still tended to be
Such lesser exercises in design
As a topiary. But the flower regarded as a symbol
Rescued our forefathers from these horticultural patterns
And brought man and flower
Into a new relation. By poets like Herbert and Vaughan
Tree and plant were recognised as having a place
In the same economy of which man was a part.
They obey the inner law of their being
And it is for man to emulate them.
"In the beauty of poems," as Whitman said,
"Are henceforth the tuft and final applause of science
. . . Facts showered over with light.
The daylight is lit with more volatile light.
The poets of the cosmos advance
Through all interpositons and coverings
And turmoils and stratagems
To first principles. . . . Beyond all precedent
Poetry will have to do with actual facts."
"The true use of the imaginative faculty of modern times
Is to give ultimate vivification
To facts, to science, and to common lives."
A poetry, therefore, that like William Morris
In his *News From Nowhere* will constantly show
"How the Change Came" *—how far more clearly
The poet may see into the nature of political reality
Than can the practical men of his day.

A poetry which in all connections will constantly render such serv-
    ices
As the protest of the nature poetry of the English poets

* The chapter in which, at the time when the Fabians thought Socialism would be
achieved by a process of cumulative reform, "at once," as John Strachey says, "so
gradual that the capitalist class would never resist it, and so thorough that nothing
of Capitalism would remain," Morris gives a most acute forecast of the rise of
Fascism.

Of the Romantic Reaction * on behalf of value,
On behalf of the organic view of nature,
A protest, invaluable to science itself,
Against the exclusion of value
From the essence of matter of fact.

Not only then a progress of poetry in relation to flowers
From Marvell's tribute to "that sweet militia"
Whose order and variety he deemed the twin pivots
About which human welfare revolves
To myself debating "whether the old escholtzia
Is any better for the scarlet, carmine and vermilion
Which have invaded the sunny golden-orange
Of its pristine splendour" †—a progress
I'd fain see it equal and far surpass
In regard to every branch of nature.

And thus a poetry which fully understands
That the era of technology is a necessary fact,
An inescapable phase in social activity,
Within which men are to rise
To ever greater mental and emotional heights,
And that only artists who build on all that men have created,
Who are infused with a sympathy and sensitive appreciation
Of the new technological order,
And all it may mean for their art,
Can play their role with any certainty
That their work will survive historically
And in doing so they will also make
Their contribution to the New Order.

And above all a learned poetry, knowing how
Taliesin received the hazel rod
From the dying hand of Virgil
Who in turn had taken it from Homer
—A poetry full of milk,
"Milk rising in breasts of Gaul,

* *Vide* A. N. Whitehead's *Science and the Modern World.*
† Quotation from the present author's long poem "In a Cornish Garden."

Trigonometrical milk of doctrine,"
In which it is more than fancy
That brings together the heroes of Arthur,
The founders of Rome and of New Rome,
Moslem and Manichean,
Joseph of Nazareth and Joseph of Arimathea,
Lupercalian and Lateran rites,
The pagan and the Christian,
And groups them kaleidoscopically
Around Taliesin, our "fullest throat of song"
—A poetry covering "the years and the miles"
And talking "one style's dialects
To London and Omsk."

A learned poetry, rich in all historical and linguistic knowledge
As can constantly educe and use such a fact
As that the ruin of a Dominant Minority
(As we discern in ranging all human history)
Takes the form of the sequence κόρος, ὕβρις, ὕτη.
(Subjectively κόρος means a psychological condition
Of being "spoilt" by success; ὕβρις means
The consequent loss of mental and moral balance;
And ὕτη means the blind headstrong
Ungovernable impulse that sweeps an unbalanced soul
Into attempting the impossible.)
There is the formula for all the great catastrophes of history
From 480 B.C. to A.D. 1939,
—A learned poetry wholly free
Of the brutal love of ignorance;
And the poetry of a poet with no use
For any of the simpler forms of personal success.

THE GLEN OF SILENCE

By this cold shuddering fit of fear
My heart divines a presence here,
Goddess or ghost yclept;
Wrecker of homes. . . .

Where have I heard a silence before
Like this that only a lone bird's cries
And the sound of a brawling burn to-day
Serve in this wide empty glen but to emphasize?

Every doctor knows it—the stillness of foetal death,
The indescribable silence over the abdomen then!
A silence literally "heard" because of the way
It stands out in the auscultation of the abdomen.

Here is an identical silence, picked out
By a bickering burn and a lone bird's wheeple
—The foetal death in this great "cleared" glen
Where the *fear-tholladh nan tighem* * has done his foul work
—The tragedy of an unevolved people.

DIREADH III

*"So, in the sudden sight of the sun, has man stopped, blinded, par-
alysed and afraid?"*

I am reft to the innermost heart
Of my country now,
History's final verdict upon it,
The changeless element in all its change,
Reified like the woman I love.

Here in this simple place of clean rock and crystal water,
With something of the cold purity of ice in its appearance,
Inhuman and yet friendly,
Undecorated by nature or by man
And yet with a subtle and unchanging beauty
Which seems the antithesis of every form of art,

Here near the summit of Sgurr Alasdair
The air is very still and warm.

* Destroyer of homes.

The Outer Isles look as though
They were cut out of black paper
And stuck on a brilliant silver background,
(Even as I have seen the snow-capped ridges of Hayes Peninsula,
Stand out stark and clear in the pellucid Arctic atmosphere
Or, after a wild and foggy night, in the dawn
Seen the jagged line of the Tierra del Fuego cliffs
Looking for all the world as if they were cut out of tin,
Extending gaunt and desolate),
The western sea and sky undivided by horizon,
So dazzling is the sun
And its glass image in the sea.
The Cuillin peaks seem miniature
And nearer than is natural
And they move like liquid ripples
In the molten breath
Of the corries which divide them.
I light my pipe and the match burns steadily
Without the shielding of my hands,
The flame hardly visible in the intensity of light
Which drenches the mountain top.

I lie here like the cool and gracious greenery
Of the water-crowfoot leafage, streaming
In the roping crystalline currents,
And set all about on its upper surface
With flecks of snow blossom that, on closer looking,
Shows a dust of gold.
The blossoms are fragile to the touch
And yet possess such strength and elasticity
That they issue from the submergence of a long spate
Without appreciable hurt—indeed, the whole plant
Displays marvellous endurance in maintaining
A rooting during the raging winter torrents.
Our rivers would lose much if the snowy blossom
And green waving leafage of the water-crowfoot
Were absent—aye, and be barer of trout too!
And so it is with the treasures of the Gaelic genius
So little regarded in Scotland to-day.
Yet emerging unscathed from their long submergence,

Impregnably rooted in the most monstrous torrents *
—The cataracting centuries cannot rive them away—
And productive of endless practical good,
Even to people unaware of their existence,
In the most seemingly-unlikely connections.
I am possessed by this purity here
As in a welling of stainless water
Trembling and pure like a body of light
Are the webs of feathery weeds all waving,
Which it traverses with its deep threads of clearness
Like the chalcedony in moss agate
Starred here and there with grenouillette.

It is easy here to accept the fact
That that which the "wisdom" of the past
And the standards of the complacent elderly rulers
Of most of the world to-day regard
As the most fixed and eternal verities—
The class state, the church,
The old-fashioned family and home,
Private property, rich and poor,
"Human nature" (to-day meaning mainly
The private-profit motive), their own race,
Their Heaven and their "immortal soul,"
Is all patently evanescent,
Even as we know our fossil chemical accumulations
Of energy in coal, peat, oil, lignite and the rest
Are but ephemeral, a transitory blaze
Even on the small time-scale of civilized man,
And that running water, though eminently convenient and practica-
    ble
For the present, will give us a mere trickle
Of the energy we shall demand in the future.

And suddenly the flight of a bird reminds me
Of how I once went out towards sunset in a boat
Off the rocky coast of Wigtownshire
And of my glimpse of the first rock-pigeon I saw,
It darted across one of the steep gullies

* See John Ruskin's description of the spring at Carshalton.

At the bottom of which our boat lay rocking
On the dark green water—and vanished into safety
In a coign of the opposite wall
Before a shot could be fired.
It swerved in the air,
As though doubtful of its way,
Then with a glad swoop of certainty
It sped forward, turned upward,
And disappeared into some invisible cranny
Below the overhanging brow of the cliff.

There was such speed, such grace, such happy confidence of refuge
    in that swoop
That it struck me with the vividness of a personal experience.
For an instant I seemed to see into the bird's mind
And to thrill with its own exhilaration of assured safety.
Why should this be? It was as though
I had seen the same occurrence,
Or some part of it, before.

Then I knew. Into the back of my mind had come
The first line of the loveliest chorus in *Hippolytus,*
That in which the Troezenian women,
Sympathizing with the unhappy Phaedra,
Who is soon to die by her own hand,
Sing of their yearning to fly away from the palace
Whose sunny terraces are haunted by misery and impending doom.
They long to escape with the flight of the sea-birds
To the distant Adriatic and the cypress-fringed waters of Eridanus
Or to the fabulous Hesperides,
Where beside the dark-blue ocean
Grow the celestial apple-trees.
It is the same emotion as filled the Hebrew poet
Who cried: "O for the wings of a dove,
That I might flee away and be at rest."
'ἠλιβάτοις ὑπὸ χενθμῶσι γενοίμαν'
The untranslatable word in that line
Is the ὑπὸ. It includes more
Than a single word of English can contain.

Up-in-under: so had the pigeon
Flown to its refuge in "steep hiding places,"
So must Euripides have seen a sea-bird
Dart to its nest in the cliffs of Attica.
For an instant, sitting in that swaying boat
Under the red rocks, while the sunset ebbed down the sky
And the water lapped quietly at my side,
I again felt the mind of the poet reaching out
Across the centuries to touch mine.
Scotland and China and Greece!
Here where the colours—
Red standing for heat,
Solar, sensual, spiritual;
Blue for cold—polar, bodily, intellectual;
Yellow luminous and embodied
In the most enduring and the brightest form in gold—
Remind me how about this
Pindar and Confucius agreed.
Confucius who was Pindar's contemporary
For nearly half a century!
And it was Pindar's "golden snow"
My love and I climbed in that day.
I in Scotland as Pindar in Greece
Have stood and marvelled at the trees
And been siezed with honey-sweet yearning for them;
And seen too mist condensing on an eagle,
His winds "streamlined" for a swoop on a leveret,
As he ruffled up the brown feathers on his neck
In a quiver of excitement;
Pindar, greatest master of metaphor the world has seen,
His spirit so deeply in tune
With the many-sidedness of both Man and Nature
That he could see automatically all the basal resemblances
His metaphors imply and suggest.
Scotland and China and Greece!

So every loveliness Scotland has ever known,
Or will know, flies into me now,
Out of the perilous night of English stupidity,

As I lie brooding on the fact
That "perchance the best chance
Of reproducing the ancient Greek temperament
Would be to 'cross the Scots with the Chinese.' " *
The glory of Greece is imminent again to me here
With the complete justification his sense of it
In Germany—his participation in that great awakening
Taking the form of an imaginative reliving,
On behalf of his people, of the glory of Athens—
Lacked in Hölderlin. I see all things
In a cosmic or historical perspective too.
Love of country, in me, is love of a new order.
In Greece I also find the clue
To the mission of the poet
Who reveals to the people
The nature of their gods,
The instrument whereby his countrymen
Become conscious of the powers on whom they depend
And of whom they are the children,
Knowing, in himself, the urgency of the divine creativeness of Na-
    ture
And most responsive to its workings in the general world.
"Wer das Tiefste gedacht, liebt das Lebendigste."
And remembering my earlier poems in Scots
Full of my awareness "that language is one
Of the most cohesive or insulating of world forces
And that dialect is always a bond of union," †
I covet the mystery of our Gaelic speech
In which *rughadh* was at once a blush,
A promontory, a headland, a cape,
Leadan, musical notes, litany, hair of the head,
And *fonn,* land, earth, a delight, and a tune in music, ‡
And think of the Oriental provenance of the Scottish Gael,
The Eastern affiliations of his poetry and his music,
". . . the subtler music, the clear light
Where time burns back about th' eternal embers,"
And the fact that he initiated the idea of civilization

* Sir Richard Livingstone.
† Sir James Crichton-Browne.
‡ Macfarlane's *English and Gaelic Vocabulary* (Constable, Edinburgh, 1815).

That to-day needs renewal at its native source
Where, indeed, it is finding it, since Georgia,
Stalin's native country, was also the first home of the Scots.

The Gaelic genius that is in this modern world
As sprays of quake grass are in a meadow,
Or light in the world, which notwithstanding
The *Fiat lux* scores of thousands of years ago,
Is always scanty and dubious enough
And at best never shares the empery of the skies
On more than equal terms with the dark,
Or like sensitive spirits among the hordes of men,
Or seldom and shining as poetry itself.
Quake grass, the "silver shakers," with their plumes shaped and
    corded
Like miniature cowrie shells, and wrapped
In bands of soft green and purple, and strung
(Now glittering like diamonds,
Now chocolate brown like partridge plumage)
On slender stems and branchlets, quick
To the slightest touch of air!

So Scotland darts into the towering wall of my heart
And finds refuge now. I give
My beloved peace, and her swoop has recalled
That first day when my human love and I,
Warmed and exhilarated by the sunny air,
Put on our skis and began
A zigzag track up the steep ascent.
There was no sound but the faint hiss and crush
Of the close-packed snow, shifting under our weight.
The cloudless bowl of the sky
Burned a deep gentian. In the hushed, empty world,
Where nothing moved but ourselves,
Our bodies grew more consciously alive.
I felt each steady beat of my heart.
The drawing and holding of my breath
Took on a strange significance.
Nor was I merely conscious of myself.
I began to be equally aware of my love;

Her little physical habits
Sinking into my mind
Held the same importance as my own.

How fragrant, how infinitely refreshing and recreating
Is the mere thought of Deirdre!
How much more exhilarating to see her, as now!

"She said that she at eve for me would wait;
Yet here I see bright sunrise in the sky." *

Farewell all else! I may not look upon the dead,
Nor with the breath of dying be defiled,
And thou, I see, art close upon that end.

I am with Alba—with Deirdre—now
As a lover is with his sweetheart when they know
That personal love has never been a willing and efficient slave
To the needs of reproduction, that to make
Considerations of reproduction dictate the expression of personal love
Not infrequently destroys the individual at his spiritual core,
Thus "eugenic marriages" cannot as a whole
Be successful so far as the parents are concerned,
While to make personal love master over reproduction
Under conditions of civilization is to degrade
The germ plasm of the future generations,
And to compromise between these two policies
Is to cripple both spirit and germ,
And accept the only solution—unyoke the two,
Sunder the fetters that from time immemorial
Have made them so nearly inseparable,
And let each go its own best way,
Fulfilling its already distinct function,
An emancipation the physical means for which
Are now known for the first time in history!

Let what can be shaken, be shaken,
And the unshakeable remain.
The Inaccessible Pinnacle † is not inaccessible.

* From a Chinese eight-line lyric, twenty-seven centuries old.
† Of Sgurr Dearg, in Skye.

So does Alba surpass the warriors
As a graceful ash surpasses a thorn,
Or the deer who moves sprinkled with the dewfall
Is far above all other beasts
—Its horns glittering to Heaven itself.*

EDINBURGH

"Most of the denizens wheeze, sniffle, and exude a sort of snozzling whnoff whnoff, apparently through a hydrophile sponge."
EZRA POUND

The capital of Scotland is called Auld Reekie,
Signifying a monstrous acquiescence
In the domination of the ends
By the evidences of effort.
—Not the mastery of matter
By the spirit of man
But, at best, a damnable draw,
A division of the honours
And, far more, the dishonours!
—Dark symbol of a society
Of "dog eat dog."
Under which the people reveal themselves to the world
Completely naked in their own skin,
Like toads!
Yes, see, the dead snatch at the living here.
So the social corpse, the dead class,
The dead mode of life, the dead religion,
Have an after life as vampires.
They are not still in their graves
But return among us.
They rise with the fumes
From the chimney of the crematorium
And again settle down on the earth
And cover it with black filth.

* See *Volsungakvida en forna,* 41 (*Saemundar Edda,* Jónsson).

To repossess ourselves of the primal power
"Let there be light" and apply it
In our new, however more complex, setting
Is all. And let us not cry
"Too difficult! Impossible!" forgetting
That the stupendous problems that obsess us to-day
Are as nothing to the problems overcome
By the miraculous achievements of men in the past
—Yes, the first problems in the very dawn of human history
Were infinitely greater, and our troubles are due
To the fact that we have largely lost
The earliest, the most essential,
The *distinctively human* power
Our early ancestors had in abundant measure
Whatever else they lacked that we possess.
Possess thanks to them!—and thanks to the primal indispensable
     power
They had and we have lost progressively
And affect to despise—
Fools who have lost the substance
And cling to the shadow.
Auld Reekie indeed!
Preferring darkness rather than light
Because our deeds are evil!

I see the dark face of an early mother of men
By a primitive campfire of history.
Her appearance is rendered all the more remarkable
Because of the peculiar performance of the smoke.
By some process, natural no doubt but mysterious to us,
She exercises a strange control over the smoke
As she shuffles round—with vast protruding lips
And with wide rings hanging from her ears,
Weaving her hands. And it is
As if the billows of thick white vapour
Are forced to follow her will
And make a magical dancing cloud
Behind her as she moves.
Learn again to consume your own smoke like this,
Edinburgh, to free your life from the monstrous pall,

To subdue it and be no longer subdued by it
Like the hand of the dyer in his vat.
So all the darkness of industrialism yet
Must be relegated like a moth that pursues
The onward dance of humanity.

So the mighty impetus of creative force
That seeks liberation, that shows even through
The scum of swinish filth of bourgeois society,
The healthy creative force will break through
—Even in Edinburgh—and good, human things grow,
Protecting and justifying faith
In regeneration to a free and noble life
When labour shall be a thing
Of honour, valour, and heroism
And "civilization" no longer like Edinburgh
On a Sabbath morning,
Stagnant and foul with the rigid peace
Of an all-tolerating frigid soul!

This is the great skill that mankind has lost,
The distinctively human power.
Lo! A poor Negress teaches this rich university city
Something more important than all it knows,
More valuable than all it has!
But Edinburgh—Edinburgh—is too stupid yet
To learn how not to stand in her own light.

GLASGOW

"It is not every poet who has the inner authority for remarking that
Glasgow contains a million slaves."
                    THE LISTENER

In a city like Glasgow, all the upper class well-to-do, and professional
people are nothing more than so many phagocytes feeding on the
pus of an abscess.

Wagner might call Berlin a city
Of sordid spaces and pretensions to greatness;
Berlioz write down Paris "the infernal city
That thinks of itself the home of art"—Glasgow
(Though Cazamian praises its *originalité puissante*
—A phrase I too might use; but only as Villon in his hymn
To the Blessed Virgin the triple invocation to Dian-Hecate!)
—Glasgow, the great city that has never had
A single poet of the slightest consequence!—
Glasgow thinks nothing, and is content to be
Just what it is, not caring or knowing what.

Crowded with *grundformen,* incommunicable as hand-writing,
It is beyond all human knowing indeed,
And that's the only knowing there is, alas!

"Let a Colgate smile get you out of it."

The houses are Glasgow, not the people—these
Are simply the food the houses live and grow on
Endlessly, drawing from their vulgarity
And pettiness and darkness of spirit
—Gorgonising the mindless generations,
Turning them all into filthy property,
Apt as the Karaunas by diabolic arts
To produce darkness and obscure the light of day.
To see or hear a clock in Glasgow's horrible,
Like seeing a dead man's watch, still going though he's dead.
Everything is dead except stupidity here.

Where have I seen a human being looking
As Glasgow looks this gin-clear evening—with face and fingers
A cadaverous blue, hand-clasp slimy and cold

As that of a corpse, finger-nails grown immeasureably long
As they do in a grave, little white eyes, and hardly
Any face at all? Cold, lightning-like, unpleasant, light, and blue
Like having one's cold spots intoxicated with mescal.
Looking down a street the houses seem
Long pointed teeth like a ferret's over the slit
Of a crooked unspeakable smile, like the Thracian woman's
When Thales fell in the well, a hag
Whose soul-gelding ugliness would chill
To eternal chastity a cantharidized satyr;
And the smell reminds me of the *odeur de souris*
Of Balzac's Cousin Pons. All the strength seems
To leave my body as I look, and a deadly
Grey weariness falls over my thoughts like dust.
A terrible shadow descends like dust over my thoughts,
Almost like reading a *Glasgow Herald* leader
Or any of our Anglo-Scottish daily papers,
Smug class organs, standardized, superficial,
Unfair in the presentation of news, and worse than useless
As interpreters of the present scene or guides to the future,
Or like the dread darknesses that descend on one
Who, as the result of an accident, sustained
In the course of his favourite recreation, tricycling,
Suffers every now and then from loss of memory.

"And she thought she had been so careful . . ."

The very thought of hurling myself once more
Against the obstacles raised by the crass stupidity
Of my opponents . . . ah, no! I am too old,
Too old, too old, too old, and as for Scott *
The only other "whole and seldom man" I know here,
Feeling independently the electricity in the air,
The cabal of his foes gives all this insensate welter
Of a city an expression of idiot fury.

* "I do not hesitate to say that no finer work than these songs has been done in these islands in our time. . . . In rhythmic flexibility and elasticity these songs recall the finest speciments of Hugo Wolf. In fact, for highly organised unity of shape, style, vocal line and expression, I should not hesitate to place them, world's asunder though they are spiritually, in the same rank."—Kaikhosru Sorabji, of the "Scottish Lyrics" of the contemporary Glasgow composer Francis George Scott.

All the fools whose jobs impinge on music here
Howl: "If *he* becomes popular, where
Will *our* compositions be—our arrangements, rather?"
(Scott popular?—Scott whose work is *di essenza popolare?*
This popular not meaning plebian or poor in content,
But *sano, schietto, realistico,*
e regligiosamente attinente al profondo spirito della razza?
Scott popular?—in Glasgow?)

What a place for bat-folding!

Whenever the faintest promise, the slightest integrity,
Dares to show in any of the arts or thought or politics
At once the jealous senile jabber breaks out
Striking with sure instinct at everything with courage and integrity
("There's nothing too cowardly for Glasgow's spokesmen
To have the courage to do.")
"Confound it all! If once we let these young folk in
What is to become of us?" An ant on a hot brick
Is a study in repose compared to these leading citizens
When any new talent's about—Haydn of Beethoven,
Grétry of Mozart, Handel of Gluck, Rossini of Weber,
Out-Haydnd, out-Grétryd, out-Handeld, out Rossinid,
By mannikins a million times pettier still
Than any of these were to their hated betters.
Scott, I say . . . but who knows in this broth-like fog
There may be greater artists yet by far than we,
Unheard of, even by us, condemned to be invisible.
In this Tarnhelm of unconscionable ignorance
Where "everybody is entitled to his own opinion."

Open Glasgow up! Open it up. It is time
It was made sun-conscious. Give every house
Ceilings and roofs of iridescent glass, windows for walls,
Let great steel-framed windows bring the blaze
Of the sky into every room; half partitions
And low divisions of polished shining wood break up
The entire sweep of the main constructions and give
A sense of great space and air; waxed floors
Reflect the window vistas. Have chairs of chromium steel

[358]

(And never ask where the money's coming from,
  It's there all right, and doing nothing else.)
Let metal ornaments and glass shelves
Catch and multiply the floods of light everywhere.
Let the eye be bewildered trying to identify
The new aspects of familiar materials, "bravely coming out of the
    ether."
—But this is modernism, Bolshie art? In other words
Those hateful things, common sense and efficiency!
("Brilliant common sense" as Orage used to call it,
In which all the essential elements of life
Are fused like the contradictory components of a lens.)
And do not fear to use new materials too. I do not fear
So much black and white and shining steel will give
A chilly effect—for colour will be everywhere,
Strange subtle colours hard to name,
—Schooner, terroco, graphite, matelot,
Sphinx-like fawn and putty, string and carbon blue—
The most utilitarian objects unrecognisable
But none the less useful, every room will be enlarged
To huge dimensions by the windows; the rippling foliage
Of the trees will dapple your tables
—Albeit a simplified forest calling for no such formula
As, say 150Ad ab (30) Fsd (2) oo Gx.
*"These trees have no zeal of tragic glory, breathe
No life, no death, in their cool dusky sprays."*

SO HERE I HAIL ALL THE FELLOW ARTISTS I KNOW

So here I hail all the fellow-artists I know
And all the singers and narrators everywhere,
*"A rum lot they are, as the Devil said when he looked over the ten
    Commandments."*
Ashugi, akyni, zhirshi, bakhshi, and other folk singers,
Minstrels, histriones, jongleurs, juglares,
Skomorohi, guslari, forsangere, recitadoras,
Kaleki, ciegos, Sidney's "blind crowder,"

And all the descendants to this day everywhere
Of Teiresias and blind Maeonides
(Fili, ollamhs, cainte, vates, and ιε ροποίοι,
And the "poluphloisboisterous" music
Of every anruth, cli, cano, and all the rest
From the ri-bhard down to the bobhard and the bhard-loirge,
And shanachie after shanachie
Down to the shanachie of the chimney-corner,
Wandering scholars, clerics of the Marbhan type,
And all the Cliar Sheanachain,*
The children of Manannan, *la binn, la searbh,* †
". . . the patron saint
Of merry rogues and fiddlers, trick o' the loop men,
Thimblemen and balladmen that gild the fair."
Ah, fain would I follow if I could
The *Imtheacht na Tromdhaimhe* ‡
Of the whole round world!)
Ashugi, akyni, zhirshi, bakhshi, and other folk singers,
Creators of the new heroic epodes of to-day.
The Turkic poems of Hussein Bozalgonly of Tauz,
Uzbek and Darginian songs,
The songs of Suleiman Stalsky, § the singer of the Daghestan people,
The blind old *kobyar,* Ostap Vyeryesai,
And Timofei Ivanitch, the old *skazitel,*
Who knew all the songs of all Russia.
The songs of the *akyn* Kenen of Kazakhstan
(Kazakhstan in renaissance, strengthened by its new "iron roads");
Taijiks from a *kishlyak* in Obi-Garma
Singing of the flaming Stalin;
The lyrics of the Mordovian minstrel Krivosbeyeva; ||
The Armenian legend *Lenin-Pasha;*
The song of Jambul . . .
    Run as a herald through our Kazakh auls,
    Make the whole steppe attend

* Strolling satirists.
† One day sweet, another sour.
‡ The Proceedings of the Great Bardic Assembly.
§ Died November 23, 1937.
|| I have elsewhere written my appreciations of such poets as the Kirghiz poet Toktogul Satylganov (born 1871); Ivan Franko (born 1860), the Western Ukrainian poet; the Bashkir poet, Mazhit Gafur (born 1880); and many others.

You, song of *Akyn* Jambul.
  "Listen, Kaskelen, Karakol, Kastek,
    Glorious is the great Soviet Law,
    It enacts joy to the peoples;
    It waters the steppe and brings fruit;
    It lifts up our hearts to sing;
    It commands all Nature to live
    In service and praise of the people;
    The song of the old Kazakh *Akyn* Jambul
    To Hassem Lakhuti, the Persian Communist poet.
    The ripened song swells in our hearts.
    Let us strike up together, *Akyn* Lakhuti . . .
    The centuries will reverberate with our song,
    And all the world's tongues will repeat it."
See . . . on the steppe, barren and waste,
A huge thousand-handed man moves in great circles
Ever wider girthing the earth,
And in his path the dead steppe comes to life,
Quivering, juicy grass shoots forth,
And everywhere towns and villages emerge;
And he strides ever on,
Further towards the edge,
Sowing what is live and human.
Then one feels towards people
A new tenderness and respect;
Feels in them an unquenchable vitality
That can vanquish death,
That eternally transforms what is dead into life,
Moving towards immortality by mortal roads.
—Death overshadows people,
But it cannot engulf them.

SCOTLAND

  Scotland! Everything he saw in it
  Was a polyhedron he held in his brain,
  Every side of it visible at once

[361]

Of knowledge drawn from every field of life!
—Polyhedrons everywhere! He knew
There was a way of combining them he must find yet
(Like the movement, almost too quick for the eye to catch,
The no-meeting—but only change upon the instant—
Of spirit and sense; the agile leaping
From the sensual plane to the spiritual,
This straddling of two universes,
This rapidity of movement and back again.
The change is instantaneous, it is dizzying.
Will it stop-stand out like a star,
This gale of crystalline mockery?)
Into one huge incomparable jewel,
Like knowing the sunlight as a living thing
(For no man can see anything, save in proportion
As he sees everything, clear and complete),
An ultimate brooch of Lorne
To hold his plaid on his shoulder.
(Though when that happened, of course,
Everybody would say it was just one-sided!)
Scotland! How he hated all those
Who said "Scotland" when they only meant,
When all they knew was only,
In their rich slug-like carneying voices,
Some little gimcrack abstraction,
Some Pisgah-vision down a city cul-de-sac
Of that made-in-England specialty, the Proletariat,
Some owl-blink of an anthropocentric routineer,
Some cheap glass bead of a single-track mentality,
Some wretched little worm-cast of their own casting,
Babes feeding a lion with spoonmeat!
Scotland—like a copy of Greek prose without any accents! . . .

THE GAELIC MUSE

At last, at last, I see her again
   In our long-lifeless glen,
Eidolon of our fallen race,

[362]

Shining in full renascent grace,
She whose hair is plaited
Like the generations of men,
And for whom my heart has waited
   Time out of ken.

Hark! hark! the *fead chruinn chruadh Chaoilte,*
Hark! hark! 'tis the true, the joyful sound,
Caoilte's shrill round whistle over the brae,
The freeing once more of the winter-locked ground,
The new springing of flowers, another rig turned over,
Dearg-lasrach bho'n talamh dubh na h-Alba,
Another voice, and another, stirring, rippling, throbbing with life,
   Scotland's long-starved ears have found.

Deirdre, Audh *—she has many names,
But only one function. Phaneromene,†
Hodegetria,‡ Chryseleusa, §
Chrysopantanasa—Golden-universal Queen—
Pantiglykofilusa, || Zoodotospygi,¶
Like the sun once more in these verses seen
The light *angelicae summeque sanctae Brigidae, #*
Goddess of poets, of whom Ultan ** sang;
The golden, delightful flame; the branch with blossoms,
The actual Air-Maiden once more we see,
Incorporated tangibility and reality,
Whose electric glance has thrilled the Gaels
Since time beyond memory.
Twelve centuries ago Scotland with her praises rang.
Mary of the Gael! Brigit born at sunrise!
Her breath revives the dead.
Your songs, my friends, are songs of dawn, of renaissance too.

* Audh—the Deep-Minded.
† Phaneromene—made manifest.
‡ Hodegetria—leading on the way.
§ Chryseleusa—golden-pitiful.
|| Pantiglykofilusa—all-tenderly-embracing.
¶ Zoodotospygi—the life-giving fountain.
# "Of the most angel-like and most saintly Brigit" (see *Leabhar Imuinn*, Dublin, 1855–69).
** Ultan of Ard Breccain, died in A.D. 656. Composed a great "Hymn in praise of Brigit."

Twigs of the tree, of which it is said
Uno avulso non deficit alter
*Aureus.** Worthy heirs and successors you
Of *Ceile De,*† of Ultan, of Broccan Cloen. ‡
 Let your voices ring
 And be unafraid.

Muscail do mhisneach a Alba! §
Set up your *Cuirt na h'eigse* ||
With a resounding Barrantas,¶ my friends!

Ah, Scotland, her footsteps, her voice, her eyes,
Agniotisa here, entire in our skies!

Too long the Bible-black gloom has spread
       Now let your red
Radiance and melody wed
Over all Scotland be shed
Till the Giants in the cave awake
And with a snap of their fingers break
Forever dull England's chains of lead
And every Scot turns from Britannia of the sugar-bowl jaws
To our own long-lost Queen of Queens instead.
 You have sounded the rallying cry.
  It cannot be long
 Till the hosts of our people hie
  On the heels of your song,
And we all make a colour to your red #
And flush redly to your Muse's fair bright cheek.
 *Ho ro** togaibh an aird!*

---

* From Virgil, *Aen.* VI, of the Golden Bough: "Though one be torn away, there fails not another, golden."
† *Ceile De,* Gaelic bard of "the time of Aengus," whose poem (sometimes ascribed to Brigit herself) is preserved in the Burgundian Library.
‡ Broccan Cloen, flourished about A.D. 500, author of chief poetic tribute to Brigit's name.
§ *Muscail,* etc.: "Waken thy courage, O Scotland!" (after Padraigin Haicead's (?1600–1656) similar cry to Banba, i.e., Eire).
|| *Cuirt na h'egise*—Court of Poetry.
¶ Barrantas—poetic summons.
# "Make a colour to your red," Gaelic idiom, meaning "match you in colour."
** *Ho ro,* make ready to go.

"Mi eadar an talamh's an t-athar a' seoladh
Air iteig le h-aighear, misg-chath', agus sholais,
Us caismeachd phiob-mora bras-shroiceadh am puirt." *
She is our Scottish Gile na Gile †—the strange pulchritude
That is the secret Scotland of the Gael,
The personification of Alba as the discrowned,
Wandering heart of beauty, our Shiela-ny-Gara,
Our Cathleen-ny-Houlihan, our *Druimfhionn Donn,*
Our *pe'n Eirinn i,* "whoe'er she be," ‡
Sean O Tuama's § Moirin-ny-Cullenan,
—And she leads us all over Scotland and the Isles
As the faery queen in Eire led Sean Clarach ||
To view the faery strongholds—Cruachain, Brugh-na-Boinne,
Creeveroe, Tara, Knockfeerin, and the rest
—The knot of white ribbon on the hair
Of the image of fine-tressed Gaelic womanhood!

Here only is there no makeshift
Of seeking intimacy with other human beings
And never finding it.
—Ah, my Queen, slender and supple
In a delightful posture
As free from self-conscious art
As the snowcap on a mountain!
—An absorbing attachment of the spirit,
Not a sexual relationship as that is generally understood,
But an all-controlling emotion
That has no physical basis,
Love resolved into the largest terms
Of which such emotions are capable,
The power of the spirit beneath that exquisite tremulous envelope

* Alexander MacDonald's lines beginning "Mi eadar . . ." mean "Between earth and heaven in the air I am sailing, on the wings of exultance, battle drunken, enraptured, while the notes of the great pipes shrilly sound out their tunes."
† *Gile na Gile,* brightness of brightness, the best of the Irish *aislingi,* or vision poems, telling of encounters with fair phantoms. By Aodhagan O Rathaille, 1670–1726.
‡ Uilliam Dall O'Heffernan's *Pe'n-Eirinn i,* "Whoe'er She Be," is "a song of rare finish . . . the poet communicates the thrill that startled him on Fionn's Hill, where he had gone to seek despairing solitude, when she, that lovelier than Deirdre, came to him—whoe'er she be. The wonder of the secret love lives across the centuries."
§ Sean O Tuama, 1708–75.
|| Sean Clarach MacDomhnaill, 1691–1754.

[365]

Possessing moral courage to a rare degree
Which can keep her steadfast in the gravest peril,
And a dignity so natural and certain
That it deserves the name of stateliness.
Death cannot intimidate her.
Poverty and exile, the fury of her own family
And the calumnies of the world
Are unable to bend her will
Towards courses she feels to be wrong
—Imparting with every movement, every look,
Some idea of what the process of literature could be,
Something far more closely related
To the whole life of mankind
Than the science of stringing words together
In desirable sequences.

(What is the love of one human being
For another compared to this?
—Yet I do not underestimate
What such love can be!
On vit plus ou moins à travers des mots
As a rule, but sometimes these moments do come
When words and thoughts are one,
And one with the receptive understanding;
And in such moments
The individual reality of two lives
—For reality is subjective, personal
To each one of us, held in
By the crystal walls of our experience—
Can be fully understood;
The crystals are broken down for a space,
And two realities mingle and become one.
There is little better.
The physical falls away,
Almost irrelevant,
When naked spirits meet in kindness.)
Alas! The thought of ninety-nine per cent of our people
Is still ruled by Plato and Aristotle
Read in an historical vacuum by the few
From whom the masses receive

A minimum of it but along with that
A maximum incapacity for anything else.
The Greek, being a Southerner, was (and still is)
By temperament excitable and easily roused
To excessive display of feeling. Greek troops, we know—unlike
    Scots—
Were peculiarly liable to sudden panic,
And the keen intelligence of the race
Was no more rapid in its working
Than was their susceptibility to passion.
Wisely, therefore, the Greek moralists preached restraint;
Wisely they gave their impressionable countrymen advice
The very opposite of that
The more steady Northerner requires,
And we in modern Scotland most of all!

From

A Kist of Whistles and Other Poems

1943

OF TWO BULGARIAN POETS *

To Dafinka L. Doganova

Todoroff exile—pent in Switzerland
And Slaveikoff in Italy
Untimely died: but left their poesy,
Rare winds of love whereby forever fanned
Bulgarian hearts will glow and understand
Th' incomparable joy of purity,
And from the pinnacles of faith foresee
The glory that the poet, Truth, has planned.

When peace returned a faithful nation brought
Their bodies to Sofia's holy spot.
Their bodies!—for the singer of "Cis Moll"
Immortal lives in our mortality,
Even as Beethoven, and Todoroff's soul,
Receiving naught, gives light eternally.

SONETO DEL SONETO

Voiture and Desmarets † in French essayed
The sonnet on the sonnet with success,
Marini in Italian. (Ah, yes!

* Pentcho R. Slaveikoff and Petko Jordan Todoroff.
† Desmarets, 1596–1676.

My first four lines are very easily made!)
Hurtado de Mendoza, it is said,
First thus displayed his ready cleverness
Although Lope de Vega's, more or less,
Has kept all other efforts in the shade.

But little trouble has my octave given!
I need not name my predecessors who
In English have tried variants of the trick.
Already, as you see, I have not striven
In vain this pleasing exercise to do
With verbal skill and just arithmetic!

IN THE GOLDEN ISLAND *

On reading the "Antología de Poetes Cataláns Moderns"

Now let us pass through Carner's † fairy wood,
Where flowers their blue eyes ope'd so very wide,
While pines told ancient tales of kingly pride
To hours and birds spelled into quietude;
Or see the peasant's door that open stood
Handlike inviting all to step inside; ‡
Or the old olives that so subtly hide
Dead men's desires in many a flying mood.

In Chopin's monastery § by candle-light
Shakespeare, Tagore or Machado we'll read,
Or walking back from Palma through the night

* Mallorca.
† Joseph Carner.
‡ Na Maria Antonia Salva's "Casa Pegesa."
§ At Valldemosa.

[369]

Know how for every guest * the roses still
Blush out, and deem us Daríos † indeed
For whom the singing fountains gravelier spill. ‡

ON READING PROFESSOR IFOR WILLIAMS'S "CANU ANEURIN" § IN DIFFICULT DAYS

"Only barbarism, villainy, and ignorance do not respect the past, cringing before the present alone."
                                        PUSHKIN

Stay me with mosses, comfort me with lichens.

Opening the Gododdin again and renewing
My conscious connection with the gwyr y gogledd ||
I who never fail to detect every now and again,
In the Hebridean and Shetland and Cornish waters I most frequent,
By subtile signs Myrddin's ship of glass ¶
Which has floated invisibly around the seas
Ever since Arfderydd a millennium and a half ago,
(Since Arfderydd—a few miles from where I was born!) #

* Joan Alcover's "L'Hoste."
† Rubén Darío.
‡ Rubén Darío says, "The olives have made the groves of the Golden Island a
Gethsemane where tortured passivity is eternal. . . . They guard the secret desires
of the dead with the wills, the gestures, the attitudes of living men." Joseph Carner,
of Barcelona, found a fairy wood where the pines told stories "De Reys i de Donzel-
les," and the flowers opened their blue eyes very wide. In his noble poem "L'Hoste"
(the guest, i.e., Rubén Darío in Mallorca) Joan Alcover sang, "Roses are redder
where he passes, and the fountain sings with more solemnity." Na Maria Antonia
Salva, who learned her craft in translating Mistral, found the real stuff of poetry in
her pictures of country life.
§ Published by the University of South Wales Press Board, Cardiff, 1939.
|| Men of the North.
¶ After the battle of Arfderydd, Myrddin, sometimes called Myrddin Wyllt or
Merlinus Sylvestris, the Merlin of the Arthurian romance, fled to the Caledonian
forest and finally escaped with his paramour, Chwimleian (Vivien), in a ship of
glass.
Arthuret, near Carlisle (A.D. 575). The author was born twenty miles away, just
over the Scottish border.

I am as one who sees again in a stark winter wood
(And the forest of Celyddon * is indeed in death's grip to-day)

The lichens and mosses, earth's first mercies, shine forth
—The dusk of Lincoln green warming the ragged tree-bole,
Dark flaked liverwort on dank cliff,
Rich velvet mosses making a base
For the old stone dykes—all glowing
In a lustrous jewel-like beauty for the enjoyment of which
One might well endure the rigours of winter!
Contrary to common belief, the lichens and mosses
Love the winter sunlight as wise human beings do.
(Thus, of two retaining walls of a sunk lane,
The lichens and mosses are most abundant and vigorous
On the side that receives the largest volume of sunlight,
And a warm stretch of dykefoot facing the low-set
Southern winter sun is the most resplendent
In fair velvet of any exposure known to me.)

Even so, at the feet of the great grim vertical problems
Of contemporary life I am sustained and cheered
By the perennial shining of a few
Little personal relationships,
Surely in these days of Massenmensch
A singularly blessed example
Of the transcendent function † emerging
From an enantiodromic movement.

Even so in these sterile and melancholy days
The ghastly desolation of my spirit is relieved
As a winter wood by glowing moss or lichen,
And the sunk lane of my heart is vivified,
And the hidden springs of my life revealed
Still patiently potent and humbly creative
When I spy again the ancestral ties between Scotland and Wales,
And, weary of the senseless cacophony of modern literature,
Recur to Aneirin's Gododdin, one of the oldest poems
In any European vernacular—far older indeed

* The forest of Celyddon, the Caledonian forest.
† C. G. Jung's term.

Than anything ever produced on the Continent
Outside Greek and Latin; and not only
Note how (great topical lesson for us to-day)
It is not the glory, but the pity and waste, of war
That inspires its highest passages, but realise
That the profoundest cause in these Islands to-day,
The Invisible War upon which Earth's greatest issues depend,
Is still the same war the Britons fought in at Catraeth *
And Aneirin sings. The Britons were massacred then. Only one
Escaped alive. His blood flows in my veins to-day
Stronger than ever, inspires me with his unchanged purpose,
And moves me alike in Poetry and Politics.

Between two European journeys of Neville Chamberlain's
And two important speeches of Herr Hitler's
I return to the Taliesin and Llywarch Hen poems,
Full of hiraeth, of angry revolt
Against the tyranny of fact, even as Malesherbes
Spent the time lesser men would have devoted
To preparing their case against the forty-three accusations
Contained in the Acte énonciatif
Of December 11, 1792,
In reading Hume's History of the House of Stuart.

So I am delivered from the microcosmic human chaos
And given the perspective of a writer who can draw
The wild disorder of a ship in a gale
Against the vaster natural order of sea and sky.
If man does not bulk too big in his rendering
He does not lose the larger half of dignity either.

Aneirin stays me with mosses
And comforts me with lichens
In the winter-bound wood of the world to-day
Where the gaunt branches rattle like gallows bones.

It is like one of the commonest and at the same time
One of the most indeterminate factors in the life of men
—An experience so intensely private

* Catterick in Yorkshire.

And so jealously guarded and protected
It scarcely reaches the level of articulation.
It is felt to be precious and indispensable.

It belongs to the very foundations
Of temperament and character,
Yet it seldom rises to the clear-cut stage
Of positive affirmation.
It lies somewhere between wistfulness and perception,
In the borderland between longing and knowing.
It is like music from some far-off shore
Or a light that never was on land or sea.

HOSTINGS OF HEROES

There are two days, two sights, I covet most
Of all in the depths of our history lost.

First, Clontarf,* where, says the Irish annalist,
Earl Sigurd in person led into battle
The wild men from the Orc Islands and the Cat Islands,
From Manaan and Sci and Leodus,
From Ceinn-Tire and from airir-gaidhed,
And "an immense army" from the Innis-Gall.

Next, that glorious scene when Dundee
Sent out the Fiery Cross, and the Chiefs
Met him in their war array,
Like the muster of the war-chiefs in the Iliad
As John Philip portrays it in his epic (in Latin)—†
The divers branches of Clan Donald, all with tufts
Of heather tied to their spear-heads, and each
Under its own chieftains
—Black Alasdair of Glengarry, young Clanranald,

* Battle of Clontarf, 1014.
† The epic *The Grameid* has been published, with a translation, by the Scottish History Society.

[373]

Glencoe huge as a giant, with his twisted beard
Curled backward, and his wild eyes rolling,
And Keppoch in gilded armour,
The two Macleans, Duart and Otter,
Macleod of Raasay, in the old Highland dress
Of saffron shirt, belted plaid, and rawhide shoes,
Raasay who could outstrip the deer
And take the wild bull by the horns and master him,
Young Stuart of Appin, MacNaughton of Dundarave,
Grant of Glenmoriston, MacAlaster of Loup, and a host of others,
And above all, Lochiel, the old Ulysses
—A helmet covers his head
A double-edged brand is girt to his side.
Blood-red plumes float on his crest,
A cuirass of leather, harder than adamant,
Girds his breast—on his left arm hangs his shield,
His tartan hose are gartered round his calf,
Mail covers his shoulders
And a brazen plate his back.
His very look, so fierce,
Might fright the boldest foe,
His savage glance, the swarthy hue
Of his Spanish countenance, his flashing eyes,
His beard and moustache
Curled like the moon's horns.

But in the place of all this
What have we to-day?
Dingy parades of vermin!
Details of the English army
In clothes the colour of excrement;
Or processions like that in Edinburgh
In honour of Sir Walter Scott's centenary,
A funeral trickle of Baillies and Lawyers,
Members of the Leith Water Board,
And, sole representative of the Republic of Letters,
Hugh Walpole!

God! What a crawl of cockroaches!

THEY KNOW NOT WHAT THEY DO

Burns in Elysium once every year
Ceases from intercourse and turns aside
Shorn for a day of all his rightful pride,
Wounded by those whom yet he holds most dear.
Chaucer he leaves, and Marlowe, and Shakespeare,
Milton and Wordsworth—and he turns to hide
His privy shame that will not be denied,
And pay his annual penalty of fear.

But Christ comes to him there and takes his arm.
"My followers too," He says, "are false as thine,
True to themselves, and ignorant of Me,
Grieve not thy fame seems so compact of harm;
Star of the Sot, Staff of the Philistine
—Truth goes from Calvary to Calvary!"

CORNISH HEROIC SONG FOR VALDA TREVLYN

Come, let us drink, beloved. You have brimmed my glass
With a supernaculum of a cherry bounce
(More *chia,* as the Chinese say, than Chian is,
Or Chianti, and beyond reckoning finer far
Than even the Coan wine my friend Sturge Moore has sung *
In one of the first longish poems my boyhood knew).
—No red Hermitage for me as long's there's this about,
Nor yet *fion geal as maith tuar* (white wine fine of hue)!
I pour you now the odhaeir you desire.
I have a *slainte churamach* † to give.

Witch, you foreknow my mood to-night. I see you wear
The golden lunula I had copied for you
From the finest of the four found in Cornwall yet,

* *Vide* "Sent from Egypt with a Fair Robe of Tissue to a Sicilian Vinedresser" by
Thomas Sturge Moore.
† A very important toast.

Linking the Early Bronze Age and the Twentieth Century,
This crescentic collar or gorget of thin gold,
Linking Scotland and Cornwall too,
For was not the lunula a Scots creation?
Linking the fogous and our "aonach" * here, with its trick drive-way
No one we do not want can ever find,
Cunningly contrived as the prehistoric communications
Between our peoples were—between
North Scotland, Ireland, and Cornwall,
The Cornwall from Chun Castle to the Stripple Stones,
The coastwise movement, from the south-west, of the Castle complex.
Presupposed in the bronze industry of Jarlshof
And illustrated by the souterrains and fogous,
Identical with the coulisses, the nervous system,
Of all my politics and my poetry now,

Strange as the catalysis by which we found each other,
Cuireideach † as the difference of one man's blood and another's;
As any Plotinus's "transition into another field";
As that secret of great men which lies in the relationship they find
Between things whose laws of continuity escape all lesser men,
So that their supreme achievements which astonish the world
Are, for them, quite simple affairs—like comparing two lengths;
And subtle as the style of jewellery to-day in which
(Subtle as your sacral dimples and lozenge of Michaelis)
A bracelet keeps its platinum to itself as though
The precious substance were a Huguenot, and stones are cut slender,
A single sliver to hold all the fires that were expected
Of a brilliant with its fifty-eight facets or of the eighteenth century
Pearshaped stone with its whole surface faceted.
—A trend, with which we are in sympathy
In all connections, to achieve something like a balance
Between Earth's own efforts and her children's work!

I sing of Cornwall.

Chip of Atlantis, that clings to England still,
Alien in its traditions, utterly different,

* Means (1) a solitary place, a mountain top, a hill; (2) a place of union. *Cf.* Latin,
unicus, single; *unire*, to unite; both from *unus*, one.
† Full of turns and twists; tricky.

This granite-bound corner, storm-washed,
With the smell of seaspray in its fields,
This boon to man, with its gentle air,
Its entrancing colours—Cornwall!
—Cha! I am no good at *natures-mortes!*

Cornwall, epic *intime!*

Cornwall and England, David and Goliath!
Not the ideal but the actual Cornwall
Full of the wandering abscess of the English influence!

It is only the initial force, *id est* temperament,
That can carry one to the goal one is seeking,
Effect the seposition of the Cornish yet
From the indiscrimminate English who make
A bolus of the whole world.
Cornwall, that little world apart, whose essence,
—Not whose existence—is to establish men
As different from those of any other land
As Chinaman from Dutchman!

Despite a branch of the League of Nations Union at Tintagel
And the whole Duchy poxed with British Legion Clubs,
Boy Scouts and Girl Guides and branches of the Junior Imperial
    League,
Despite—nay, because, and in the teeth of these.

Easy to cry: "And shall Trelawny die?"
Impossible to ask: "And shall Cornwall die?"
And count on forty Cornishmen to know the reason why.
Yet the form abides, the function never dies
And perhaps we are not alone in again
(Though little resipiscence can yet be seen
In this xenomorphic and stasimorphic land,
Caught in England's sarmentous toils, every strand of which
Is hairier than the sarothrum on the leg of a bee,
Reptant strands more numerous than the thalline hyphae
And deadlier far, making an accursed raphe
Between these two unrabbetable lands,

A pour rough reseau with no lacework on it,
A monstrous irregular retitelarian web,
The Anglo-Cornish border, rempli
With khaki instead of with sericon,
A hideous symphysia, a foul cinenchyma,
All Cornish life there like deadhead in a sprue.

Sprue? Rhabdite! England's ovipositor!)
In relation to the genius of Cornwall
Entertaining something of the great Aristotelian insight
Into the metaphysical basis
Of the concepts of Formal and Final Cause,
While, alive as we are to the entire multitudinous world,
(Northern Europeans are at their best by day;
Latins, nocturnal, only come to life
By artificial light; being Gaels
We are at home with either)
Our stand for Cornwall involves not "criticism,"
It is just "selection," the root motive of κρινκ that informs us,
Rather than "condemnation," or even "judgment"
—Phacoids of Cornwall as the new world shapes!

I sing of Cornwall, not of Lyonesse,
(Though I too cherish that pre-Arthurian Celtic flicker of being
Which has seemingly disappeared so entirely
Of bare, dark, and elemental Tristan's land—old
Celtic, pre-Christian—Tristan and his boat and his horn.
—If that is only in my life like the quotation
From *Tristan und Isolde* in Berg's *Lyric Suite,*
Which nevertheless does not seem out of place,
And I know King Arthur—*pace* Layamon,
Chaucer, Malory, Spenser, Dryden, Wordsworth,
Tennyson, and all the rest of the romancing bards—
Is none other than Thor, Her-Thor, Ar-Thur,
Thor Eindri of the Edda, the Indian Indra,
And realise the full relation of this
To "Poesy's unfailing river
Which through Albion winds forever")
Of Cornwall (that land without imagination, being poetless),
And of art as the knowledge of the noumenal world,

Of Cornwall, and of that old *scat bal,** her speech,
—Scat *bell* rather! Buried in its fallen cleghty from the reach
Of all the braced farcers of the Arthurian Congress!—
(I fear no sudden sound of it behind me
—If I have nerves, they are like veins in rock!—
When I survey with full content my infinite world,
No ringing, hellish wounding like a treacherous shot,
No envious noise declaring my possessions impure.
Since we have passed all that has been, is, and will be
Through the Athanor of our love.
Nay, now, if I am vulnerable to any attack it is
But slowly as Cornwall's bastions to the sea,
And from forces as different from anything human
As salt-water is from basalt.)

Her speech, her condition, her *Ur*-motives, her all, complete and
    clear,
    A necklace for my love appear
    Moniliform in my verses here,
My little lusty broadbrowed strong-necked love;
And down the shining stream awakens every here and there,
Among the other lights and hues, the ancient dark-red flame,
(The Celtic genius—Cornwall, Scotland, Ireland, Wales—
Is to the English Ascendancy, the hideous khaki Empire,
As the white whale is to the killer whale,
The white whale displaying in its buccal cavity
The heavy oily blood-rich tongue which is the killer's especial de-
    light.
The killer slips his head into the behemoth's mouth
And rives away part after part of the tongue until
Nothing remains in the white whale's mouth but a cicatrised stump.
Yet to-day we laugh gaily and show our healthy red tongues,
Red rags to John Bull—the Celtic colour flaunting again
In a world where the ravening sub-fusc more and more
Prevails. We young Celts arise with quick tongues intact
Though our elders lie tongueless under the ocean of history.
We show ourselves as ever and again through great grey volumes of
    smoke
Red blasts of the fire come quivering—yes, we dare

* Disused mine.

To shoot out our tongues under the very noses of the English,
The fate of our forefathers has not made us afraid
To open our mouths and show our red glory of health,
Nay, we sail again, laughing, on the crown of the sea,
"Not so much bound to any haven ahead
As rushing from all havens astern,"
The deepest blood-being of the white race crying to England
"Consummatum Est! Your Imperial *Pequod* is sunk."
We young Celts disport ourselves fearlessly
Knowing that we are the units
Of a far greater cycle than Melville's great Northern cycle
And that in us it completes its round.)
The Aldebaran light as in the hollows of your stroked hair's curves,
Stroked till the unsufflaminate dye comes up like suffioni,
"Like little lamb-toe bunches springs
In red-tinged and begolden dye
Forever,"
Gleaming from honey-colour to tangerine
("Gold for goodness and copper for cleverness")
Like the *caoir* of the very *clanna-speura* in your *clannfhalt*
—Or like the witch of Atlas's crimson well of refuge
Whence came constant impulsion to the beautiful
To new intensities, to priests to renounce their idols,
Kings their regalia, soldiers their armament,
Gaolers to set their prisoners free, lovers to defy convention.
The weight of your dresses, as Damodaragupta says,
Like the cloud of smoke ascending from the furnace of Love,
Your Meliboean tresses, for the hair of thine head is purple
As the Song of Songs which is Solomon's says.
Dense pillars of dusk through which every now and again
Glows a deeper undershade of crimson as though
Some trapped genius almost thrusts itself out
Of the moving prism that holds it, colour of *fion na Spaine,*
Or like Fate's message to me in the sympathetic ink
That turns purple with tin in the same acid.
Your hair, for an omen, is the very colour of the Phoenix's wings,
Or like Typhoean breathing winning free through all its overburden
Than which no vastier deep, no heavier handicap,
Occludes the Cornish genius and holds it from its triumph,

Coming out slowly, slowly, buldering and heavily,
The lazy cordial colour, banner of red moccado and locram,
The arcane colour of Cornwall's number
And basic shibboleth glory-hue of true Cornish things!

No poet worth his salt, amid the press
Of Earth's accabling problems, has time, far less
Desire, to waste on skiascoped mythologies
The prepotent, rare, and priceless energies
Filially, and protoparentally, true History's
Whose issues, in proseuchae such as these
—Else Cornish religion, *ionraic* religion, is to seek; the common
Religiosity is all a horrible departure from the idiom
Of Cornish genius, as UnEnglish even as UnChristian too,
Irreconcilable with sovereign life, mongrel, base, awry—
Can be my prayers' only addresses,
Maugre voices off, "Rex quondam, rexque futurus."
                                    Fables! Faiblesse!
Though such multivious falsity's the strongest power one sees
In the world to-day; even as "fairy rings" kill trees
So collapsed Cornwall's veridical qualities
In Wesleyans and myxoedematous sectaries like these
Felled by the abundant centrifugally-spreading hyphae
(Terrible as an army without banners, appalling
As summer visitors, or as "for dullness, the creeping Saxons,"
Or as, to Occidentals, the reeling ant-heap East's nimieties.
—Thicker, my darling, than your head of hair
The inexorable threads fare,
Kill the grass here, then, beyond the ring
                                    Stimulate it there
Even as where chalcopyrite is changed to chalcocite,
At greater depths, beyond the reach of concentrating waters,
The original chalcopyrite may remain, or in opposite wise
To those curious Hollywood types who are pretty and can act
But who, mysteriously enough, seem paralysed
So far as all other mental development is concerned
—On the screen charming, even convincing artists,
Off it, collapsing into nothingness)
Of the responsible fungi. Toadstools! Toad's tales!

How Cornwall has suffered from this disintegrity!
The wine gone and nothing but the bagasse left.

Horrible fog-cowls of fungi everywhere, umbrella-like phallic sym-
    bols,
Or in crescent thick ears or in hoof-like shapes,
As with the Birch Polypore, *Polyporus betulinus*—
Whose powder-like spores gain entry to trees
Through wounds and kill them—fungus bodies in themselves
Of little use, save, trimmed, to sharpen razor blades,
Or serve as substitutes for cork, or, cut in strips,
Do insect-collectors to pin their captures on!
Our love is free of all such mushroom growths,
Local morals, fashions of feeling, and blind-spot science
And of all fear of fungus-wrought overthrows.
His attitude towards woman is the basic point
A man must have thought out to know
Where he honestly stands.
Since praise is well, and compliment is well,
But affection—that is the last and final
And most precious reward any man can win.
I remember when you were like that shrub
Which is smothered with carillons of little brick-red bells
Finely striped with yellow lines;
That, when the sun shines through them,
Glow like hot blown glass.
But ah! now, beloved, it is as when on the Carmine Cherry,
A hundred feet high and with a spread
Coinciding with the circumference of the earth,
The ruby-red flowerbuds open, and the whole tree
Bursts into carmine flame, a mass of blossom, stark crimson.
To see the sun through its branches
When the tree is in full bloom
Is a thing that can never be forgotten.
Nor the sight of your eyes now, Valda,
Through the toppling wave of love.
Love's scarlet banner is over us.
We conquer chaos, a new Creation.

THE DIVIDED BIRD

Ah! Peirce * was right. His "minuter logic"
Could only avail towards what he sought
As the scrawl on an infant's slate
To a cartoon of Raphael.

The alethetropic barrenness of a Formal Logic,
The characteristic vice of mathematicians,
Of taking any hypothesis that seems amusing
And deducing its consequences, can do no more
Than pluck our bird and scatter its feathers.

Silly as the peacock's feather Lord Kames † declared
Not specified so would leave us at a loss to form
An accurate image of the fanciful feat
Described in *Henry V* ‡ to exemplify what
A poor and private displeasure can do against a king:
"You may as well go about to turn the sun to ice
With fanning in his face with a peacock's feather"
. . . . "Plume yourself upon it as much as you like,
But what will that do to the king?"

                    Let us rather
Be with the bird as we are with the full-blown
Yellow rose of Space and Time whose petals we've counted
But will not pluck for our answer
Since it would work out "No!"
Tyun, tyun, tyun, tyun
    Spi tui zqua
Tyo, tyo, tyo, tyo, tyo, tyo, tyo, tyo, tix;
    Qutio, qutio, qutio, qutio,
    Zquo, zquo, zquo, zquo.
Tzy, tzy, tzy, tzy, tzy, tzy, tzy, tzy, tzy, tzy,
Quorrox tui zqua pipiquisi.

* Charles Sanders Peirce, the American philosopher.
† Lord Kames (1696–1782), Scottish judge and author, wrote *Elements of Criticism* (1762), and other legal, historical, philosophical, and aesthetic works.
‡ Act IV, Scene 1. See discussion of this, and of Kames' contention, in Professor I. A. Richards' *The Philosophy of Rhetoric*.

Into the innermost core of my life
Flock the quick shadows; and now I know
Wings are spread over the world to-day
Only conceived in the depths of darkness so.
From the stream of intuition rises a truth
That reason, since it lacks it, denies the name;
More august than reason, more enduring, outsoaring it
With Earth's loveliest song, and amplest pinions aflame.

And here in the shadows in my thalamus * now
The bird has disclosed all its secrets to me;
I know the destiny of man, the call
Of the Seraphim to the life that's to be,
That still, like the pure birdliness I now hold,
Only in the darkest depths of intuition lies;
In poverty and peace and selfless love
. . . From these alone can humanity rise.

Tell me no more that proud ambition,
Material means, the lusts of the eye,
All we can see and feel and take apart,
Are the stays of mankind, or the power to fly
Of birds is born of their feathers and shape.
I know that nothing like these in myself at all,
No erudition or effort, will enable me to sing
. . . Or men to make a better world withal.

The world in which nothing will evade us
Having cause to mistrust the limitations of our love,
We who, since Elijah, should no more halt
Between two opinions than that bird above!
The obscure sense of value does not discriminate
The principle. . . . Justice, sympathy, are of no avail;
All divisions disappear before love alone
. . . It means we have too little love if in aught we fail.

I am as one who is still pursuing
The bird behind all I can think of it

* The poet here expresses his agreement with those brain physiologists who find
intuition—as distinct from cortical understanding, which is what he calls "mere
reason"—localised in the thalamus.

[384]

And see and hear and feel . . . as one
Who faithfully quests the Holy Grail yet,
Priesthood within priesthood, mass behind mass,
Without sodality, or institution, or order,
Heard only in the heart's silence. . . . Now the bird stoops;
With its eyes filling mine, I tremble on the border

With its eyes filling mine . . . O would I could go
To Everyman with the power of the Age of Plenty so!
The bird is in them all if they'll liberate it
From the cage of vain reason that holds it yet.
That is, reason better; for true reason knows
The abyss it rests on, and distinguishes with fairness
Between the pseudo-simplicity of perceptual acceptance
And the genuine simplicity of immediate awareness.

BALLAD OF AUN, KING OF SWEDEN

Surely Hell burns a deeper blue
With each noble boast of men like you.

With each noble boast of men like you
—Such men as all but all men it's true.

See what I'm doing for England, you cry,
Or for Christendom, civilisation, or some other lie.

And no one remembers the story of Aun,
The Swedish king, who sent son after son

To death, buying with each another span
Of life for himself, the identical plan

All governments, all patriots, self-righteously pursue.
How many sons have *you* given, and *you,* and you?

Nine sons in succession was the grim
Record of Aun, till the people rose and slew *him*.

But when will the people rise and slay
The ubiquitous Aun of State Murder to-day?

Realising murder is foulest murder no matter
What individual or body for what end does the slaughter!

A GOLDEN WINE IN THE GAIDHEALTACHD

To W. D. MacColl and our hosts and hostesses in Arisaig, Eigg, South Uist, Raasay, Skye, Barra, and Mull

In Scotland in the Gaidhealtachd there's a golden wine
Still to be found in a few houses here and there
Where the secret of its making has been kept for centuries
—Nor would it avail to steal the secret, since it cannot be made else-
    where.

In Scotland in the Gaidhealtachd there's a golden wine.
Carelessly and irreligiously quaffed it might be taken
For a very fine Champagne. But it is not an effervescing wine
Although its delicate piquancy produces a somewhat similar effect
    upon the palate.

In Scotland in the Gaidhealtachd there's a golden wine,
A wine that demands so deliberate a pause,
In order to detect its hidden peculiarities
And subtle exquisiteness of its flavour, that to drink it
Is really more a moral than a physical delight.
There is a deliciousness in it that eludes analysis
And like whatever else is superlatively good
Is better appreciated by the memory
Than by present consciousness.

In Scotland in the Gaidhealtachd there's a golden wine.
One of its most ethereal charms lies
In the transitory life of its richest qualities,
For while it requires a certain leisure and delay

Yet if you linger too long upon the draught it becomes
Disenchanted both of its fragrance and its flavour.

In Scotland in the Gaidhealtachd there's a golden wine.
The lustre should not be forgotten among the other
Admirable embodiments of this rare wine; for, as it stands in a glass
A little circle of light glows round about it,
The finest Orvieto or that famous wine,
The Est Est Est of Montefiascone,
Is vulgar in comparison. This is surely
The wine of the Golden Age such as Bacchus himself
First taught mankind to press from the choicest of his grapes.

In Scotland in the Gaidhealtachd there's a golden wine.
There is a tradition that if any of it were sent to market
This wine would lose all its wonderful qualities.
Not a drop of it therefore has ever been sold,
Or ever will be. Indeed the wine is so fond
Of its native home that a transportation
Of even a few miles turns it quite sour.
Yet the custom of those who have it has always been and still is
To let it flow freely whenever those
Whom they love and honour sit at the board.
But it cannot be drunk in all the world
Save under these particular roofs in Arisaig and Eigg,

In Tobermory, South Uist, Barra, Raasay and Skye,
Nor can they see or smell or taste it who are not
Competent receivers—nor could they bestow
Who lack the sense of operative form—this consecrated juice
Symbolising the holy virtues of hospitality and social kindness.

Through what else can Scotland recover its poise
Save, as Very Hope believes, this golden wine yet?

Shetland (West side) herring fishing, June, 1936.

Written during a week aboard the
sailing ship *Valkyrie*

To Skipper John Irvine, of Saltness, Whalsay

Twenty miles out to the main deep
Due west o' the Ramna Stacks
And sou-west o' the Flugga Light
I ha'e a' that my pleasure lacks.

Gannet, haud wide. Seek the bush-raip alang
Till aiblins at last you may sight
A single white cork amang a' the broon
On which you may like to alight.

But awa' doon here on the inshore grunds
Twenty miles sou-west o' the Flugga Light
I row at ease on a broon mysel'
And ha'e nae need to seek for a white.

For shootin' oor nets parallel to the Ramna Stacks
I think o' the sixareens * o' the auld Fiedeland fleet
And their hardy fishermen a' langsyne in the mools,
And life ony auld gait is fell sweet.

Rinnin' oor nets oot in line wi' the Stacks
Wi' oor ain broon sails clashed doon at oor feet
There's nae white to be seen save yon toom face o' a mune
Till we haul up syne, when oor shot † may compete.

Gannet, haud wide. Swing awa' roon' the buoys.
It's my watch tonight while we lie to the nets,
And I'm blithe to be whaur the hert o' darkness
Wins back sae muckle day aye needs forgets.

* Sixareens—the old square sailboats.
† Shot—haul of herring.

My een compete wi' the Aeschiness Light,
There's little else to be seen wi' the ootward eye,
But it's no' the ootward eye that contents my mind,
Nor yet that difference, gannet, 'twixt you and me.

And I ken the morn we'll pit in at North Roe *
And I'll see wi' the lassies in the guttin' ranks there
The wee Whalsay lassie I lo'e best o' a'
Wi' a wreath o' white gulls roond her bonnie broon hair
—Aye, when her skinklan' tresses she combs
She's bonnier than ocht on the Floo'ery Holms.

Fillin' oor cran-baskets and swingin' them up
And alang on the trollies, a look and a smile,
A word in the bygaein', and, if I'm lucky, a touch,
'll haud me gaein' again for anither while.

Praise be, it's only a plain Shetland lad
At whom ony sweet Shetland lass e'er keeks.
God or the King or Heaven kens wha
If they tried to butt in 'ud be deemed juist freaks.
Ony fisher lad 'ud hae them beat to the wide
If they cam' here ettlin' to find a bride.

Syne we'll bear awa' yont the Stacks aince mair
Till I'll feel like a "reincandescent" again,
But whaur the white light that glows in me's frae
Only mysel', and the lassie at North Roe, ken.

Oh, awa' yont the Ramna Stacks again
For anither night on the edge o' the Main Deep there!
—Lassie, I doot I never saw afore
Hoo bright the gowd glints in your bonnie broon hair.

Furth frae your breists and oot through the ocean
Pearl-white stream ne'er confused in the maelstrom o' waters.
As the needle to the Pole my hert to you,
Fairest 'mang the haill o' Hialtland's daughters!

* Roe—pronounced Rew.

[389]

Seaward again yont the Erne's Crag
And the horns o' the neeps o' Greevlan',
And I praise the Lord that your love for me
In the weavin' waters needs nae unreevlin'!

Look, there's a tystie fleein' wi' his boat full! *
But I've dipped a raip owre and sprinkled oor deck
Wi' the sparklin' saut draps for luck's sake again
Or the tystie's gobbled the fish doon his neck.

Ho, there Jimmy! Jimmy Williamson, ho!
Sing to the herrin' as you used to do.
I'll go in wi' the chorus, but there's twa bright herrin'
Loupin' in my chest'll no answer to you!

Sing: *"Come on, peerie † fish. Fill the hungry hold.
I see a straggle. I see white in the lum.
I see faither awa' there at the back o' the bed.
Here's a better bit strollie. Let her come. Let her come.
The seals are snuffin' a' alang the tow-heid,
Hannah ‡ abune is squealin' wi' greed.
Come on in. You're safer wi' us indeed,
Bonxie § and maulie ‖ are seekin' their feed.
There she's again. I see her. I see her.
Toddle up, toddle up. You're far better here."*
I hear the tirricks ¶ roarin' astern.
*"I'll sing to the herrin' in the mornin', lad.
I'll tell her to shiver her noses then
When she's taen the best cravat ever she's had."*

The fish Christ Jesus and my ain bonnie lass
Flash sidewise in my blood-pool a' the time.
There's twa fish loupin' in my bosem, Jimmy,
Wi' an ever-mair glorious skyme after skyme.

* Tystie (Black Guillemot)—with his boat full—with a fish in his mouth. (The following three lines refer to an old fisherman's superstition.)
† Peerie—little.
‡ The herring gull (the little black-backed gull).
§ The great skua.
‖ The Fulmar petrel.
¶ Arctic terns.

Flickerin' birds fade into the grim rocks where they nest
As the starry hosts in the sunrise fade.
My body may swing on the fishin' grunds here
But my spirit in the light o' her love is stayed.

Let the night darken. They'll brighten the mair,
My een and the Aeschiness Light and them.
And *them,* I say—but in the howe o' the night
Guid kens they shine like a single flame.

Borin' its way through the hert o' the dark
And bearin' me wi't—till we come aince mair,
Tackin' up the Soond to the Biorgs again
And I see her standin' in the guttin ranks there
Wi' a wreath o' gulls like wavin' white lilies
Plaited aboot her bonnie broon hair
—Sae I'll see her again in the first o' the day
Till she and I blend in yae flame tae,
Fairer than yon that's erst seemed sae fair!

Certes if she * rises to soom the night
There'll be something to meet her afore her face!
Mair than sixty vessels shootin' their nets
In the light o' the sunset a' roond oor place.
Yet aiblins the morn I'll hae white in my net
Purer than ony the ocean's gien yet.

White as driven snaw and warmin' as wine
And mine, my sweethert, mine—mine!
Witch that I burn in my hert ilka night,†
The *Valkyrie*'s luck and my pride and delight!

Nae lass in the crews ‡ at the Shetland stations
Can gut herrin' mair deftly and quickly than you.
But, certes, you've put the guts *into* me,
And I'd sail for you into Hell's reid mou'.

* "She" here—also "her" in stanza 17—refers, of course, to the herring.
† Refers to another old fisherman's superstition.
‡ Three girls constitute a gutting crew.

It's a fine clear trusty sky the night,
The fires o' the sunset are playin' reid yet
Roond the Blue Mull, Valleyfield and the Pobie astern
—Like the fires o' my hert roond you, my pet.

An' I'll sail Earth's seas as lang as I maun
Mixin' my blood wi' the bitterest brine
If that is the only airt I can win
At last to mixin' my blood wi' thine.

For a workin' lad and a workin' lass
Can lo'e each ither juist at least as weel
As Royalty or the walethiest folk
Or onybody trained in a public skeel.

It's a perfect miracle, lassie, hoo near
You can seem to me whiles even awa' oot here
On the edge o' the main deep. It was ill to ken
It was only a dream I had o' you then.

When the kaim o' Foula lifts on the Smew
My peerie lass I'm aye thinkin' o' you,
And aye I'd leifer see yours instead
O' even the finest dry weather heid,
And when there's nocht else in the warld in sight
You're aye in view.

O Love that pours oot through the welterin' sea
In a constant inviolable muckle moonpath to me
Frae my lass at North Roe, I'se warrant that current
'll find a' life's troubles, and Death itsel', nae deterrent!

Grain o' wind now, boys, and the auld boat
In through its blasts like a greyh'und coorses
Doon the tricky tideways o' Yell Soond, fu'
O' sunshine noo—on white horses!

Three reefs and nae comfort up or doon
Where I'm still thinkin', my love, o' you
While we play Lant * in an air smoke, steam,
And sweaty socks mak' like an Irish stew.

* An old and complicated card game much favoured by Shetland fishermen.

THE WRECK OF THE *SWAN*

Even so—as a man at the end tries no more
To escape but deliberately turns and plunges
Into the press of his foes and perishes there—
I remember the lesson of the wreck of the *Swan,*
Within her own home harbour and under the lights
Of her crew's native city, swept to doom on Christmas Eve.

The lights were warm on happy family parties
In hundreds of homes. —One wonders
If a man or woman here and there did not part
The curtains to look out and think how black
Was the night, and foul for men at sea.

Few could know that quite near at hand, just beyond
The bald fisher-rows of Footdee, the crew
In the lifeboat *Emma Constance* were fighting to save
Five men in the wheelhouse of that trawler, the *Swan,*
That wallowed in broken seas.

It was not what a seaman would call rough in the channel
But there was a heavy run of broken water
Along the inside wall of the North Pier
And for some reason unknown the *Swan* grounded
Two hundred yards within the pier-head,
Swung round, held fast, and took to labouring
In a swelter of breakers and spray.

Less than ten minutes later a gun
Fired a rocket from the Pier and a line
For the breeches-buoy was across the *Swan.*
Had it been accepted that would have ended the tale.
But the men of the *Swan*—who knows why?—
Refused that line of safety.

Meanwhile, with the celerity of firemen, the lifeboat crew,
Had assembled and tumbled into their powerful sixty-foot boat,
And she was off, and, in a few minutes, alongside the *Swan*
Between that helpless ship and the pier.

Again the door of safety was wide open to the men of the *Swan*
And again they refused to pass through it.

The coxswain of the lifeboat roared at them,
Through his megaphone, to jump; but the five men
Of the *Swan* turned away and took refuge
In their doomed ship's wheelhouse instead.
There is a dark fascination in trying to appreciate
The spiritual inwardness of that strange situation.
Five men, for their own good reasons, refusing
To leave the shelter of their wheelhouse, while the lifeboat laboured
In the seas and the darkness, its crew dedicated to rescue,
Shouting to them in vain to come out and be saved.

A great wave hissing angrily came down on the lifeboat
And broke her adrift from the wreck.
Wielding the force of many tons it threw her
Against the foundations of the pier.
Along the length of 100 feet of solid masonry
She was flung like a piece of stick.

But the coxswain got her out again—a feat of seamanship
To hold the imagination in itself!—
And back alongside the *Swan* the *Emma Constance* went,
And again the lines were thrown,
But none of the men in the wheelhouse
Would come out to make them fast.

This time they had refused their last chance,
A sea of enormous weight broke over the wreck.
It carried away the upper part of the wheelhouse.
It swept the *Emma Constance* once more
Against the adamant wall of the pier.

This is the story of the men who wouldn't come out.
They were never seen alive again—and the coxswain and crew of
    the lifeboat
Carry the dark knowledge that up against
Something more formidable, more mysterious even,
Than wind and wave they battled largely in vain.

Four times they had gone back to that tragic wreck,
Manoeuvred with high skill in the cauldron 'twixt ship and pier,
Played the searchlight continuously on the battered bridge,
Cruised about for an hour,
But the men of the *Swan* refused to come out!

No dreamers these but hard-bitten men
Used to all the tortures of Old Feathery Legs
—The black villain who rides every crested wave
North of 65 degrees—he and his accursed legions,
The fog, the blizzard, the black-squall and the hurricane.

Up to their waists in water on the foredeck,
Gutting fish in the pounds, a black-squall
Screaming around, and the temperature 40 degrees below,
Working like automatons, 30 . . . 40 . . . 50 hours,
Grafting like fiends, with never a break or blink of sleep between.
A wave as high as the mast-heads crashing on deck
And sweeping all hands in a heap in the lee-scuppers,
Their arms and hands clawing up through the boiling surf
Still grasping wriggling fish and gutting knives.
And every now and then a message like this
Throbbing out of the black box.

    "VALKYRIE calling all trawlers! . . . He's got us . . . Old
Feathery's got us at last. . . . We can see the rocks now . . . just
astern. . . . Another minute, I reckon! . . . We're on! . . . Good-
bye, pals. . . . Say good-bye to my wife . . . to my kiddies! . . .
Good-bye, Buckie. . . . Good-bye, Scotland!"

In 31 years at sea, he'd spent less
Than four years ashore, mostly in spells
On an average of 36 hours
Between trips—that's the price
His wife and kids had to pay for fish.

Time the public knew what these men have to face.

Nearly 100,000 of them at sea.
Nor are they the only men concerned.

[395]

Shipbuilders, rope, net and box manufacturers,
Fish-friers, buyers, retailers, salesmen,
Railways and road transport,
Coal, salt, and ice industries,
—About 3,000,000 folk would have to look elsewhere
For their bread and butter
If there were no trawlermen—or fish.

"Stand by all hands!" Down below
The lads along the starboard scuppers,
Backs bent, hands clawing the net,
Long as the ship, wide as a street,
Keyed to high-tension point,
Every muscle tense and taut.
"Shooto!" Over she goes.

Off the South-East coast of Iceland,
The East Horns, a famous landmark,
About five miles off the port-quarter.
All along the coast the great, barren, sullen mountains,
Eternally snow-crested, and shaped
Like monstrous crouching animals,
Sweep down to the water line,
And many a brave ship lies
Under the lowering evil shadows
Of the terrible rocks.

The successful skippers read the "fish sign"
In a thousand different ways.
The gulls, the wind, currents, tides,
The depth of water, the nature of the bottom,
The type of fish caught in certain patches,
The nature of the food in their stomachs
Exposed by the gutting knife,
These factors and a thousand others
Supply information to be had or read
Only after years of battle and bitter experience.

Trawling along the lip of a marine mountain,
Covered by 200 fathoms of water,

On what is veritably a narrow mountain pass,
Scooping up hard "sprags" (cod)
And "ducks" (haddocks),
Each net sweeping up fish in hundreds of thousands,
Towing for miles over an area wide as a town.

The skipper has been on the bridge
For nearly 60 hours on end,
Down below, in the fish-pounds for'ard,
The lads are reeling like drunken men,
The decks awash, swirling high
As their arm-pits, and icy-cold.

These men are no dreamers.

Rex est qui metuit nihil.

A true man chooses death as he can in no part lie to a girl
But will put himself conscientiously into the worst possible light.

Töten ist eine Gestalt unseres wandernden Trauerns . . .
Rein ist im heiteren Geist,
Was an uns selber geschieht.*

(Killing is only a form of the sorrow we wander in here . . .
The serener spirit finds pure
All that can happen to us.)

"Death is ugly.
Tomato is crashing too." †

The Gaels never die! They either "change" or "travel."

"Happy the folk upon whom the Bear looks down, happy in this
    error,
whom of fears the greatest moves not, the dread of death. Hence
    their warrior's
heart hurls them against the steel, hence their ready welcome of
    death." ‡

* Rainer Maria Rilke.
† Tio Nakamura.
‡ Lucan, *Pharsalia*.

[397]

"It was possibly the inculcation of these doctrines that moved the Celtic warriors to hurl their bodies against cold steel—a characteristic the world is only too familiar with in the conduct of our Highland regiments. They can still listen to the battle-songs of a thousand ages, with a susceptible mood nowise estranged amid the crumbling foundations of a former sovereignty. A German military authority—Clausewitz, I think—said that the Highlander is the only soldier in Europe who, without training, can unflinchingly face the bayonet."

For now I see Life and Death as who gets
The first magical glimpse of Popocatepetl,
Its white cone floating in the rare winter air,
Incredibly near, . . . incredibly unreal,
And its sister peak which the Indians call
"The sleeping woman," like a great prone goddess,
Above her circlet of clouds,
Or like Mount Elbruz's mile-apart twin breasts of snow!

I don't look the kind of guy, do I,
Who aches to get away from the high truth
Of the passing mountains into the close heat
Of the Pullman again, and the company of his pals
—Into a small enclosed space where I can feel
Confident and important again?
I am accustomed to the altura, believe me.
I am what the guides call schwindelfrei.
This is not the poetry of a man with such a grudge against life.

That a very little of it goes a long way with him.
No great barbaric country will undermine and ruin me,
Slowly corroding my simple unimaginative qualities,
Rob me of my conventions, of my simple direct standards,
Who have no undefeatable inner integrity to take their place.
I love this country passionately, expanding
To its wild immensity as a flower opens in the sunshine,
I am the last man in all the world to hate these great places
And depend for my only comfort on the theatres and cafés,
The wide, well-lit avenidas, the scandal and gossip of the cabarets,
The emotion and danger of the bull-ring.

I would not rather be sitting in the closed comfort of the Pullman,
A drink before me, surrounded by people I know,
And things I can understand.

I feel with life
As a man might towards a little child,
But towards Death, as towards one of my own contemporaries
Whom I have known as long
As I have known myself.

From

In Memoriam James Joyce

1955

IN THE FALL

Let the only consistency
In the course of my poetry
Be like that of the hawthorn tree
Which in early Spring breaks
Fresh emerald, then by nature's law
Darkens and deepens and takes
Tints of purple-maroon, rose-madder and straw.

Sometimes these hues are found
Together, in pleasing harmony bound.
Sometimes they succeed each other. But through
All the changes in which the hawthorn is dight,
No matter in what order, one thing is sure
—The haws shine ever the more ruddily bright!

And when the leaves have passed
Or only in a few tatters remain
The tree to the winter condemned
        Stands forth at last
   Not bare and drab and pitiful,
But a candelabrum of oxidised silver gemmed
By innumerable points of ruby
Which dominate the whole and are visible
Even at considerable distance
As flame-points of living fire.
That so it may be
With my poems too at last glance
Is my only desire.

All else must be sacrificed to this great cause.
I fear no hardships. I have counted the cost.
I with my heart's blood as the hawthorn with its haws
Which are sweetened and polished by the frost!

See how these haws burn, there down the drive,
In this autumn air that feels like cotton wool,
When the earth has the gelatinous limpness of a body dead as a
    whole
While its tissues are still alive!

Poetry is human existence come to life,
The glorious energy that once employed
Turns all else in creation null and void,
The flower and fruit, the meaning and goal,
Which won all else is needs removed by the knife
Even as a man who rises high
Kicks away the ladder he has come up by.

This single-minded zeal, this fanatic devotion to art
Is alien to the English poetic temperament no doubt,
"This narrowing intensity" as the English say,
But I have it even as you had it, Yeats, my friend,
And would have it with me as with you at the end,
I who am infinitely more un-English than you
And turn Scotland to poetry like those women who
In their passion secrete and turn to
Musk through and through!

So I think of you, Joyce, and of Yeats and others who are dead
As I walk this Autumn and observe
The birch tremulously pendulous in jewels of cairngorm,
The sauch, the osier, and the crack-willow
Of the beaten gold of Australia;
The sycamore in rich straw-gold;
The elm bowered in saffron;
The oak in flecks of salmon gold;
The beeches huge torches of living orange.

Billow upon billow of autumnal foliage
From the sheer high bank glass themselves
Upon the ebon and silver current that floods freely
Past the shingle shelves.
I linger where a crack willow slants across the stream,
Its olive leaves slashed with fine gold.
Beyond the willow a young beech
Blazes almost blood-red,
Vying in intensity with the glowing cloud of crimson
That hangs about the purple bole of a gean
Higher up the brae face.

And yonder, the lithe green-grey bole of an ash, with its boughs
Draped in the cinnamon-brown lace of samara.
(And I remember how in April upon its bare twigs
The flowers came in ruffs like the unshorn ridges
Upon a French poodle—like a dull mulberry at first,
Before the first feathery fronds
Of the long-stalked, finely-poised, seven-fingered leaves)—
Even the robin hushes his song
In these gold pavilions.

Other masters may conceivably write
Even yet in C major
But we—we take the perhaps "primrose path"
To the dodecaphonic bonfire.

They are not endless these variations of form
Though it is perhaps impossible to see them all.
It is certainly impossible to conceive one that doesn't exist.
But I keep trying in our forest to do both of these,
And though it is a long time now since I saw a new one
I am by no means weary yet of my concentration
On phyllotaxis here in preference to all else,
All else—but my sense of sny!

The gold edging of a bough at sunset, its pantile way
Forming a double curve, tegula and imbrex in one,
Seems at times a movement on which I might be borne
Happily to infinity; but again I am glad

When it suddenly ceases and I find myself
Pursuing no longer a rhythm of duramen
But bouncing on the diploe in a clearing between earth and air
Or headlong in dewy dallops or a moon-spairged fernshaw
Or caught in a dark dumosity, or even
In open country again watching an aching spargosis of stars.

LET US ARISE

Let us arise,
We whose "calf-country" is *Siksha,*
The science of proper pronunciation, and the grammar of Panini.
Beyond all grammars for originality of plan
And for analytical subtlety—Panini
Fabled to have *seen* rather than composed
This "natural history of the Sanskrit tongue"
In Sūtras which are perfect miracles of condensation,
The maximum abridgement being effected by the coining
Of an arbitrary symbolical language,
The key to which must be acquired
Before the rules themselves can be rendered intelligible.
—The closing *Sūtra* shows the consummate brevity attained.
It reads merely "a a," which is said to mean
"Let short *a* be held to have its organ of utterance
Contracted, now we have reached the end of the work
In which it was necessary to regard it as otherwise."
—Grammar regarded as we should regard the natural sciences,
Something to be studied and elaborated for its own sake
—And so on to Kātāyana's Vārttikas
Or "supplementary rules and annotations"
And to Patanjali's Mahabhashya or "great commentary"
And to the hundred and fifty grammarians and commentators
Who followed in the footsteps of that great triumvirate,
Each criticising or commenting on his predecessors—
Kaiyata, Vamanan, Bhattoji-dīkshita,
To Madhyama-kaumudī, the laghu-kaumudī of Varada-rāja,
Vopadeva—we know them all

[403]

And every detail of their works
Even as in our own Europe we know
How what was once the dialect of Burgos
Was acquired by Aztecs, Mixteks, Zapoteks,
Aimaras, Quechuas, Araucanians, Guaranies and Tagalogs,
And we know the clear, well-balanced Castilian,
The explosive concentration of Portuguese and Extremenan,
The thin pliancy of Galician,
The soft vigour and luminousness of Valencian and Mallorcan,
The bitter and sincere harshness of Catalan,
Even as we know Greek, from Homer to modern Greek,
Including the Koinê and the dialects, ancient and modern,
And rejoice over how κάμνω found in Homer
In the sense of "make" survived in popular speech
For 3000 years, though it did not get into books,
And how the third plural οντι is used in Cos
Where also survives the Doric form πόκα
And in Astypalaea the true aspirate survives
As t-th (like pot-hook) for Θ
Even as we know how
Costa i Llobera's *Pi de Formentor*
Is not Catalan but Majorcan,
Not Majorcan but of Pollensa,
Not Pollensan but a specific pine-tree
Hanging in verdure over the rocks by the sea,
And have understood the need of definitely fixing the meaning of a
    word,
Now so important, once in fairly common use
Both in Jewish and Christian literature
Down to the eleventh century A.D.
And to that end have traced the usages
In "The Oracles of Papias," Sophocles' Greek Lexicon
Josephus, Philo, Clement of Rome, Polycarp, Irenaeus,
Noting the cunningly concocted plausibilities
With which heretics have misled the minds of the simple
And all the distortions of those who have proved
Incompetent exegetes of noble utterances,
And so tried to trace the exact meaning of this word
Whether in the form of τὰ λόγια or τὰ λόγια τοῦ θεοῦ
Or τὰ λόγια αὐτοῦ, or κυριακά

Or τὰ λόγια αὐτοῦ, or ἐκείνου
Or, lastly, as θεῖα λόγια and ἱερὰ λόγια

Even as we know that in B.C. 500
The Chinese symbol meaning "moon" was pronounced "ngiwpt"
But in Peiping to-day is read "yueh," "ut" in Canton,
"Ngwok" in Foochow, and "yö" in Shanghai,
While the Japanese read it as "gestu"
And it is called "saran" in Mongolia
And "biya" in Manchuria,
While in Tibet, Korea, Annam, and other places
Still other sounds are attached to it
But in each case the meaning is perfectly clear
And its use through many centuries by the literate sections
Of so many linguistically different peoples
Surely proves there must be something in it,
Quite aside from its sound,
That is universally accessible;
Loving to trace back the doctrine of *amor intellectualis Dei*
To its fountain-head,
To find a 13th-century anticipation
Of the Pound-Eliot *olla podrida* of tongues
In the *descort* of Raimbaut de Vaqueiras,
Or, brooding over the world history of the dance,
Review with the mind's eye all the forms,
Passecaille, chaconne, sarabande,
The dances of the Dinka, the Naura, the Nilotic Nanda,
The Toba of the Grand Chaco,
To the maxixe, tango, charleston,
Shag and big apple, and, *en route,*
Rejoice, in a philological parenthesis,
To analyse the Hebrew verb *raḳad*
And find thence that King David *skipped*
Rather than *danced* before the Ark.
The Russian *Trepaḳ* and the Georgian *Leḳuri,*
The French *Bourrée* and Spanish *Fandango,*
The dizzy *Moldavanesca* with its circular movements,
The slow *Hora* languid as the strains of the Moldavian *doina,*
The men's fiery *Ciocarlia* dance, the *Coasa suite,*
And the charming Tajik *Non-Boza.*

[405]

(Compare the dance passages in Dynnik's *Shazanniya o Nartakh*
And in Dozon's *B'lgarski Narodni Pesni*)

Even as we delight in the letter of Aristeas
Which contains less than 2000 words
(All listed in Wendland's *Index Verborum*)
Of which more than 500 are various forms
Of twenty-eight words only;
—Apart from the interests of its contents
This short treatise is of unique value to men like us
Because it contains no fewer than thirty-two hapex legomena
And thirty-seven other words which can be described as rare.
We who have sat with Kurds in their appalling cellars,
With Kazaks in their round igloo-like huts,
With Persians in their earth-floored hovels,
And talked with Uzbeks, Tadjiks, Tartars,
We, who know intimately *meddah, karagön,* and, above all
Orta oyunu, that imitation of peasants and of all
The various nationalities composing the Ottoman Empire,
Are coming now to the *orta oyunu* of all mankind.

And even as we know Shelta, Hisperic Latin, and Béarlagair na
        Sāer,
(Knowing them as a farmer surveying his fields
Can distinguish between one kind of crop and another
At a stage when that is a mystery to the unskilled eye
—Knowing that wheat has a deeper green,
Barley a twisting blade that gives it a hazy look,
Oats a blue, broad blade.
The beans blossom, and the cloverfields also,
Now the valley becomes clothed as with diverse carpets
—Red clover, white clover,
The silver blue of beans,
And occasionally
The wine-glow of a field of trefolium).

Even as we know
The Cretan Mantinades (or Chattismata as Cypriots call it),
The "poe etarides" going on for hours at fairs and rural banquets,
Instantly improvised pendeca-syllabic couplets

(Much like *puirt a beul* at Hebridean ceilidhs
Or like the Welsh pennillion)
Each one capping its forerunner to a ritual tune;
Or the similar performance of two Basque Bersolaris
Involving, with more than Finnish *sisu,* the whole being,
All the senses at once, and not merely
A St. Vitus' dance of head, shoulders and arms,
Like the top dissection of a chicken;
Or, best of all, Valéry's *nuit de Gênes,*
The painful and ecstatic awareness
Of language as the central mystery
Of the intellectual life, the great obsession
With language and the point of consciousness.

Or even as we know
Schweitzer and Cappelletti on the Cimbric language *
Of the last descendants of the old Lombobards;
Tibetan influences on Tocharian;
Glottalized Continuants in Navaho, Nootka, and Kwakiutl,
A doctrinal dissertation on the Takelma language;
Studies in the language of the Kharosthi documents
Written in a variety of Indian Prakrit
Used as the administrative language
Of Shan-Shan or Koraina in the third century A.D.;
A practical introduction to Ruq'ah script;
And Pirandello's treatise in German on the Sicilian dialect,
Laute und Lautentwicklung der Mundart von Girgenti.

And rejoicing in all those intranational differences which
Each like a flower's scent by its peculiarity sharpens
Appreciation of others as well as bringing
Appreciation of itself, as experiences of gardenia or zinnia
Refine our experience of rose or sweet pea.

Or even as, in the Shetland Islands where I lived,
I know, in the old Norn language, the various names
Applied to all the restless movements of the sea

* Tautsch (*Lehrbuch des Cimbrischen Dialekts von Giazza*) Bolzano, Ferrari—Auer
1945. *Die Herkunft der Zimbern (Jahrbuch für vergl. Volkskunde: Die Nachbarn,*
Band, 1) Göttingen: Vandenhoek and Rupprecht.

—*Di*, a wave; *Da mother di*, the undulations
That roll landward even in calm weather;
Soal, swell occasional by a breeze,
Trove, a short, cross, heavy sea,
Hak, broken water, *Burrik*, a sharp sea or "tide lump,"
Bod, a heavy wave breaking on the shore,
Brim, sound of sea breaking on the shore,
Especially when land could not be seen, as in a fog,
Brimfooster, sea breaking on a sunken rock or *baa*,
Faxin, a *baa* threatening to break,
Overskud or *votrug*, broken or spent water or backwash,
Gruttik, ebb-tide, *Grinister*, ebb during spring tide,
Draag, the drift of a current,
Sokin or *Saagin*, short period of still water between tides,
Snaar, a turn or whirl in a current,
Roost, a rapid flowing current,
And the several names applied to the sea bottom
Flör, maar, jube, graef and *ljoag*

Or like the differences between the writers
Of one province and those of another in Italy
—The Venetians, as Raffaello Barbiera has pointed out,
Have an expansive and brilliant note; the Lombards
Are more prone to reflection and to brooding
Over the eternal tears of mankind; the Piedmontese
Have been noted for their fervour of patriotic and liberal
    enthusiasm,
The Neapolitans, again, burn with the fire of extemporisation
And sing of their flaming mountain and of their sunlit seas . . .

We commend two passages—as clues to possible method.
The first is this from Mallarmé:
"To evoke in a deliberate shadow the unmentioned object
By allusive words, never direct words,
Which may be reduced to an equal silence.
That means an attempt very near creation."

The other is from a book on Buddhism:
"It would be possible to write a learned book
On Buddhism which should recite

The various facts with scholarly exactness
Yet leave the reader at the end
Wondering how intelligent and spiritual men and women
Of our day could really be Buddhists.
One must seek to avoid this effect
And try to enable the reader to understand
A little *how it feels to be a Buddhist*.
To give the feelings of an alien religion
It is necessary to do more than expound
Its concepts and describe its history.
One must catch its emotional undertone,
Enter one's way into its symbols, its cult, its art,
And then seek to impart these not merely
By scientific exposition
But in all sorts of indirect ways."
The way is the way of Rozanov's *Solitaria*
Or Kierkegaard's dialogues of "indirect impartation."
There is urgent need for a new humanism.
(And to that end we must have a language
As personal as Chinese calligraphy
—When a Chinese calligrapher "copies"
The work of an old master it is not
A forged facsimile but an interpretation
As personal within stylistic limits
As a Samuel or Landowska performance
Of a Bach partita
—A language in which it is easy to see
The bibulous genius of the inspired monk, Huai Si,
The cultured and carefree personality
With the tastes of an antiquarian of President Yu,
The rather effeminate grace of Chao,
The obstinate resolution of Huang, the rare energy,
The consummate control, of Wang Shi-Chih,
The ostentatious vulgarity of the Emperor Chien Lung,
And, in the plump and chirpy strokes of Su Tung-po,
The loose flesh and easy manner of a fat person.)
The real humanity of the humane is departing from the world.
I am troubled by the tendency in science to-day
For the law to be derived from limited groups of observations
Rather than from the wide generalisations of understanding.

And I am haunted by the masses
In our great industrial centres,
Greedy for productivity and neglecting fertility.
The fertility and potential abundance of life
Is a gift so strange to their minds that they feel in themselves
No responsibility towards it—they hold it something
That rises of itself, not an achievement
Which nothing but adequate effort can keep alive.

SILENCE

With Hölderlin's later and greatest poems,
Poetry leaves its articulate German tradition,
Achieving the miracle of speechlessness
Bursting into speech.
If Goethe had the gift of his Tasso
To say what he suffered
And say it at a level of realisation
Where others would be silenced by agony,
Then Hölderlin sought,
And often miraculously found,
The word with which silence speaks
Its own silence without breaking it.

(Silence supervening at poetry's height,
Like the haemolytic streptococcus
In the sore throat preceding rheumatic fever
But which, at the height of the sickness,
Is no longer there, but has been and gone!
Or as "laughter is the representative of tragedy
When tragedy is away.")

Short of miracles surpassing that miracle
From Hölderlin's poetry the way leads
Either to silence itself or to poetic mischief,
The verbose stammer of those who have never learned
To speak or to be silent,

Or the professional ecstasies of souls
That, only because they are uninhabitable,
Are constantly beside themselves.

So beyond all that is heteroepic, holophrastic,
Macaronic, philomathic, psychopetal,
Jerqueing every idioticon,
Comes this supreme paraleipsis,
Full of potential song as a humming bird
Is full of potential motion,
When, as we race along with kingfisher brilliance,
Seeking always for that which "being known,
Everything else becomes known,"
That which we can only know
By allowing it to know itself in us,
Since "determinatio est negatio,"
Suddenly "chaos falls silent in the dazzled abyss."
Ciò che lo mio intelletto non comprende
"Thin, thin the pleasant human noises grow
And faint the city gleams."
(O poet, hold thy peace and be content!)
Like the amount of material never heard at all
In the six *dumky* of Dvorak's Opus 90,
Possibly a third of the music never heard at all
Yet the *Trio* is one of his most remarkable works
Though I doubt if any performance
Can realise all that's implicit in the score.
Or like Monsieur Teste who "dies without confessing,"
Or Olivier Messiaen's *Antienne du silence*
(*Pour le jour des Anges gardiens*)
Or the blanks and spaces in Mallarmé's *Coup de Dés*
Showing the retractions, prolongations, flights of the thought,
"L'attente, le doute, la concentration étaient choses visibles
Ma vue avait affaire à des silences
Qui auraient pris corps,"
Or like Hindemith questioning the importance
Or even the relevance, to music, of sound itself.
Sound shrinks to nothingness and musical composition
Becomes an abstract philosophical activity,
So we become intolerant of lesser music,

Idle tinkling, uncontrolled and unskilled composition,
And our minds are opened to music
Using symbols that are yet unknown to us,
Wrapped in strange sounds we must first learn to decipher.
Even so, Conscience calls the self of *Dasein*
Out of the state in which it is lost
In the "one like many." The caller
Is unfamiliar to "oneself" in its everydayness
And speaks in the uncanny mode of silence
To call the self back into the silence
Of the "existent" potentiality of being.

IN MEMORIAM DYLAN THOMAS

I rejoiced when from Wales once again
Came the ffff-putt of a triple-feathered arrow
Which looked as if it had never moved.*

But now the bowman has fitted one more nock
To his string, and discharged the arrow straight up into the air
Partly as a gesture of farewell, partly of triumph,
And beautiful!—I watched the arrow go up.
The sun was already westing towards evening
So, as the arrow topped the trees
And climbed into sunlight,
It began to burn against the evening like the sun itself.
Up and up it went, not weaving as it would have done
With a snatching loose, but soaring, swimming,
Aspiring towards heaven, steady, golden and superb.

Just as it had spent its force,
Just as its ambition had been dimmed by destiny
And it was preparing to faint, to turn over,
To pour back into the bosom of its mother earth,
A terrible portent happened.

* With acknowledgments to T. H. White, *The Sword in the Stone*. The reference
here is to the author's friend, Dylan Thomas.

A gore crow came flapping wearily
Before the approaching night.
It came, it did not waver, it took the arrow,
It flew away, heavy and hoisting,
With the arrow in its beak. I was furious.
I had loved the arrow's movement,
Its burning ambition in the sunlight,
And it was such a splendid arrow,
Perfectly-balanced, sharp, tight-feathered,
Clean-nocked, and neither warped nor scraped.

I was furious but I was frightened.
It is a very old and recurring portent in our history.
We remember the story of Valerius Corvus
(Ah, would my bowman had been saved like Valerius
By a crow which hid him from the foe with its wings!)
And the famous episode in the great Irish epic of Ulster,
The *Táin Bó Chuailgné,*
In which the goddess Morrigu attacks Cuchulainn,
Who scorned her love,
In the form of a crow.
(A like episode is depicted on one of the decorated faces
Of an Etruscan alabaster vase in the Florence Museum,
Among scenes of the Trojan War).
The crow is not a mere flight of fancy.
It is the creature which stands for battle
And the gods and goddesses of war.

But the crow cannot quench the light
With its outstretched wings forever
Nor break the law of gravity
Nor swallow the arrow.
We shall get it back. Never fear!
And how I shall rejoice when the War is over
And there comes from Wales once again
The fff-putt of a triple-feathered arrow
Which looks as if it had never moved!

WE MUST LOOK AT THE HAREBELL

We must look at the harebell as if
We had never seen it before.
Remembrance gives an accumulation of satisfaction
Yet the desire for change is very strong in us
And change is in itself a recreation.
To those who take any pleasure
In flowers, plants, birds, and the rest
An ecological change is recreative.
(Come. Climb with me. Even the sheep are different
And of new importance.
The coarse-fleeced, hardy Herdwick,
The Hampshire Down, artificially fed almost from birth,
And butcher-fat from the day it is weaned,
The Lincoln-Longwool, the biggest breed in England,
With the longest fleece, and the Southdown
Almost the smallest—and between them thirty other breeds,
Some whitefaced, some black,
Some with horns and some without,
Some long-wooled, some short-wooled,
In England where the men, and women too,
Are almost as interesting as the sheep.)
Everything is different, everything changes,
Except for the white bedstraw which climbs all the way
Up from the valleys to the tops of the high passes
The flowers are all different and more precious
Demanding more search and particularity of vision.
Look! Here and there a pinguicula eloquent of the Alps
Still keeps a purple-blue flower
On the top of its straight and slender stem.
Bog-asphodel, deep-gold, and comely in form,
The queer, almost diabolical, sundew,
And when you leave the bog for the stag moors and the rocks
The parsley fern—a lovelier plant
Than even the proud Osmunda Regalis—
Flourishes in abundance
Showing off oddly contrasted fronds
From the cracks of the lichened stones.

It is pleasant to find the books
Describing it as "very local."
Here is a change indeed!
The universal *is* the particular.

PLAITED LIKE THE GENERATIONS OF MEN

Come, follow me into the realm of music. Here is the gate
Which separates the earthly from the eternal.
It is not like stepping into a strange country
As we once did. We soon learn to know everything there
And nothing surprises us any more. Here
Our wonderment will have no end, and yet
From the very beginning we feel at home.

At first you hear nothing, because everything sounds.
But now you begin to distinguish between them. Listen.
Each star has its rhythm and each world its beat.
The heart of each separate living thing
Beats differently, according to its needs,
And all the beats are in harmony.

Your inner ear grows sharper. Do you hear
The deep notes and the high notes?
They are immeasurable in space and infinite as to number.
Like ribbons, undreamt-of scales lead from one world to another,
Steadfast and eternally moved.
(More wonderful than those miraculous isles of Greece
"Lily on lily, that o'erlace the sea,"
Than the marvellous detailed intensity of Chinese life,
Than such a glimpse as once delighted me of the masterly and ex-
        haustive
Classification of psychical penetrations and enlacements
On which von Hartmann relied, giving here some slight dissection
Of the antinomies underlying ethical thought, discussing there the
        gradations

Of the virtues, the stratifications of axiology, with an elaborate power
And beauty—but there!—Oh, Aodhagán O Rahaille meets again
The Brightness of Brightness in a lonely glen
And sees the hair that's plaited
Like the generations of men!).

From

The Battle Continues

1957

THE SPANISH WAR

Ah, Spain, already your tragic landscapes
And the agony of your War to my mind appear
As tears may come into the eyes of a woman very slowly,
So slowly as to leave them CLEAR!

Spain! The International Brigade! At the moment it seems
As though the pressure of a loving hand had gone,
(Till the next proletarian upsurge!)
The touch under which my close-pressed fingers seemed to thrill,
And the skin to divide up into little zones
Of heat and cold whose position continually changed,
So that the whole of my hand, held in that clasp,
Was in a state of internal movement.
My eyes that were full of pride,
My hands that were full of love,
Are empty again . . . for a while.
                    For a little while!

From
Impavidi Progrediamur *

BRITISH LEFTISH POETRY, 1930–40

Auden, MacNeice, Day Lewis, I have read them all,
Hoping against hope to hear the authentic call.
"A tragical disappointment. There was I
Hoping to hear old Aeschylus, when the Herald
Called out, 'Theognis, bring your chorus forward.'
Imagine what my feelings must have been!
But then Dexitheus pleased me coming forward
And singing his Bœotian melody:
But next came Chaeris with his music truly
That turned me sick and killed me very nearly.
And never in my lifetime, man nor boy,
Was I so vexed as at the present moment;
To see the Pynx, at this time of the morning,
Quite empty, when the Assembly should be full" †
And know the explanation I must pass is this
—You cannot light a match on a crumbling wall.

VERSES WRITTEN DURING THE SECOND WORLD WAR

At last! Now is the time with due intensity
To hew to what really matters—not
"Making the world safe for democracy,"
"Saving civilisation," or any such rot.

* Not yet published. One of the four volumes of the huge poem of which "In Memoriam James Joyce" (1955) was the first.
† Aristophanes, *The Acharnians*.

[418]

But what there was about the Welsh handling, say
Of Arthur and Merlin (as good an example as may be got),
That conquered the imagination of Europe in a way
Conchobar and Cuchulainn did not.

Let it at least be said of us when we die:
"Of all the slogans to which mass-man clings
Only a Chinese could have thought more lightly than they
—They had so much love for real things."

TO NEARLY EVERYBODY IN EUROPE
TO-DAY

A war to save civilisation, you say?
Then what have *you* to do with it, pray?
Some attempt to acquire it would show truer love
Than fighting for something you know nothing of.

HAPPY ON HEIMAEY

Meanwhile the last of the human faculties
To be touched by the finger of science,
Still unanalysed, still immeasurable,
The sense of smell is the one little refuge
In the human mind still inviolate and unshareable
Because communicable in no known language.
But someday this the most delicate of perceptions
Will be laid bare too—there will be
Chairs of osmology in our universities,
Ardent investigators searching out, recording, measuring,
Preserving in card indexes
The departing smells of the countryside,
Hayfields will be explained in terms of Coumarin,

Beanfields in Ionome, hedge-roses in Phenyl-Ethyl-Propionate,
Hawthorn as Di-Methyl-Hydroquinone.
(But will they ever capture the scent of violets
Among the smoke of the shoeing forge, or explain
The clean smell of a road wet with summer-rain?)
Until that day on Heimaey, 400 miles due North-West
Of Rona in the Hebrides, I am content to walk out
Into an unreal country of yellow fields
Lying at the foot of black volcanic cliffs
In the shadow of dead Helgafell,
And watch a few farmers scything
(Careful of the little birds' nests,
Iceland wheatear, snow bunting, white wagtail, meadow pipit,
And leaving clumps of grass to protect them)
A sweet but slender hay-crop
And tell its various constituents for myself
. . . White clover, chickenweed, dandelion,
A very large buttercup, silverweed, horsetail
Thrift, sorrel, yellow bedstraw,
Poa, carex, and rushes . . .
Or look out of my bedroom window
In the farmhouse near Kaupstadur
On a garden planted with angelica,
Red currant, rhubarb, and the flower of Venus,
Or at midnight watch the sun
Roll slowly along the northern horizon
To dip behind the great ice-caps
And jokulls of distant Iceland.
"Mellach lem bhith ind acht ailiuin for beind cairrge
Conacind and ar a mheinci feth na fairrci."
Ah, me! It is a far better thing to be sitting
Alive, on Heimaey, bare as an egg though it were,
Than rolled round willy-nilly with yonder sun.

FROM "ONCE IN A CORNISH GARDEN"

"A spray of red rose berries flung against the blue Cornish sky—
what more does man want here below?"
STEPHEN MACKENNA

> *"Even as St. John could not depict*
> *The glories of the New Jerusalem without*
> *Recourse to gold and precious stones, so we*
> *Our spirits' perfect state in terms*
> *Of Cornish geology."*

"Il y a deux sortes d'élaborations géologiques: L'une qui est un
procès de désintégration: le granit, par exemple, qui devient argile.
L'autre—et c'est comme le philosophe qui, par le brassage d'une mul-
titude de faits, arrive à un concept, au joyau abstrait d'une définition
irréprochable—est une espèce de création ou de parturition, quelque
chose à quoi aboutir qui échappe à la décomposition par la sim-
plicité. Les entrailles de la nature en travail ont enfanté ce bezoard.
Il a fallu la presse cosmique, l'action qui est passion d'un monde en
révolte contre sa propre inertie, l'épreinte tellurique, le vomissement
du feu intérieur, ce qui de plus central est capable de jaillir sous une
main inexorable, l'écrasement millénaire de ses conches qui se com-
prénètrent, tout le mystère, toute l'usine métamorphique, pour
aboutir à ce brillant, à ce cristal sacré, à cette noix parfaite et trans-
lucide qui échappe à la pourriture du brou. Parfaite, pas encore!
Il faut que la main de l'homme s'ajoute à ce caillou que l'invite. Il
faut qu'un lent polissage vienne dissiper l'obscurité inhérente, effacer
la rugosité adventice, accentuer le clivage, éliminer le défaut, éveiller
l'œil secret, compléter la rose ébauchée. Il faut que la facette mul-
tiplie le prisme. Il faut user le refus. Il faut que naisse ce prodige
minéral qui est un nombre solide; il faut qu'apparaisse enfin sous
la main de l'ouvrier ce soleil miniscule qui doit ses rayons à la géo-
métrie. (Ainsi cette pierre merveilleuse dont parle Buffon, et que
j'aime autant ne pas identifier, et qu'il appelle le girasol.) Non plus
un miroir seulement, mais un foyer."
PAUL CLAUDEL, *La Mystique des Pierres Précieuses*

There is no outline of the landscape here.
No element in the objective world,
You have not vitalised for me,

(*Sprys kernow,** be with me now!)
At every turn establishing some original confrontation
Of Cornwall and myself as pure and as immediate
As on Creation's Day.
(And how you suit your setting at every point!
Cornwall incarnate, costumed by Aage Thaarup,
With your little nigger felt cap, its forward poke
Accentuated by fringed grosgrain ribbon;
Dress and coat in the new Persian brown,
The coat generously trimmed with lamb to tone,
And with large antique bronze buttons
To finish the draped neckline of the dress.
Or, at night, in "Nitchevo," the little Ardanse black crêpe dress,
Its intricate and unusual cut blazoned by
A waist-coat bodice of white and gold lamé.
These are your colours—sultan-red, rich gold, gold brown,
Black, scarlet, nut-brown and sunrise pink,
Copper glance, purple, peach, and cream,
Cherry, geranium, coral flame, and blush,
Wheatgold, sun-orange, and harlequin red,
Just as the right cosmetic chart for your type is this—
Carmine rouge, used high on the cheeks and skilfully shaded;
Brown eye-shadow; black eyelash make-up;
Black eyebrow pencil very carefully applied
Not to give a harsh line.
A rachelle powder, dusted lightly over
To soften the whole make-up; carmine lip-stick,
And a rachelle make-up blender for your arms and neck;
And for the evening under artificial lights
You'll change your powder to the flesh colour
And your eye-shadow to a glorious violet
And use a vermilion lip-stick.
Even as in our garden all the flowers have
Colours like these and look
Like isolated moods of yours, particular memories of you,
Gestures and smiles of yours that have somehow taken root
And flourish here for ever
Oh, all the colour in this golden moment
Seems to flow from you!

* Cornish Gaelic, meaning "Spirit of Cornwall."

[422]

—The brilliant red supergiant El Monte asters,
Double petunias in fringed, ruffled, and laciniate forms,
Rose of Heaven and Little Star petunias,
And, among the roses, the flaming yellow
And copper-toned Feu Pernet-Ducher, the coral-petaled
Carrie Jacobs Bond, the orange-overcast
Carillon, and the brilliant deep-red Dickson's Centennial.
Then the sweet-scented Golden Gleam nasturtiums,
The great clusters of glorious fiery red Russian lilies,
—Like the reflection of my own heart's blood—
And the rainbow show of giant Zinnias
Burnt orange, deep salmon, rose and purple
(And these be your words, beloved,
In so far as earth-speech may avail,
That sight or sound of you always
May conjure up without fail—
Coinnealta, solasta, croidhearg, cunbalach,
Eireachdail, taiceil, gloir-ghlaasta, fionfhuil, gniomh-luaineach.*
And for the phrase that matches you best
"The mile-great sheaf-like blast of purple-glowing and red flames,"
Or Meredith's "her pomp of glorious hues, her revelry of ripeness,
    her kind smile").

SCOTLAND SMALL?

Scotland small? Our multiform, our infinite Scotland *small?*
Only as a patch of hillside may be a cliché corner
To a fool who cries "Nothing but heather!" Where in September
    another
Sitting there and resting and gazing round
Sees not only heather but blaeberries
With bright green leaves and leaves already turned scarlet,
Hiding ripe blue berries; and amongst the sage-green leaves
Of the bog-myrtle the golden flowers of the tormentil shining;
And on the small bare places, where the little Blackface sheep

* These Scottish Gaelic words mean: bright, brilliant, blood-red, constant, handsome, staunch, of tuneful speech, of deft deed, and "wine-blood" (i.e., noble).

Found grazing, milkworts blue as summer skies;
And down in neglected peat-hags, not worked
In living memory, sphagnum moss in pastel shades
Of yellow, green, and pink; sundew and butterwort
And nodding harebells vying in their colour
With the blue butterflies that poise themselves delicately upon them,
And stunted rowans with harsh dry leaves of glorious colour
"Nothing but heather!" —How marvellously descriptive! And in-
complete!

ESPLUMEOIR

"He's chain lightning. Brains count in this business."

*"It was an amazing discovery, like the inside of your head being
painlessly scraped out. There was an amazing clarity, like the brilliant moon falling into it and fitting it neatly."*

But shairly, shairly, there maun be
Or sae, of course, it seems to you—
Some instinct o' black waters swirlin'
And dangerous images juist oot o' view
Ettlin' to spoil happiness and pu' apairt
Dreams that ha'e become realities?

I tell you, No! There's naething—naething o' the kind.
Nae ootward things, shapes, colours, soonds, or memories o' these
To strike in on and move and muddle the mind;
Nae *sombra do tempo* cast
By comin' events or present or past,
And least o' a' ony *Scheinprobleme* here!
I ken fu' weel for a man like you
To think o' this maun be as when
On the wa' abune your heid
Shiftin' prisms o' licht frae the water
May dance a fandango
Unutterably free and airy

In a squalid wee ship's-cabin
While you couldna hit the wa'
If you were locked in a wardrobe, you fool.
But as for me I canna mind a time
When the mere thocht o't didna mak' me
Licht up like a match!

"Aloof as a politician
The first year efter election"
You grumble, "There's naething to see.
It's a' expressionless as tho' it micht be
Enamelled wi' an airbrush that tawnish grey
Nae-colour sae common on motors—wasn't only yesterday?—
Yet bricht as when the stars were glowin'
Wi' sic a steady radiance that the lift
Seemed filled to overflowin'—I wadna hae't in a gift.
It mak's me feel upon my word
Like a fly on the edge o' a phonograph record."
(A phrase divertin'ly *vergeistigt* here)

The Leisure State! Fell dreich, you think? Intelligence is character-
    ised
By a natural lack o' comprehension o' life
But here intelligence is a', and a'thing devised
To favour "life" and its expense excised,
Naething left in human nature cybernetics
Can ever delegate to electronic tricks;
Tint, clean tint, as gin it had never been
A' that could be touched or tasted, heard or seen.
We' nae mair expression that a china settin' egg.

The utter stillness o' the timeless world!
The haill creation has vanished forever
Wi' nae mair noise or disturbance than a movie fade-out,
The expression o' blankness which sae often
Distinguishes the profound thinker.

Naething to see—you sudna ha'e far to gang
For an analogy frae your Earth experience thl',
Sin' at winter's edge when a'thing's gone sere

[425]

Emptied o' a' Simmer's routh and bare as a bane gey near
Bacteriologists say the soil's teemin' mair thrang
Wi' life than at ony ither time, yet wi' nocht to show.
Like cricket's deceptive impression o' slowness
Tho' the split-second decisions sae often required
Ha'e to be made quicker than in ony ither game;
Or like the sleepy een o' a great detective
Wha misses nocht and canna be fooled
But's aye maist, when he looks least, alert.
Or as a day that was gaen to be
Oppressively het wi' thunder later
Used to stimulate a'thing to live
Brimmin'ly afore the cataclysm
Till a'thing that ran or flew or crawled
Abune or aneth was filled pang-fu' wi' life
Like yon cicada shrillin' piercin'ly
Try'in to stert up the haill chorus.
He'd been underground an 'oor ago
And micht be doon a bird's throat by nicht.
That he was alive richt then was reason eneuch
For singin' wi' a' his micht.
Eternity's like that—a'thing keyed up
To the heichest pitch as if
A cataclysm's comin'—only it's no!

Eternity is like an auld green parrot
I kent aince. Its conversational range was sma'
Yet when it tilted its heid and cocked
A beady eye at you, you got the feelin'
That, if it chose, it could tell you a thing or twa;
That, as the French pit it,
Il connût le dessous des cartes.
Eternity is like an obstinate jellyfish
That comes floatin' back as soon as you've scared it off
But, if you try to seize it, reverses its tactics
And jouks awa' like a muckle dawd o' quicksilver.

Or pit it like this—Eternity's
Twa doors frae the corner a'whaur
A sma', demure white biggin'

Wi' shutters and a canopy.
The canopy's royal blue
And it says *Eternity*
In discreet soap-glass letters
On ilka-side. Under the canopy
You walk up and the front door
Is a' mirror wi' a cool strip
O' fluorescent light on top.
You push the pearl button,
And listen to the delicate chimes
And adjust your tie in the mirror
And fix your hat—but the guy
Ahint the bullet-proof mirror
Sees a' that too,
Only you canna see him.
The guy ahint the mirror
Is Tutti-Frutti Forgle,
A muckle nigger wi' fuzzy-white hair
Wha kens his business.
Aince past Tutti, you check your hat
In a quiet soft-lit anteroom,
Syne the haill place is yours.

Sae cool and sculptured in its lack o' detail,
Its quiet reserve, its expensive simplicity,
Sae couthily different frae earth's nerve-frayin' emotionalism,
Coolness, stillness, nae silly vivacity,
Nae spillin' owre and showin' feelin's here,
Like a wumman wha's daurk hair disna reflect the licht.
Tho' her grey een reflect far mair than their share o't.
Yon cauld snake. Yon *nymphoea tuberosa!*
Water-lillies hae sic a strong urge to live
They can get unco teuch wi' obstacles in their way.

Aye, dreich eneuch, at first sicht—I ken fu' weel
Hoo efter pursuin' his quarry furiously
Mony's the keen hunter feels his spirit unaccoontably
Sag when at last it's wi'in easy reach;
Staleness clamps on him syne like a muckle leech.
Staleness? —the Deil!

Juist as intense desire whiles mak's a man
Impotent at the richt (or wrang) minute!

That's why a poet like Valéry tried
Frae his poetry to haud a' "life" ootside
"You're deid. You've nae mair to day wi' the warld again."
Its's neist to impossible for onybody to be
Circumcised frae the warld like this,
Hyne away frae its pleasures, sorrows, comforts—free
O' the haill damned thing as a corpse is.
Of course you canna understand, canna grasp the connection
For *this,* you fool, *this* is to ken the resurrection!

BAGPIPE MUSIC

Let me play to you tunes without measure or end,
Tunes that are born to die without a herald,
As a flight of storks rises from a marsh, circles,
And alights on the spot from which it rose.

Flowers. A flower-bed like hearing the bagpipes.
The fine black earth has clotted into sharp masses
As if the frost and not the sun had come.
It holds many lines of flowers.
First faint rose peonies, then peonies blushing,
Then again red peonies, and, behind them,
Massive, apoplectic peonies, some of which are so red
And so violent as to seem almost black; behind these
Stands a low hedge of larkspur, whose tender apologetic blossoms
Appear by contrast pale, though some, vivid as the sky above them,
Stand out from their fellows, iridescent and slaty as a pigeon's breast,
The bagpipes—they are screaming and they are sorrowful.
There is a wail in their merriment, and cruelty in their triumph.
They rise and they fall like a weight swung in the air at the end of a
    string.
They are like the red blood of those peonies.
And like the melancholy of those blue flowers.

[428]

They are like a human voice—no! for the human voice lies!
They are like human life that flows under the words.
That flower-bed is like the true life that wants to express itself
And does . . . while we human beings lie cramped and fearful.

TO A FRIEND AND FELLOW-POET

It is with the poet as with a guinea worm
Who, to accommodate her teeming progeny
Sacrifices nearly every organ of her body, and becomes
(Her vagina obliterated in her all-else-consuming
Process of uterine expansion, and she still faced
With a grave obstetrical dilemma calling for
Most marvellous contrivance to deposit her prodigious swarm
Where they may find the food they need and have a chance in life)
Almost wholly given over to her motherly task,
Little more than one long tube close-packed with young;
Until from the ruptured bulla, the little circular sore,
You see her dauntless head protrude, and presently, slowly,
A beautiful, delicate, and pellucid tube
Is projected from her mouth, tenses and suddenly spills
Her countless brood in response to a stimulus applied
Not directly to the worm herself, but the skin of her host
With whom she has no organised connection (and that stimulus
O Poets! but cold water!) . . . The worm's whole musculocutane-
    ous coat
Thus finally functions as a uterus, forcing the uterine tube
With its contents through her mouth. And when the prolapsed
    uterus ruptures
The protruded and now collapsed portion shrivels to a thread
(Alexander Blok's utter emptiness after creating a poem!)
The rapid drying of which effectually and firmly
Closes the wound for the time being . . . till, later, the stimulus
    being reapplied,
A fresh portion of the uterine tube protrudes, ruptures, and col-
    lapses,
Once more ejaculating another seething mass of embryos,

[429]

And so the process continues until inch by inch
The entire uterus is expelled and parturition concluded.
Is it not precisely thus we poets deliver our store,
Our whole being the instrument of our suicidal art,
And by the skin of our teeth "flype" * ourselves into fame?

GLASGOW 1960

Returning to Glasgow after long exile
Nothing seemed to me to have changed its style.
Buses and trams all labelled "To Ibrox"
Swung past packed tight as they'd hold with folks.
Football match, I concluded, but just to make sure
I asked; and the man looked at me fell dour,
Then said, "Where in God's name are *you* frae, sir?
It'll be a record gate, but the cause o' the stir
Is a debate on 'la loi de l'effort converti'
Between Professor MacFadyen and a Spainish pairty."
I gasped. The newsboys came running along,
"Special! Turkish Poet's Abstruse New Song.
Scottish Authors' Opinions"—and, holy snakes,
I saw the edition sell like hot cakes.

REFLECTIONS IN A SLUM

A lot of the old folk here—all that's left
Of them after a lifetime's infernal thrall
Remind me of a Bolshie the "whites" buried alive
Up to his nose, just able to breathe, that's all.

Watch them. You'll see what I mean. When found
His eyes had lost their former gay twinkle.
Ants had eaten *that* away; but there was still
Some life in him . . . his forehead *would* wrinkle!

* *Flype* (Scots)—turn inside out.

And I remember Gide telling
Of Valéry and himself:
"It was a long time ago. We were young.
We had mingled with idlers
Who formed a circle
Round a troupe of wretched mountebanks.
It was on a raised strip of pavement
In the boulevard Saint Germain,
In front of the Statue of Broca.
They were admiring a poor woman,
Thin and gaunt, in pink tights, despite the cold.
Her team-mate had tied her, trussed her up,
Skilfully from head to foot,
With a rope that went round her
I don't know how many times,
And from which, by a sort of wriggling,
She was to manage to free herself.
Sorry image of the fate of the masses!
But no one thought of the symbol.
The audience merely contemplated
In stupid bliss the patient's efforts.
She twisted, she writhed, slowly freed one arm,
Then the other, and when at last
The final cord fell from her
Valéry took me by the arm:
"Let's go now! She has ceased suffering!"

Oh, if only ceasing to suffer
They were able to become men.
Alas! how many owe their dignity,
Their claim on our sympathy,
Merely to their misfortune.
Likewise, so long as a plant has not blossomed
One can hope that its flowering will be beautiful.
What a mirage surrounds what has not yet blossomed!
What a disappointment when one can no longer
Blame the abjection on the deficiency!
It is good that the voice of the indigent,
Too long stifled, should manage
To make itself heard.

But I cannot consent to listen
To nothing but that voice.
Man does not cease to interest me
When he ceases to be miserable.
Quite the contrary!
That it is important to aid him
In the beginning goes without saying,
Like a plant it is essential
To water at first,
But this is in order to get it to flower
And I *am concerned with the blossom.*

OF MY FIRST LOVE

O my first love! You are in my life forever
Like the *Eas-Coul-aulin* * in Sutherlandshire
Where the Amhainnan Loch Bhig burn
Plunges over the desolate slopes of Leitir Dubh.
Silhouetted against grim black rocks
This foaming mountain torrent
With its source in desolate tarns
Is savage in the extreme
As its waters with one wild leap
Hurl over the dizzy brink
Of the perpendicular cliff-face
In that great den of nature,
To be churned into spray
In the steaming depths below.
Near its base the fall splits up
Into cascades spreading out like a fan.
A legend tells how a beautiful maiden
In desperation threw herself
Over the cataract—the waters
Immediately took on the shape
Of her waving hair,
And on moonlight nights she is still to be seen
Lying near the base of the fall,
Gazing up at the tremendous cascade
Of some six hundred feet!
O my first love! Even so you lie
Near the base of my precipitous, ever lonelier and colder life
With your fair hair still rippling out

* Name of waterfall, meaning, in Gaelic, tresses of hair.

As I remember it between my fingers
When you let me unloosen first
(Over thirty chaotic years ago!)
That golden tumult forever!

LISTENING TO A SKYLARK

Are you, bricht sangbird, o' the earth or sun?
Or baith? and tell me, gin the last, O! can
A like sublime duality—in life,
No' daith!—no whiles be won to by a man?

For when, as noo, you soar in silence 'gainst the clear
Plate o' the midday sun I only ken
You're there gin you ootshine its licht
Wi' some quick move, syne melt into't again.

Yet when your gowden sang comes glitterin' doon
I ken at aince that oor puir human clay
Can whiles, unlike a' ither mortal life but yours,
Tak' fire and soar and sing divinely tae.

Even as, O bird! your fedderome can tak' on
The *haill* sun's licht, shine ane wi't, or ootshine,
Oor lourd flesh, God, has poo'ers to mak' oors tae
Maist o' the glory that else 'ud still be nocht but Thine.

CORONACH FOR THE END OF THE WORLD

Mony a piper has played himsel
   Through battle and into daith,
And a piper'll rise to the occasion still
   Whan the warld is brakin' faith!

A trumpet may sound or harps be heard
   Or celestial voices sweet,
But wi nocht but the cry o the pipes can Earth
   Or these . . . or silence . . . meet.

The pipes are the only instrument
   To soond Earth's mortal hour;
But to greet what follows, if onything does,
   Is no in even *their* power.

BONNIE BIRDIE A' AFLOCHT

Bonnie birdie a' aflocht!
What's in me to gar ye dreid
Till affward frae the earth it seems
Your wings athwart the sun maun spreid.

Aswaip the lift ye drop again
To tak anither keek at me.
Or was't the sun I dinna fleg
That smilingly encouraged ye?

I wad that like the sun and you
I had aa Space for awmous tae,
And wore it wi a gallant cant
In sic a bricht astalit way.

Adist, ayont, you come and gang
Inerrand in abandon.
Men say that God's awhaur at aince.
Then you're his imitation!

Ah, no! blithe bird, man's thocht is that,
Invisible as God himsel!
Wad else 'twere mair like you or him
—Or baith, you aefauld miracle!

THE AERIAL CITY

From the Russian of Afanasy Shensin-Foeth

At the peep o day in the lift forgether
    Bonnie cloods like a steepled toun,
Wi mony a dome like a bubble o gowd
    And white roofs and white waas blinterin doun.

O yon is my ain white city—
    Or I cam to the earth I bade there!
Abune the derk warld quhile it sleeps
    In the reid lift skinklan fair.

But it hauds awa to the North,
    Sails saftly, saftly, and high—
And a voice is fain that I'd join it—
    But gies me nae wings to try.

CRYSTALS LIKE BLOOD

I remember how, long ago, I found
Crystals like blood in a broken stone.

I picked up a broken chunk of bed-rock
And turned it this way and that,
It was heavier than one would have expected
From its size. One face was caked
With brown limestone. But the rest
Was a hard greenish-grey quartz-like stone
Faintly dappled with darker shadows,
And in this quartz ran veins and beads
Of bright magenta.

And I remember how later on I saw
How mercury is extracted from cinnabar
—The double ring of iron piledrivers
Like the multiple legs of a fantastically symmetrical spider
Rising and falling with monotonous precision,
Marching round in an endless circle
And pounding up and down with a tireless, thunderous force,
While, beyond, another conveyor drew the crumbled ore
From the bottom and raised it to an opening high
In the side of a gigantic grey-white kiln.

So I remember how mercury is got
When I contrast my living memory of you
And your dear body rotting here in the clay
—And feel once again released in me
The bright torrents of felicity, naturalness, and faith
My treadmill memory draws from you yet.

From

The Golden Treasury of Scottish Poetry

1940

BIRLINN CHLANN-RAGHNAILL *

The Birlinn of Clanranald

Being a ship-blessing, together with a sea-incitement
made for the crew of the Birlinn of the Lord of
Clanranald

God bless the craft of Clanranald
When brangled first with the brine,
Himself and his heroes hurling;
The pick of the human line!

The blessing of holy Triune
On the fury of the air;
The sea's ruggedness smoothed away
Ease us to our haven there!

Father who fashioned the ocean
And winds that from all points roll,
Bless our lean ship and her heroes,
Keep her and her whole crew whole!

Your grace, O Son, on our anchor,
Our rudder, sails, and all graith
And tackle to her masts attached,
And guard us as we have faith!

Bless our mast-hoops and our sail-yards
And our masts and all our ropes,

* Translated from the Gaelic of Alexander MacDonald, 1700?–1780?.

Preserve our stays and our halyards,
And confirm us in our hopes!

Holy Ghost, be you our helmsman
To steer the course that is right.
You know every port under Heaven.
We cast ourselves on your sleight!

The Blessing of the Arms

God's blessing be on our claymores
And flexible grey toledos
And heavy coats of mail-harness
Through which no dull blade can bleed us.

Bless our shoulder-belts and gorgets
And our well-made bossy targes,
Bless each and all of our weapons,
And the man who with it charges.

Bless our gleaming bows of yew-wood
Good to bend in battle-melee,
And birchen arrows, not to splinter
In the surly badger's belly.

Bless every dirk, every pistol,
Every kilt of noble pleating,
Every martial apparatus
With us under this ship's sheeting.

Lack no knowledge then or mettle
To do brave deeds with hardihood
While still four planks of her remain
Or pair of overlaps holds good.

With her drowned boards yet for footstools
Or a thole-pin above water
Let ocean not numb your resource,
Your hearts inchoate horror shatter.

Keep up a herculean struggle.
If the sea detects no weakness,
Her pride at last will be overcome
And reward your prowess with meekness.

As your foe in a land battle
Seeing your strength is left untouched
Is more apt to weaken in onslaught
Than be in fiercer furies clutched,

So with the sea; if you maintain
Set resolve and dauntless spirits
She will at length, as God's ordained,
Humble herself to your merits.

Incitement for Rowing to Sailing-Place

To put the black well-fashioned yewship
   To the sailing-place
Thrust you out flexible oarbanks
   Dressed to sheer grace;
Oars smooth-shafted and shapely,
   Grateful for gripping,
Made for lusty resolute rowing,
   Palm-fast, foam-whipping;
Knocking sparks out of the water
   Towards Heaven
Like the fire-flush from a smithy
   Updriven,
Under the great measured onstrokes
   Of the oar-lunges
That confound the indrawn billows
   With their plunges,
While the shrewd blades of the white woods
   Go cleaving
The tops of the valleyed blue-hills
   Shaggily heaving.
O stretch you, pull you, and bend you
   Between the thole-pins,
Your knuckles snow with hard plying

The pinewood fins;
All the big muscular fellows
   Along her lying
With their hairy and sinewy
   Arms keep her flying,
Raising and lowering together
   With a single motion
Their evenly dressed poles of pinewood
   Mastering the ocean.

A Herculean planked on the fore-oar
   Roaring: "Up, on with her!"
Makes all the thick shoulder muscles
   Glide better together,
Thrusting the birlinn with snorting
   Through each chill sea-glen;
The hard curved prow through the tide-lumps
   Drives inveighing,
On all hands sending up mountains
   Round her insistence.
Hugan, the sea says, like Stentor;
   Heig, say the thole-pins.
Rasping now, on the timbers,
   Of the shirred surges!
The oars jib; blood-blistering
   Slowly emerges
On each hard hand of the rowers
   In berserk fettle
Hurling on the trembling oakplanks,
   Caulking, and metal,
Though nailheads spring with the thunder
   Thumping her thigh.
A crew to make a right rocking
   The deeps to defy,
Working the lean ship like an auger
   Through walls of water,
The bristling wrath of blue-black billows
   No daunting matter.
They are the choice set of fellows
   To hold an oarage

Outmanoeuvring the dark swirlings
    With skill and courage,
Without a point lost or tiring,
    Timely throughout,
Despite all the dire devilment
    Of the waterspout!

(Then after the sixteen men had sat at the oars to
row her against the wind to a sailing-place, Calum
Garbh, son of Ranald of the Seas, who was on the
fore-oar, recited an iorram (or rowing song) for her,
as follows:)

And now since you're selected
—No doubt true choice effected!—
Let rowing be directed
            Bold and set.

Give a rocking pointedly,
Without lapse or lack of netteté,
So all sea-problems set yet be
            More than met.

A well-gripped stubborn rocking
From bones and sinews yoking,
The steps from her oarbank knocking
            Foam to fire.

Incite each other along
And a good so-go-all song
From the fore man's mouth fall strong
            To inspire.

Oar's sawdust on the rowlocks,
Hands run with sores like golochs,
Waves' armpits like any mollusc
            Screw the oars.

Cheeks be lit all blazing red,
Palms of skin all casing shed,

While sweat off every face and head
            Thumping pours.

Stretch you, pull you, and bend you
The blades the pine-trees lend you,
Ascend, descend, and wend you
            Through the sea.

Banks of oars on either side
Set your labour to her tide
And spray on ocean's thorter-pride
            Throw freely.

Row as one, cleanly, clearly;
Through flesh-thick waves cut sheerly;
A job that's not done wearily
            Nor snail-wise.

Strike her evenly without fluther.
Often glance at one another
So in your thews still further
            Vim may rise.

Let her oak go skelping through
Big-bellied troughs of swingeing blue;
In their two thighs pounding too
            Each spasm down.

Though the hoary heaving ocean
Swell with even more commotion,
Toppling waves with drowning notion
            Roar and frown,

And incessant wash pour in
O'er her shoulders and the din
Groan all round and sob to win
            Through her keel,

Stretch you, pull you, and bend you.
The red-backed sleek shafts tend you.

[443]

With the pith strong arms lend you
    Victory feel.

Put that headland past your prow
Where you strain with sweat-drenched brow
And lift the sails upon her now
    From Uist of the sheldrakes!

> (Then they rowed to a sailing-place. They took in the sixteen oars which were swiftly pruned down against her thigh to avoid sheet-ropes. Clanranald ordered his gentlemen to see to the disposition in the places for which they were qualified of men who would not be daunted by any spectre from the deep nor any chaos in which the ocean might involve them. After the selection every man was ordered to take up his appointed place, and accordingly the steersman was summoned to sit at the rudder in these words:)

Set at the rudder a brawny
    Grand fellow,
Top nor trough of sea can unhorse,
    Coarse skelp nor bellow;
Broad-beamed, well-set, full of vigour
    Wary withal;
Who hearing the shaggy surges
    Come roaring
Her prow expertly to the rollers
    Keeps shoring;
Who will even keep her going
    As if unshaken,
Adjusting sheet and tack—glances
    Windward taken;
Yielding no thumb-long deviation
    Of her true course
Despite the bounding wave-summits'
    Opposing force;
Who will go windward so stoutly
    With her when needed,

Though nailhead nor rib in her oak
But shrieks—unheeded;
Whom no spectre sprung from the abyss
    Could shift or dismay,
Or grey sea to his ears upswoln
    E'er tear away
From his set place while yet alive
    Helm under armpit!
Under his charge whatever's been placed
    Nothing has harmed it.
A match for old ocean rough-glenned
    With inclemency!
Who no rope strains tackwindwarding
    But easily
Lets run and tacks under full canvas
    None so meetly
And her tacking on each wavetop
    Binds so featly,
Straight harbourwards under spray-showers
    Running so sweetly!

        (There was appointed a shrouds-man.)

Set another stalwart fellow
    For shrouds-grasping;
With finger-vices, great hand-span,
    For such clasping;
Sage, quick; to help with the yard's end
    When that's needed,
With masts and gear, leave no neighbour
    Task unheeded;
Wind-wise, and aptly adjusting
    With shrouds-manning
The sheet's-man's slackings—and t'assist
    In all ways scanning.

        (A sheet's-man was set apart.)

Set too on the thwart a sheet's-man
    With great arms ending

In horny compulsive fingers
   For the sheet-tending;
Pull in, let out, as is wanted,
   With strength of grabbing;
Draw in when beating to windward,
   The blast crabbing;
And release when the gust again
   Ceases rending.

     (There was ordered out a tacksman.)

Dispose another sturdy sailor,
   Masterfully
To keep the tack to her windward,
   And deal duly;
The tack to each cleat his changing
   Up and down bringing,
As a fair breeze may favour
   Or ill come swinging;
And if he sees tempest threaten
   Against the shock
Let him shear the tack without mercy
   Down to the stock.

     (There was ordered to the prow a pilot.)

A pilot in the prow be standing.
   Let him afford
Us ever reliable knowledge
   Of what's toward
And keep confirming the steersman
   In our right going,
For he is the veritable Pole Star
   We must have showing;
Suresightedly taking a landmark
   With the trained vision
That is the God of all weathers
   On such a mission.

     (There was set apart a halyard-man.)

Take place at the main halyard
   A clear-headed
Athletic fellow, with vigour
   And care wedded,
An able fellow without flurry,
   Grim and alert,
To take from her and give to her
   Just and expert,
To lie with hand of due power
   There on the halyard,
The weight of his grasp decisive
   Rive oakwoodward;
Not tie the halyard about the cleat
   Tight beyond use
But fix it firmly, cunningly,
   With running noose;
Thus over the pin squirting, humming,
   Now as it's roped,
Yet should perchance the prop be sundered
   It may be stopped!

     (There was set apart a teller-of-the-waters, since the
     sea was becoming too rough, and the steersman said
     to him:)

I'll have at my ear a teller
   Of the waters;
Let him keep close watch windward
   On these matters;
A man somewhat timid, cautious,
   Not altogether
A coward however!—Keeping
   Stock of the weather,
Whether in his fore or stern quarter
   The fair breeze is,
Blurting out without hesitation
   Aught he sees is
Peril-spelling to his notion;
   Or, should he spy
The likeness of a drowning sea

Roaring down, cry
To put our stem swiftly to it.
　　Insistently
Clamorous at the least threat of danger
　　This man must be,
And not fear to give the steersman
　　Any hint of hazard.
—But let him be the one teller
　　Of the waters heard,
And not the whole of you bawling
　　Advices mixed,
A distraught steersman not knowing
　　Who to heed next!

　　(There was ordered out a baler, since the sea was
　　rushing over them fore and aft:)

Let attend on the baling space
　　A hardy hero
Not to be cramped or benumbed
　　By cold at zero,
Raw brine or stinging hail dashing
　　In thrashing showers
Round his chest and neck,—but armoured
　　In dogged powers,
A thick round wooden baling-can
　　In his swarthy hands,
Throwing out the sea forever
　　As soon as it lands;
Never straightening his lithe backbone
　　Till his task's o'er,
Not one drop left in her bottom
　　—Or keelson-floor!
Were her planks holed till for a riddle
　　She well might pass
He'd keep her all dry as a bottle's
　　Outside glass!

　　(Two men were appointed for hauling the peak-
　　downhauls, since it appeared that the sails would be

torn from them by the exceeding boisterousness of
the weather:)

Put a pair of hefty fellows
  Thick-boned, strong-thewed,
To take charge of her peak-downhauls
  With force and aptitude;
With the power of great fore-arms
  In till of need
To haul them in or let them run,
  But always lead
When wayward back to the middle;
  For this two men
Of the Canna men, Donnchadh Mac Chomaig
  And Iain Mac Iain,
Were chosen—deft and definite fellows
  In brawn and brain.

  (Six men were chosen to man the ship's floor as a
  precaution against the failing of any of those mentioned, or lest the raging of the sea might pluck one
  overboard, one of these six might take his place:)

Let's have six men, quick and clever
  To give a hand,
Going through the ship in all directions,
  A nimble band,
Each like a hare on a mountain top
  And dogs copping him,
Dodging this way and that, and having
  Nothing stopping him;
Handy men, quick in the uptake,
  Spry and observant,
To fill any breach as needed
  Are who we want;
Men who can climb the hard smooth ropes
  Of the slender hemp
As in May trees of a thick-wood
  Only squirrels can attempt;

Gleg fellows, shrewd to take from her
  As desired
Or give respite meet and restful;
  Keen, untired.
Such the six the ship of MacDonald
  Has now acquired.

(Now that every convenience pertaining to sailing
had been put in good order and every brave depend-
able fellow had taken up the duty assigned to him,
they hoisted the sails about sunrise on St. Bride's Day,
beginning their course from the mouth of Loch Ain-
ort in South Uist.)

The Voyage

The sun bursting golden-yellow
  Out of his husk,
The sky grew wild and hot-breathing,
  Unsheathing a fell tusk,
Then turned wave-blue, thick, dun-bellied,
  Fierce and forbidding,
Every hue that would be in a plaid
  In it kneading;
A "dog's tooth" in the Western quarter
  Snorters prophesied;
The swift clouds under a shower-breeze
  Multiplied.
Now they hoisted the speckled sails
  Peaked and close-wrought,
And stretched out the stubborn shrouds
  Tough and taut
To the long resin-red shafts
  Of the mast.
With adroit and firm-drawn knotting
  These were made fast
Through the eyes of the hooks and rings;
  Swiftly and expertly
Each rope put right of the rigging;
  And orderly

The men took up their set stations
  And were ready.
Then opened the windows of the sky
  Pied, grey-blue,
To the lowering wind's blowing,
  A morose brew,
The sea pulled on his grim rugging
  Slashed with sore rents,
That rough-napped mantle, a weaving
  Of loathsome torrents.
The shape-ever-changing surges
  Swelled up in hills
And roared down into valleys
  In appalling spills.
The water yawned in great craters,
  Slavering mouths agape
Snatching and snarling at each other
  In rabid shape.
It were a man's deed to confront
  The demented scene,
Each mountain of them breaking
  Into flamy lumps.
Each fore-wave towering grey-fanged
  Mordantly grumps
While a routing comes from the back-waves
  With their raving rumps.
When we would rise on these rollers
  Soundly, compactly,
It was imperative to shorten sail
  Swiftly, exactly.
When we would fall with no swallowing
  Down into the glens
Every topsail she had would be off.
  —No light task the men's!
The great hooked big-buttocked ones
  Long before
They came at all near us were heard
  Loudly aroar
Scourging all the lesser waves level
  As on they tore.

It was no joke to steer in that sea
    When the high tops to miss
Seemed almost to hear her keel scrape
    The shelly abyss!
The sea churning and lashing itself
    In maniacal states,
Seals and other great beasts were even
    In direr straits,
The wild swelth and the pounding waves
    And the ship's nose
Scattering their white brains callous
    Through the billows.
They shouted to us loudly, dreadfully,
    The piteous word:—
"Save us or we perish. We are subjects.
    Take us aboard."
Small fish that were in the waters,
    Murderously churned,
Floated on the top without number
    White bellies upturned.
The stones and shells of the floor even
    Came up to the top
Torn up by the all-grabbing motion
    That would not stop.
The whole sea was a foul porridge
    Full of red scum
With the blood and ordure of the beasts,
    Ruddy, glum,
While screaming with their gill-less mouths,
    Their jaws agape,
Even the air's abyss was full of fiends
    That had no shape.
With the paws and tails of great monsters
    Gruesome to hear
Were the screeching towerers. They would strike
    Fifty warriors with fear.
The crew's ears lost all appetite
    For hearing in that din,
Rabble of mad sky-demons,

And their watery kin
Making a baying so unearthly,
    Deeper than the sea-floor,
Great notes lower than human hearing
    Ever heard before.
What then with the ocean's turmoil
    Pounding the ship,
The clamour of the prow flenching whales
    With slime-foiled grip,
And the wind from the Western quarter
    Restarting her windward blast,
Through every possible ordeal
    It seemed we passed.
We were blinded by the sea-spray
    Ever going over us;
With, beyond that, like another ocean,
    Thunders and lightnings to cover us,
The thunderbolts sometimes singeing
    Our rigging till the smoke
And stench of the reefs smouldering
    Made us utterly choke.
Between the upper and lower torments
    Thus were we braised,
Water, fire, and wind simultaneously
    Against us raised.
—But when it was beyond the sea's power
    To make us yield
She took pity with a faint smile
    And truce was sealed,
Though by that time no mast was unbent,
    No sail untorn,
Yard unsevered, mast-ring unflawed,
    Oar not shag-shorn,
No stay unstarted, halyard or shrowd unbroken.
    Fise. Faise.
Thwart and gunwale made confession
    In similar wise.
Every mast-rigging and tackle
    The worse of wear;

Not a beam-knee or rib of her
  Unloosened there;
Her gunwale and bottom-boards
  Were confounded;
Not a helm left unsplit,
  A rudder unwounded.
Every timber creaked, moaned, and warped.
  Not a tree-nail
Was unpulled, no plank had failed
  To give in the gale.
Not a part that pertained to her
  But had suffered
And from its first state and purpose
  Sadly differed.
The sea proclaimed peace with us
  At the fork of Islay Sound
And the hostile barking wind
  Was ordered off the ground.
It went to the upper places of the air
  And became a quiet
Glossy-white surface to us there
  After all its riot.
And to God we made thanksgiving
  That good Clanranald
Was spared the brutal death for which
  The elements had wrangled.
Then we pulled down the speckled canvas
  And lowered
The sleek red masts and along her bottom
  Safely stored,
And put out the slender well-wrought oars
  Coloured, and smooth to the hand,
Made of the pine cut by Mac Bharais
  In Finnan's Island,
And set up the right-royal, rocking, rowing,
  Deft and timeous,
And made good harbour there at the top
  Of Carrick-Fergus.
We threw out anchors peacefully
  In that roadstead.

We took food and drink unstinting
   And there we stayed.
                ALEXANDER MACDONALD
        (ALASDAIR MACMHAIGHSTIR ALASDAIR)

THE PRAISE OF BEN DORAIN *

Urlar

Over mountains, pride
Of place to Ben Dorain!
I've nowhere espied
A finer to reign.
In her moorbacks wide
Hosts of shy deer bide;
While light comes pouring
Diamond-wise from her side.

Grassy glades are there
With boughs light-springing
Where the wild herds fare
(Of these my singing!),
Like lightning flinging
Their heels on the air
Should the wind be bringing
Any hint to beware.

Swift is each spirited one
Clad in a fine fitting
Skin that shines like the sun
Of its glory unwitting.
Like a banner when they run
Of flame-red is their flitting.
A clever deed would be done
A shot in these small bellies getting.

It calls for a prime gun
In a young man's gripping

* Translated from the Gaelic of Duncan Bán MacIntyre, 1724–1812.

—A flint with a breach-run
And trigger hard-clipping
On the hammer with none
Of hesitation or slipping;
A sound-stocked eight-sided one
To catch a stag skipping.

Yet one born for the game,
The man to outwit them,
Who whene'er he took aim
Was certain to hit them,
Lived here, Patrick by name,
Swiftly though when he came
With his boys and dogs they might flit them.

Siubhal

Keenest of careering
Of smelling and hearing
Is the little hind rearing
Among the peaks, peering
Along the wind, fearing
Whatever is nearing,
Lightly the ground clearing
'Mid summits sky-shearing,
But never descending
Where a ball might be rending
Past mending, or ending,
The grace she is tending
Here where it's blending
With the light to which, wending,
She seems to be lending
More than the sun's sending.

She makes no complaining
Of any speed straining
The mettle obtaining
In one that's not waning
From the standard pertaining
To a breed that has lain in

These high tops each aeon in
Since Time began feigning
Eternity's reign in
A separate rule to be gaining.

I love when she stretches
Her breath and the wind fetches
A ghost of her bellowing,
But it's not for us wretches
Of men that the mellowing
Call sounds o'er the vetches
As she seeks her listening
Lover in rutting-time, glistening
With loving-kindness.
His no deafness nor blindness,
The stag of the proud head tapering,
White-flash-buttocked one, capering,
High-stepper showing his paces
With reverberant roaring.
He's always on Ben Dorain
And knows all her choice places.

It would be a masterpiece
To tell all the stags one sees
Here on Ben Dorain, and with these
Every hind going at ease,
Slim, neat, a sight to please,
With her fawns by her knees,
Or all with white tails on the breeze
Filing up through the passes.

Start yon one on the edge
Of Harper's Corrie; I'll pledge
Hardly a man in the kingdom
But would need to sing dumb
Telling truth of his trying
To follow her fast flying
That of her hoofs on the grass
Puts scarce a flick as they pass.

On a lush level straying
A fair band of them playing,
Quick-footed, cunning,
Restless, age on their running
No weight will be laying,
No sorrow essaying
To shadow their sunning;
No mental troubles are theirs,
Aching hearts or sad cares.
They owe their glossy
Coats to the cosy
Forest quiet and mossy
So broad and bossy.
—At peace there toss you
Where scarce man knows you
Nor dangers engross you,
Free heads and clean bodies
Wholesome as the sod is
To whose bounty all owed is
Your sleek flesh that no load is!

It's lush asainn that's keeping
The breast to the fawns—leaping
Speckled ones!—heaping
Them invisibly deep in
Warmth that, though sleeping
In the rude waste, can creep in
No least twinge of cramp
From the cold wind or damp.

To milk of the club-rush they're owing
What keeps their lives going
Pure as the hill-streams' flowing.
It holds their hearts glowing;
Even in nights of wild snowing
In no house they'd be stowing
But in Corrie Altrum, showing
There's still snug beds for knowing
Among the bare jutting rocks

For creatures the right food stocks;
Finding by the Fall of the Fairies
What subtle shelter there is
No one less groundwise and windwise
Than they ever descries.

Urlar

The hind as she should be
   Is in the forest
Where there's plenty free
   Of the food that's fittest.
Hill-grass bladed cleanly
   She will eat with zest;
Club-rush, heath-rush, juicy,
   Of rare virtues possessed,
Cunning with right fat to see
   Her kidneys drest;
Watercress more highly
   Than wine assessed.
She fares contentedly
   On all that is best;
Cultivated grass would be
   A plague and a pest
To her so amply and meetly
   Nourished and blest
On crisp herbs of purity
   No manure has messed;
With many a tit-bit too
   Of St. John's wort, primrose,
Daisy-tops the greenswards strew,
   And orchid that grows
—Towers with flowers that as fawns do
   Have speckles in rows—
In boglands she goes to
   That no man knows.
These are the tonics true
   To which instinct goes
In trying times; they endue

Lean frames with fat that glows
Prettily on them, without rue
   From any weight it throws.

There's no more pleasing fellowship
   Than theirs at gloaming-tide
And when through deepening shades they slip
   In safety they'll abide
Long though the night, sharp the wind's nip,
   Well sheltered by a hillside
In the place that's deemed their agile trip
   For centuries its greatest pride
—Not preferring hardship or want,
But Ben Dorain, their beloved haunt!

   Siubhal

The mountain high-towered,
Well-turfed and flowered,
Stream-lit and bowered,
None other is dowered
Like her in Christendom.
I'm overpowered as I roam
Bemused by her beauty
That the maps don't acclaim
Her transcending fame
As is their bare duty
With a special sign
As the queen of her line.
All the storms that have lowered
Have found her no coward
And whatever is toward
Will find her the same.

She's exuberant in fruits
Far beyond the measure
Usually found
On like areas of ground,
And rich in rare roots
And the tenderest of shoots

[460]

And has many a treasure
Of light-woven woodlands.
Oh, hers are the good lands
For all kinds of pleasure.
The cock is high-breasted
That on her has nested
With splendid torrent invested
Of music that springs unarrested
Between him and the sun,
And other birds, many a one,
A full repertoire run.
And hers is the brisk little buck
Who could have no better luck
With such greenswards for prancing on
Without slipping or mishap,
Without failing or falling, yon
Cloven-hoofed clever chap!
Then deep corries for ranging
To the heights, or, changing,
Dallying in copsewood and bracken
Of variety there's no lack in
Ben Dorain for all his wants.
Every winding gully he haunts
On every crag-top balances
With audacious curtsies,
And has ample distances
To put behind him should
Aught to startle him intrude.
Every second tussock he takes
As over the moss-quakes he makes
On hoofs nonpareil thin
In his eagerness to win
To where his love will be found
Come up from the low ground
—Every second tussock, or third;
Light and easy as a bird!

As for the little growling doe
And her young fawns who bide
In a hidden glen ill to know

High up the mountain side,
The ear she has! And the eye!
And the quick deft feet to ply
Over the boggling peat-hags!
Lightning behind her lags.
Though Caoilte and Cuchullin
Sought her they'd be fooling.
The sight would not daunt her
Of them and every hunter,
With all the men and horses
Hire-bound by King George; their forces
Would include nothing to catch her
If she wished to escape; watch her,
Gallant, long-legged, swift-turning,
Incalculable, her white-flared hips burning
Like stars in the distance! No matter
How precipitous the uplands may be
Lured by no level land she'll be
Where they might win at her.
She is the incarnate spirit
Of the heights her kind inherit,
Analysing every breath of air
With instant unerring nose.
Volatile, vigilant, there
One with the horizon she goes
Where horizons horizons disclose,
Or lies like a star hidden away
By the broad light of day.
Earth has nothing to match her.

Urlar

The hind loves to wander
Among the saplings yonder.
The passes of the braes
Are her dwelling-place.
The leaflets of the trees
And fresh heather-stems—these
Are the fare she prefers,
To cattle-fodder averse.

Blithe and gentle her nature,
A glad gloomless creature,
Mercurial and thoughtless,
Going like a knotless
Thread through the landscape,
Yet bearing herself always
Circumspect and comely in shape,
With the hues of health ablaze;
Knowing precisely how far to press
Her vital force to fill out,
Without straining, her formal niceness,
At rest or in revel or rout.
In the glen of the sappiest
Green copsewood she's happiest,
Yet often goes by the Great Rock
Where bush-clumps break the shock
Of the North Wind and let
No icy jet of it get
On her slumbering there
In some favourite lair;
Or she trips up the dell
Of the hazels to the well
She loves to drink at; cold and clear,
Far better than beer.
No one could think of
Better for her to drink of.
It inspires her lithe wiles,
Her sheer grace that beguiles,
Her constant strength and speed
In every hazard of need.
The honour of the best ears
In all Europe is hers!

Siubhal

Graceful to see to me was a group
Lined up in the order of march to troop
Down by the Sron rock south through the loop
'Twixt Craobh-na-h-ainnis moor and the scoop
Of Corrie-dhaingean; no goog on that herd,

And none with a staring hide covered,
That for bite and sup never begged or chaffered
Nor yet lacked though to that they'd not stoop.
That was the fine line to be watching oop
The seen parts of a path between noop and noop.
Then along Corrie Rannoch's either side
About the wing of the pass and the wide
Corrie of Ben Achalader and over
By Conn Lonn on the Laoidhre's spur,
What a host to delight a deer-lover,
Everyone in a radiant red jupe!
On to the hollow of the Feinne there
And in the Creag-sheilich beyond that
Where gather the winsome hinds that care
Nothing for grass that dunghills begat,
But whose joy it is to be strutting
On a grassy level, butting
And playing with each other or in
The rutting-bogs make a right din
Of spirited lewdness, keen, wanton,
Lusty, with no care or cant on.

No tongue could keep on thirsting
On the lower side of Meall Eanail where spring
The wine-streams of Annet, honey-tasted to drink;
A flow efficacious, white, narrow,
Filtering over sand, brim to the brink,
Sweeter than cinnamon, a draught to make marrow.
This is the water to cure all thirst
That from the bottom of the earth has burst.
There's plenty of it here on the mountain top,
Free—not for sale in a shop!
This is the loveliest thing to see
In all this quarter of Europe to me,
The fresh water, mild with limpidity,
Welling so pure and harmless
From the dark roots of the watercress,
With various mosses waving about the lips
Of every ripple as it slips
From the wards of the rock and swells the pool

Uninflaming, delicious, and cool,
Coming in an eddy from the gravel,
On the shoulder of Ben Dorain,
The great demesne where you have all
The good life can set store in.

The hither side of the hill slope
Has goodliness without stint or stop;
The tumultuous tumbled moor-corrie
Opens by it—a corrie of glory.
Grouty through-other rocks, all points and pits
Shaggy and counter and ravelled—oh, it's
Easy enough for me to praise
Steep defiles such variety arrays,
For there's felicity enough on them,
All manner of fine stuff on them.
One could spend endless love on them.
Full of bells, full of buds, they are,
With everywhere the dainty clear star
Of the daisy so ruddy and fair
Twinkling in the tapestry there,
And the moorland busked in a great
Rough-figured mantle that suits her estate
What tongue can ever hope
For words with the like to cope?—
The grandest scene in all Europe!

Urlar

The lonely moorland ringed round
With glen-mouths and hill-ends,
Corrie Fraoich, will be found
Best of all. Fawns' presence lends
It that smiling look that ground
They favour aye commends.
Its southerly setting defends
It from cold; hence they abound.
Glad is the little hind here.
Pure her body, healthy, clear,
True womanly in virtue she.

Taintless her breath would appear
To anyone who might kiss her.
It is here that, once they see
It, young men always wish to be.
Like pipes' sticks are its fanwise
Ravines through which the wind sighs.
Stags' chief meeting-ground and place
That's source of every great chase.
Rich in all that comes out with rain,
Wild berries and flowers perfume this plain.
There's heaps of fish in near-by streams
To get with a torch's gleams
And the narrow pine-shafted spear
Plied by men used to such gear.
Fine to see the trout leaping
Light flies in clusters catching
On waters so smoothly sweeping!
I've said as I stood watching,
The best things in land or sea found
All in you, Ben Dorain, abound!

Crunn-Luth

Who would stalk the hind in this glen
   Needs good knowledge and cunning
To steal softly within her ken
   Without starting her running,
Carefully and cleverly inveigling
   Himself forward, her notice shunning,
Using each least thing in turn then
   To hide himself and his gun in.
Bush, rock, and hollow all intaken,
   Vastly ingenious, there's great fun in.

Details of the land all well gauged,
   Clouds' direction duly noted,
His wits are thenceforth all engaged
   In covering the space allotted,
And getting the finale staged

Before the hind can have thought it
Enplotted—aye, all the campaign waged
   Ere hint of danger is brought it.

The hind's own instincts outplaying,
   In spite of herself she's taken
By the stalker, not without paying
   Full due to her wits wide-waken,
With tribute of stilly delaying
   And coolness never forsaken
And frame to wriggle a worm's way in
   Without affront or aching.

At last he puts the eye steadily
   To the hind on the stag still intent,
And the peg is drawn out readily
   The butt-iron's kick to relent.
A new flint's just tightened, and deadly
   The down-blow of the hammer's sent.
The spark to the packed powder flies redly
   And the hail from the barrel is sprent.

It was well loved by the quality
   To be up Ben Dorain's passes
In the hey-day of their vitality
   Where the deer troop by in masses,
While hunters of such judicality
   In the sport where nothing crass is
Stalk them with the right mentality
   That alone their wariness outclasses.

And the brisk keen dogs behind them,
   Creatures so surly and slaughtering,
Frantic at jaws' grip to find them
   With the herd like wild-fire scattering,
Till speed it seems has combined them
   —Their hair-on-end howling, shattering
The golden silence of deer-flight, entwined them
   With the foes their rabid foam's spattering.

[467]

Furious in high career that conjunction
    Of leaping dogs and fugitive deer,
And the peaks and passes echo with unction
    The baying of the hounds exciting to hear
As they drove down their quarries without compunction
    In to the icy pools that bottomless appear
And rocked on their necks in relentless function
    While they floundered and bloodied the waters there!
. . . Though I've told a little of Ben Dorain here,
    Before I could tell all it deserves I would be
In a delirium with the strange prolixity
Of the talking called for, I fear.

                                    DUNCAN BÁN MACINTYRE

THE GLASS OF PURE WATER

"In the de-oxidisation and re-oxidisation of hydrogen in a single drop of water we have before us, truly, so far as force is concerned, an epitome of the whole life. . . . The burning of coal to move an iron wheel differs only in detail, and not in essence, from the decomposition of a muscle to effect its own concentration."
JAMES HINTON

"We must remember that his analysis was done not intellectually, but by an immediate process of intuition; that he was able, as it were, to taste the hydrogen and oxygen in his glass of water."
ALDOUS HUXLEY (of D. H. Lawrence)

"Praise of pure water is common in Gaelic poetry."
W. J. WATSON, "Bardachd Ghaidlig."

Hold a glass of pure water to the eye of the sun!
It is difficult to tell the one from the other
Save by the tiny hardly visible trembling of the water.
This is the nearest analogy to the essence of human life
Which is even more difficult to see.
Dismiss anything you can see more easily;
It is not alive—it is not worth seeing.
There is a minute indescribable difference
Between one glass of water and another
With slightly different chemical constituents.
The difference between one human life and another
Is no greater; colour does not colour the water;
You cannot tell a white man's life from a black man's.
But the lives of these particular slum people
I am chiefly concerned with, like the lives of all
The world's poorest, remind me less
Of a glass of water held between my eyes and the sun
—They remind me of the feeling they had

[469]

Who saw Sacco and Vanzetti in the death cell
On the eve of their execution.
—One is talking to God.

I dreamt last night that I saw one of His angels
Making his centennial report to the Recording Angel
On the condition of human life.
Look at the ridge of skin between your thumb and forefinger.
Look at the delicate lines on it and how they change
—How many different things they can express—
As you move out or close in your forefinger and thumb.
And look at the changing shapes—the countless
Little gestures, little miracles of line—
Of your forefinger and thumb as you move them.
And remember how much a hand can express,
How a single slight movement of it can say more
Than millions of words—dropped hand, clenched fist,
Snapping fingers, thumb up, thumb down,
Raised in blessing, clenched in passion, begging,
Welcome, dismissal, prayer, applause,
And a million other signs, too slight, too subtle,
Too packed with meaning for words to describe,
A universal language understood by all,
And the angel's report on human life
Was the subtlest movement—just like that—and no more;
A hundred years of life on the Earth
Summed up, not a detail missed or wrongly assessed,
In that little inconceivably intricate movement.

The only communication between man and man
That says anything worth hearing
—The hidden well-water; the finger of destiny—
Moves as that water, that angel, moved.
Truth is the rarest thing and life
The gentlest, most unobtrusive movement in the world.
I cannot speak to you of the poor people of all the world
But among the people in these nearest slums I know
This infinitesimal twinkling, this delicate play
Of tiny signs that not only say more
Than all speech, but all there is to say,

All there is to say and to know and to be.
There alone I seldom find anything else,
Each in himself or herself a dramatic whole,
An "agon" whose validity is timeless.

Our duty is to free that water, to make these gestures,
To help humanity to shed all else,
All that stands between any life and the sun,
The quintessence of any life and the sun;
To still all sound save that talking to God;
To end all movements save movements like these.
India had that great opportunity centuries ago
And India lost it—and became a vast morass,
Where no water wins free; a monstrous jungle
Of useless movement; a babel
Of stupid voices, drowning the still small voice.
It is our turn now; the call is to the Celt.
This little country can overcome the whole world of wrong
As the Lacedaemonians the armies of Persia.
Cornwall—Gaeldom—must stand for the ending
Of the essential immorality of any man controlling
Any other—for the ending of all Government
Since all Government is a monopoly of violence;
For the striking of this water out of the rock of Capitalism;
For the complete emergence from the pollution and fog
With which the hellish interests of private property
In land, machinery, and credit
Have corrupted and concealed from the sun,
From the gestures of truth, from the voice of God,
Hundreds upon hundreds of millions of men,
Denied the life and liberty to which they were born
And fobbed off with a horrible travesty instead
—Self-righteous, sunk in the belief that they are human,
When not a tenth of one per cent show a single gleam
Of the life that is in them under their accretions of filth.

And until that day comes every true poet's place
Is to reject all else and be with the lowest,
The poorest—in the bottom of that deepest of wells
In which alone is truth; in which

Is truth only—truth that should shine like the sun,
With a monopoly of movement, and a sound like talking to God. . . .

THE NORTH FACE OF LIATHACH

The North Face of Liathach
Lives in the mind like a vision.
From the deeps of Coire ne Caime
Sheer cliffs go up
To spurs and pinnacles and jagged teeth.
Its grandeur draws back the heart.
Scotland is full of such places.
Few (few Scots even) know them.

I think of another
Stupendous wall of rock
On the West coast of Foula
Rising eleven hundred feet from the sea.

Keep all your "kindly brither Scots,"
Your little happinesses,
Your popular holiday resorts,
Your damned democracy.
This is no place for children
Or for holiday dawdling.
It has no friendly sand or cove.
It is almost frightening
In its lack of anything in common
With Dunoon or Portobello or Aberdeen.
It has no modern conveniences at all
—Only its own stark magnificence
Overwhelming the senses.
Every Scot should make pilgrimage here
Just once, and alone.

And thereafter pick shells at Montrose,
Or admire our rich Hebridean rock pools,

Or go to "the island that likes to be visited"
In the Loch of Voshimid in Harris
Or seek like Selma Lagerlöf
For "the butterfly changed into an island"
And is "pervaded ever since with an intense yearning
To be able to fly again
And go with the birds beyond the horizon."
And so regain the proper holiday feelings
The proper human feelings,
Surprised at no wildness of belief among
A people who can swallow the Incarnation theory,
The Christian feelings of those of whom Meredith said
"If you can believe in God
You can believe in anything."

Seen through a murky patch of fog,
Violent, ruthless, incalculable.
I have seen a head blood-drained to this hue.
But this cliff is not dead.
It has an immense life of its own
And will loom, as if it could come rushing
To beat, to maim, to kill
(Damned anti-climax of a notion!)
Just as it looms to-day
After every human being now alive
Has returned, not to rock but to dust.

What does it remind me of?
Why, since extremes meet,
Of the life of a great city perhaps,
The compelling sense of the *vécu ensemble*
The *Zusammenerlebt*,
Any of man's great *unanimes*
And their place in the history
Of human stupidity.

No flower, no fern,
No wisp of grass or pad of moss
Lightens this tremendous face.
Otherwise it might remind me of my mother.

[473]

The education she gave me was strict enough,
Teaching me a sense of duty and self-reliance
And having no time for any softness.
Her tenderness was always very reserved,
Very modest in its expression
And respect was the foremost of my feelings for her.
No. Not of my mother.
But of many other women I have known
As I could not know her.
It is with them I have found the soul most exposed,
Some thing not of this world,
Which makes you tremble with delight and repulsion
When you see it so close.

OLD WIFE IN HIGH SPIRITS

In an Edinburgh Pub

An auld wumman cam' in, a mere rickle o' banes, in a faded black
    dress
And a bonnet wi' beads o' jet rattlin' on it;
A puir-lookin' cratur, you'd think she could haurdly ha'e had less
Life left in her and still lived, but dagonit!

He gied her a stiff whisky—she was nervous as a troot
And could haurdly haud the tumbler, puir cratur;
Syne he gied her anither, joked wi' her, and anither, and syne
Wild as the whisky up cam' her nature.

The rod that struck water frae the rock in the desert
Was naething to the life that sprang oot o' her;
The dowie auld soul was twinklin' and fizzin' wi' fire;
You never saw ocht sae souple and kir.

Like a sackful o' monkeys she was, and her lauchin'
Loupit up whiles to incredible heights;

Wi' ane owre the eight her temper changed and her tongue
Flew juist as the forkt lichtnin' skites.

The heich skeich auld cat was fair in her element;
Wanton as a whirlwind, and shairly better that way
Than a' crippen thegither wi' laneliness and cauld
Like a foretaste o' the graveyaird clay.

Some folk nae doot'll condemn gie'in' a guid spree
To the puir dune body and raither she endit her days
Like some auld tashed copy o' the Bible yin sees
On a street book-barrow's tipenny trays.

A' I ken is weel-fed and weel-put-on though they be
Ninety per cent o' respectable folk never hae
As muckle life in their creeshy carcases frae beginnin' to end
As kythed in that wild auld carline that day!

A MOOLIE BESOM

Wi' every effort to be fair
And nae undue antagonism
I canna but say that my sweethert's mither
Is a moolie besom, a moolie besom,
        Naething but a moolie besom!

Am I no' feart Jean'll turn the same?
Her mither was aince as bonny as her.
Sae what's mair likely she'll become in turn
Her vieve een dull, face lourd that's noo kir,
        Naething but a moolie besom?

[475]

AUDH AND CUNAIDE

Two women I think of often.
Audh the deep-minded, mother
Of Hebridean chiefs,
Who, widowed, went to Iceland
And sleeps in one of its cold reefs.

And Cunaide, a spinster of thirty-three,
Buried fifteen centuries ago near the west end
Of the railway viaduct at Hayle in Cornwall
—Cunaide, no more unapproachable
In death than she was in life,
In Eternity than she was in time.
Oh, the cry might be found even yet
To bring Audh back to life again.
To quicken that resourceful heroic old body
Lying there like a cameo under glass.
A cry might be found to bring back
Audh, wife and mother, whose intrepid blood
Still runs in far generations
Of her children's children.
But Cunaide? . . . Who can imagine
Any appeal that would stir Cunaide
Who died, a virgin, so long ago
She might have been the sole inhabitant of another star,
Having nothing to do with human life
And Earth and its history at all?
Audh lies like a cameo under glass
Cunaide is an unmined diamond.

There is hope for one buried in ice,
But by a railway viaduct? . . . No!
"Come back to life, Cunaide!," we cry.
But if the answer comes: "To life? What's that?"
How could we tell one who doesn't know
What life is? What is it anyway?
. . . Audh knew!

THE BOBBIN-WINDER

Not even the fine threads in a lace factory,
Coming, like rays from the sun, towards the woman
Winding the bobbins, can vie
With that miracle now on the river.

Look! Where the bowls of yon water-lilies
And the threads they send down to the depths
Are so elfin it seems only a chord struck
On a piano could have given them birth.

THE CALEDONIAN ANTISYZYGY

I write now in English and now in Scots
To the despair of friends who plead
For consistency; sometimes achieve the true lyric cry,
Next but chopped-up prose; and write whiles
In traditional forms, next in a mixture of styles.
So divided against myself, they ask:
How can I stand (or they understand) indeed?

Fatal division in my thought they think
Who forget that although the thrush
Is more cheerful and constant, the lark
More continuous and celestial, and, after all,
The irritating cuckoo unique
In singing a true musical interval,
Yet the nightingale remains supreme,
The nightingale whose thin high call
And that deep throb,
Which seem to come from different birds
In different places, find an emotion
And vibrate in the memory as the song
Of no other bird—not even
The love-note of the curlew—
                        can do!

Glossary of Scots Words

abaws	abash, appal
abies	except
abordage	the act of getting on board
aft'rins	the remainder, offscourings
agley	off the right line
ahint	behind
aiblins	perhaps
aidle	foul slop
aiker	motion or break, made in water by fish swimming rapidly
airgh	lack, or what anything requires to bring it up to the level
airts	directions
alist	to come alist; to recover from faintness or decay
aroint	clear away
arrears	goes backward
atour	out from
aucht-fit	eight-foot
aumrie	cupboard
awn (to)	to own
avizandum (to take to)	to defer decision
back-hauf (to be worn to)	practically worn out
Backlands	Glasgow slum tenements
baggit	enceinte
bairn-time	a woman's breeding time
barkin' and fleein'	on the verge of ruin
barley bree	whisky
barrowsteel (to take my)	to cooperate
ba's	balls
bauch	dull
bawaw	an oblique look of contempt or scorn
beanswaup	the hull of a bean; anything of no value
beddiness	silly importunacy

beeks	shows
belly-thraw	colic
belth	sudden swirl
ben (to gang)	to go in
benmaist	inmost
biel	shelter
bien	complacent, snug
blash	sudden onset
blate	bashful
blebs	drops
blethers	nonsense
blinnin' stew	storm through which it is impossible to see
blinterin'	gleaming
Blottie O	a school game
bluffert	squall
bood to	must
boss (of body)	torso
boss	hollow
bratts	scum
braw	handsome
breenge	burst
brough	ring (round moon)
buddies	folks
buff nor stye	one thing or another
buick	trunk (of body)
buss	bush
cairn	pile
camsteerie	perverse, unmanageable
carline	old woman, witch
cavaburd	dense snowstorm
chafts	jaws
cheatrie	deceit, fraud
chitterin'	trembling violently, shivering
chowed	chewed
chowl (to)	twist, distort
chuns	sprouts or germs
clapt	shrunken
claith	cloth
claught (to)	to grab at
cleg	gadfly
cleiks	the merest adumbration
clints	rocky shelves at the sides of a river
clyre	tumor, gland

clytach	balderdash
cod	pillow
come-doon	degradation
connached	abused, spoiled
coom	comb
coonter	counter
corbaudie comes in	that is the obstacle
cordage	tackling of a ship
corneigh	enough (*lit.*: cœur ennuyé)
cottons	cottar houses
coupin	overturning
courage-bag	scrotum
couthie	comfortable
coutribat	struggle
cree (legs wi')	compete with
creel	in a state of mental excitement or confusion or physical agony
crockats up	on (one's) dignity
cross-brath'd	braided
cross-tap	mizzenmast
crottle	crumble away
cuckold	hoodwinked, diddled
cude	barrel
cull	testicle
cullage	genitals
dander	temper
datchie	sly, secret
daunton	to overawe
deef	deaf, unimpressionable
deemless	countless
derf	taciturn, cruel
dern	hide
ding	bang down
doited	mad
donnert	dazed, stupefied
dottlin'	maundering
doup	backside
dour	intractable
dowf	hollow, gloomy, inert
dowless	imponderable
dowse	quench
dozent	stupid

drobs	falls like hail
drookit	soaked
drumlie	troubled, discolored
dumb-deid	midnight
dwamin'	overpowering
dwinin'	dwindling
eel-ark	breeding ground for eels
eemis	ill-poised, insecure
e'en	eyes
eident	busy
eisenin'	lustful
elbuck	elbow
ettle	attempt, aspire
fanerels	accessories
fank o' tows	coil of ropes
fankles	traps
farles	filaments of ash
fash	trouble
feck	majority
fecklessly	impotently
ferlies	marvels
fey	fated
fidge	move
file	defile
flauchters	flutters
flech	flea
fleg	frighten
flet	flit
farfochen	completely tired out
forgether	meet
fork-in-the-wa'	means of diverting labor pains to husband
fou'	drunk
foudrie	lightning
fousome	disgusting
fratt	fretwork
fraucht	cargo
freaths	plumes of foam or froth
fremt	friendless, isolated
foziest	most stupid
fullyery	(*lit.*: foliage)

[481]

gaadies	howlers, gaffes
gaff	cleek for fish
galliard	rapid dance
gallus	reckless
gammons	feet
gangrel	wanderer
ganien	rodomontade
gantin'	yawning
gantrees	planks for putting barrel on
gausty	ghastly, ascetic
gaw (to have a)	to have a catch upon
gealed	congealed
geg	trick, deception
gell (on the)	on the go
gey	very
geylies	very much
gird	hoop
glaur	mud
gleg	eager
gleids	sparks
glisk	gleam, glance
glit	slime
gloffs	dark patches appearing denser than other parts of the atmosphere
glower	gaze at
goam	gaze stupidly at
gordet	frosted
goustrous	frightful
gowk-storm	storm of short duration (not sense, foolish fuss)
gowls	hollows (opposite of gloffs)
gree (to bear off the)	carry off the palm
grieshuckle	embers
grue	revulsion
grugous	ugly
gruntle	pig's nose
gurly	savage
guts	bowels
gy	spectacle
hain	preserve
hair (kaimed to lift)	on the go
hairst	harvest
happit	covered

harns	brains
harth	lean
hauflins	adolescent boys
haw	hollow
heich-skeich	irresponsible
hod'n	hidden
howd	shorn down
howe	hollow
how-dumb-deid	midnight
howff	public house
hwll	ululation
ilka	every
ingangs	intestines
ingles	hearths
inklins	intuitions
jag	prick
jalouse	guess
jaup	splash
jizzen	childbed (*lit.:* in the straw)
jouk	dodge
kaa	drive
kaim	comb
keethins	circles betraying fish's movements
kelter	waggle
keltie	bumper
kilted (in a tippet)	hung in a noose
kink (to)	bend or twist
kirk or mill (to mak'a)	to do one's best
kist	chest, breast
kittle	ticklish
knool	pin or peg
kyths	appears, shows
larochs	foundations
lave	rest
lear	learning
leed, or leid	language
liddenin'	going backward and forward
lift	sky
lochan	little loch
loppert	coagulated

lourd	heavy, overcharged, cloudy
lowe	flame
lowse	free, loosen
lozen	window
lugs	ears
maikless	matchless
mapamound	map of the world
marrow (winsome)	a creditable limb
mells	mixes
mirlygoes	dazzles
mochiness	closeness
moniplies	intestines
moosewab	spider's web
muckle	big
mum	silent
munkie	rope with a noose at end
munks	swings away
mutchkin	liquor measure, half-bottle
nae mowse	perilous
natheless	nevertheless
natter	rant, nag
neist	next
nesh	full of awareness
nocht	nothing
oorie	weird
ootby	outside
ootcuissen	outcast
ootrie	outré
orra	not up to much
peepy-show	cinema
peerie	spinning top
penny wheep	small ale
pickle	small quantity
pirn	reel
plumm	deep pool
pokiness	congestion
quean	lass, woman

ramel	branches
rex	strain
reishlin'	rustling
reistit	dried
ripe	search
rippit	rumpus
ripples	diarrhea
rit	scrape
rived	torn
rooky	misty
root-hewn	awkward
rouk	smoke, mist
row'd	rolled, wrapped up
rowin'	rolling
rumple-fyke	itch in anus
runkled	wrinkled
samyn	deck of ship
scouth	scope
scunner	disgust
scunnersome	repulsive
seilfu'	blissful
sentrices	scaffolding
ser'	serve
shasloch	loose straw, litter
sheckle	wrist
sibness	relationship
siccar (to mak')	to make certain
sinnen	sinew
shoon	shoes
skime	gleam
skinklan'	shining, twinkling
skirl-i-the-pan	fried oatmeal
slorp	lap up; slobber over
slounge	sharp fall
sonsy	contented
spalin'	burning away
splairgin'	spluttering
stang	paroxysm
sta'-tree	pole for tethering cattle to
steekin'	shutting
stegh	glut
stented	appointed

stertle-a-stobie	exhalations
stour	dust
stramash	rumpus
stramulyert	panic-stricken
strawns	strings or chains
swack	active, supple
swaw	ripple
swippert	lively
swith wi' virr	vehement
swither	hesitate
syne	thereafter
taigled	entangled
tapsalteerie	topsy-turvy
thieveless	impotent
thorter ills	obstructions
thow	thaw
thowless	impotent
thrang	busy
thring	shrug
toom (to)	empty
toories	pom-poms
twaesome	the two of them
tyauve (to)	struggle
ugsome	ugly, horrid
ullage	deficiency in contents of barrel
unco	very
unkennable	unknowable
vennel	lane, narrow street
vieve	vivid
wab	web
wae	woeful
waesome	woeful
waesucks	alas
wanchancy	unfortunate
waun'ert	confused
waur	worse
weird	fate
weirdless	worthless
wheengin'	complaining
wheesht	hush

whummle	overturn
widdifow	perverse
windlestrae	straw
wizened	shrunk
worm-i-the-cheek	toothache
wuppit	wound round
yabblin'	gabbling
yauk	throw
Ygdrasil	(Celtic) Tree of Life

Index to Titles

Index to First Lines